THE EVERYTHING
GUIDE TO
ANGELS

Dear Reader,

There is no such thing as a coincidence. This book is in your hands because you called it forth and the angels want to be a part of your life. I assure you, if you invite the angels into your life, you will never feel alone again and you will realize the true meaning of unconditional love.

My guardian angel appeared to me during a very challenging time when I was being treated for thyroid cancer. My journey with cancer was a spiritual awakening and a blessing in disguise. It guided me back "home" to a spiritual connection that was missing in my life. Since then the angels have become my best friends and my spiritual guides.

My passion for the angels and the miraculous gifts of transformation I received inspired me to become a messenger for the angels. This book is filled with the gems of wisdom you need to invite divine miracles and magic into your life. The angels are excited and eager to assist you in any way they can.

So get ready for a magical ride. Open your heart—invite the angels into your life—and expect miracles!

Blessings,

Karen Paolino

Welcome to the EVERYTHING® Series!

These handy, accessible books give you all you need to tackle a difficult project, gain a new hobby, comprehend a fascinating topic, prepare for an exam, or even brush up on something you learned back in school but have since forgotten.

You can choose to read an *Everything*® book from cover to cover or just pick out the information you want from our four useful boxes: e-questions, e-facts, e-alerts, and e-ssentials.

We give you everything you need to know on the subject, but throw in a lot of fun stuff along the way, too.

We now have more than 400 *Everything*® books in print, spanning such wide-ranging categories as weddings, pregnancy, cooking, music instruction, foreign language, crafts, pets, New Age, and so much more. When you're done reading them all, you can finally say you know *Everything*®!

QUESTION

Answers to
common questions

FACT

Important snippets
of information

ALERT

Urgent
warnings

ESSENTIAL

Quick
handy tips

PUBLISHER Karen Cooper

DIRECTOR OF ACQUISITIONS AND INNOVATION Paula Munier

MANAGING EDITOR, EVERYTHING® SERIES Lisa Laing

COPY CHIEF Casey Ebert

ACQUISITIONS EDITOR Lisa Laing

SENIOR DEVELOPMENT EDITOR Brett Palana-Shanahan

EDITORIAL ASSISTANT Hillary Thompson

EVERYTHING® SERIES COVER DESIGNER Erin Alexander

LAYOUT DESIGNERS Colleen Cunningham, Elisabeth Lariviere, Ashley Vierra, Denise Wallace

Visit the entire Everything® series at *www.everything.com*

THE EVERYTHING®

GUIDE TO ANGELS

Discover the wisdom and healing power
of the Angelic Kingdom

Karen Paolino, CHT, ATP

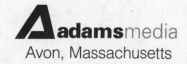

Avon, Massachusetts

*Blessings and gratitude to each and every one of you
who read this book and may you open your heart to the
angels. Together we can co-create heaven on earth and
with the help of the angels; we can all experience love,
peace, and harmony.*

Published by Adams Media, a division of F+W Media, Inc.
57 Littlefield Street, Avon, MA 02322 U.S.A.
www.adamsmedia.com

ISBN 10: 1-60550-121-2
ISBN 13: 978-1-60550-121-5

Printed in the United States of America.

J   I   H   G   F   E

Library of Congress Cataloging-in-Publication Data
is available from the publisher.

This publication is designed to provide accurate and authoritative information with regard to the subject matter covered. It is sold with the understanding that the publisher is not engaged in rendering legal, accounting, or other professional advice. If legal advice or other expert assistance is required, the services of a competent professional person should be sought.

—From a *Declaration of Principles* jointly adopted by a Committee of the American Bar Association and a Committee of Publishers and Associations

Many of the designations used by manufacturers and sellers to distinguish their products are claimed as trademarks. Where those designations appear in this book and Adams Media was aware of a trademark claim, the designations have been printed with initial capital letters.

*This book is available at quantity discounts for bulk purchases.
For information, please call 1-800-289-0963.*

Contents

Acknowledgments

A special thank you to my earth angels, Louie, Joelle, and Justin for your loving support and encouragement. Rita, thank you for believing in me and sending me this amazing opportunity to write this book. Dottie, I am very grateful for your expertise in editing and your encouraging words every step of the way. Thank you, Lisa at Adams Media, for your guidance and your support throughout this entire process.

I am grateful to all my students and clients. By sharing their experiences with me, they taught me what's truly possible when you invite the angels into your life. Last but not least, thank you, angels, for all the blessings you've brought into my life, including this incredible opportunity to write this book. Now, others can be touched by your unconditional love and support.

The Top 10 Things You Will
Accomplish by Reading This Book

1. Discover how to lift the veil between heaven and earth to see, feel, and hear the angels by practicing meditation, journaling, affirmations, and chanting.

2. Learn the history of the angels and discover what roles they played and their significance in the different religions throughout time.

3. Answer the big question: Is it just my imagination or is it the voice of my angels?

4. Learn how to use angel cards to receive messages of divine guidance and gain insight into different aspects of your life.

5. Discover the magic of signs, synchronicities, and coincidences, and learn how to interpret their meaning as a message from your angels.

6. Experience how the angels can help you release worry, gain patience, let go of guilt, and live in the present moment with a positive attitude.

7. Have fun with the angels—they can help you locate the perfect parking spot, find lost objects, bargain shop, and experience smooth travel and great weather.

8. Develop and enhance your intuitive and psychic abilities so you can see into the future, interpret your dreams, and communicate with angels and loved ones in spirit.

9. Receive help from the angels to heal physically and emotionally, find a soul mate, enhance relationships, create prosperity, find the perfect job, and manifest your dreams.

10. Be inspired and believe the angels are real. Read stories about real people who have been touched by the angels and experienced miracles of healing, help, and transformation.

Introduction

THE WORLD AROUND YOU is constantly changing. Through mass media and the Internet you have a conscious awareness of how humanity is challenged every day. Because of this, people are nervous and confused and they are searching for answers. Intuitively many find themselves on the spiritual path trying to find the answers and the support they need. This is exactly why the angels are more present than ever before. They want you to feel more peaceful and they are honored to help you in any way they can. Their mission is to help you discover the answers you seek.

The angels were gifted to you by God since the beginning of time. They are messengers of love and light who act as intermediaries between heaven and earth. They have appeared throughout history and in many different cultures, most often portrayed as friendly spirits who walk among the people.

God knew that when you were born into this human experience you might forget your connection to the divine and how loved you really are. So He sent the angels to help you. The angels have different roles and assignments to help you in every possible way you can imagine. God also gave you another significant gift, the gift of free will and free choice. This is a very important point to remember when working with the angels. Because of free will, you need to *ask* the angels for their help and guidance. Once you ask, the angels get to work behind the scenes and you begin to witness miracles unfolding in your life.

This book is true to its title; you are going to learn everything you need to know about the angels and how to work with them. You will receive all the tools you need to bridge the connection between you and the divine. With practice, you will walk over the bridge and become one with the reality of heaven on earth. You will communicate with the angels and they will respond, with peace, clarity, encouragement, and wisdom. There is no previous experience required and you don't have to be "gifted" or psychic to communicate with the angels. They will hold your hand every step of the way. They know you better than you know yourself and they know exactly how to help you. Just be curious and open your heart to receive.

God and the angels want you to experience heaven on earth. When you develop a deep desire to experience it, the divine says, "Yes! She's finally ready. Let's step in and help." The cocreation begins and everything naturally falls into place to bring about its manifestation. With faith, trust, and belief in the impossible, miracles can happen. You will begin to experience more joy, happiness, and peace in every aspect of your life: your relationships, your home, your career, your finances, and overall well being.

The angels are ready to help you remember your true potential as spirit, living in the human experience. It's time to wake up and lift the veil between heaven and earth. Just remember these two truths as you embark on the journey: One, you are never alone; and two, you are always loved unconditionally by God and the angels.

CHAPTER 1

What You Need to Know about the Angels

Angels are messengers of love who serve as guardians and helpers between heaven and earth. The more you open your awareness to who they are and why they are here, the more you can invite their miracles of love and support into your everyday experience. You don't have to be psychically gifted to connect or communicate with angels; they are here to serve all of humanity. Just affirm your desire and open your heart to them.

What Are Angels?

Angels are messengers from God. They can act as the link through which you can communicate between heaven and earth. Their role is to watch over you, protect you, and guide you along your human journey. The word "angel" comes from Greek word *angelos,* which means "messenger." Angels are divine celestial beings who have not experienced living in a human body on the earth plane. God gave you the angels so you would never feel alone or abandoned by God. They vibrate in the same loving energy as God, and they are here to serve and help humanity with compassion, grace, joy, playfulness, and peace.

Throughout history, in almost every culture and religion, there have been stories and validations of the angels and their roles as messengers from heaven to earth. Their presence is portrayed in many different forms. In different religious scripture such as the Bible, the Koran, and the Kabbalah, the angels have been described as healers, messengers, and guides. Artists throughout time have been inspired by angels. Their paintings depict angels in various forms—a glowing light and aura surrounding them, human-like beings with glorious wings, some with a halo above their head or a musical instrument in their hands. Their appearance and purpose may vary throughout the world and its history, but their universal influence over mankind is a presence of love, guidance, and a reminder that we are not alone.

The Bible affirms God's love for all in Psalms 91:11–12 "For he will command his angels concerning you to guard you in all your ways; they will lift you up in their hands, so that you will not strike your foot against a stone."

One important reminder: You were given two gifts to experience in this lifetime: free will and free choice. Whatever choices you make and however those choices play out, the angels are there to watch over in unconditional love. One important point about this gift of free will is that the angels will not interfere in your life unless you ask them. The only time they will intervene is if there is a life-threatening situation and it's not your time to leave this earth plane. This is called divine intervention, and they will do whatever it takes to save your life. Many have shared their personal experiences of divine intervention when they were miraculously saved from a life-threatening situation. So the most important thing to remember when working with these divine celestial beings is to ask for help and guidance when you need it. This opens the doors to invite miracles into your life and to receive clear communication from God and the angels.

How Many Angels Are There?

There is a great curiosity among adults and children about how many angels there are. Scripture does not quote the exact numbers, but it does allude to their massive presence. For example in Daniel 7:10: "A fiery stream issued and came forth from before him: thousand thousands ministered unto him, and ten thousand times ten thousand stood before him: the judgment was set, and the books were opened." And in Matthew 26:53: "Thinkest thou that I cannot now pray to my Father, and he shall presently give me more than twelve legions of angels?"

Everyone has at least two guardian angels assigned to her by God, and they will be with you from birth to the time of death. So to get an idea about how many guardian angels there are in heaven, think about the number of human beings that have existed throughout time and multiply that number by two. Add that number to the divine helpers from the hierarchy of angels which will be discussed later in the book. These include the Seraphim, Cherubim, Thrones, Dominions, Virtues, Powers, Principalities, Archangels, and the other ministering angels who have their individual roles in God's divine order.

Needless to say, one cannot even imagine how many angels there are, and yet it is evident that there are more than enough to go around. You have your personal guardian angels that were specifically assigned to you and later on you will learn about the specific angels you can call upon to help you in different aspects of your life. There are angels in abundance everywhere; just remember to ask for their help and guidance. They will rush to your side and you will feel their presence embrace you in love and protection.

What Do the Angels Look Like?

This is a very important question for those seeking to know more about the angels and how to connect with them. Angels have been portrayed in many forms: with wings and without, male and female, human and child, with a sword or trumpet, radiating in pure light or even appearing in multiple colors of light. This opens discussion to the possibility that everyone may have a different perception of angels. Many interpretations of the angels and what they look like are based on a person's viewpoint, their culture, religious upbringing, belief system, and even their strongest intuitive senses. For example, if a person uses his sense of feeling to experience his surroundings he will most likely feel the presence of the angels around him. He may experience chills down his spine or warmth surrounding him. If someone uses this form of extrasensory perception it's called clairsentience. A more visually oriented person may have an easier time seeing the angels through his inner vision or imagination. This form of extrasensory perception is called clairvoyance.

Clairsentience comes from the French word *clair*, meaning "clear," and sentience, meaning "feeling." This is a form of extrasensory perception where a person uses their sense of feeling to obtain psychic knowledge.

Clairvoyance originated from the seventeenth-century French word *clair* and *voyances* meaning "visibility." It is the apparent ability to gain information about an object, location, or physical event through means other than the known human senses. This is a form of extrasensory perception where a person has the ability to obtain information about a person, an event, or even an object using their sense of inner sight. A clairvoyant is "one who sees clear."

As you seek your own path of spiritual growth and intuition development, you will learn to trust your own experience of the angels and what they look or feel like to you. The angels know you better than you know yourself; be reassured that if you ask them; they will make their presence known to you.

Who Sees the Angels?

The angels are all around you and they appear in many forms. A veil separates you from the ability to see heaven and earth as one. For children, the veil is thinner and their beliefs are not clouded with fear, so many of them can naturally see the angels. Sometimes parents will witness their children interacting with "imaginary friends." This could very possibly be their guardian angels communicating and playing with them.

FACT

In a 2005 Harris Poll, 68 percent of the people polled believed in angels. The number increased to 79 percent for those polled with an education of high school or less. Children tend to be more open and the veil seems to be thinner when you're younger; therefore, there is an increased possibility of experiencing the angelic realm.

When close to the moment of death, some patients have reported witnessing an apparition of an angel or loved one coming to escort them back home. Those who are grieving from the loss of a loved one are also more open to receiving a visitation from the angels. One way the angels can appear to them is during their dream state. Many who have had this experience share that it seemed so real, even though they knew it was a dream.

Have you ever seen flashes or sparkles of light around you? Or have you ever seen a shadow of someone or something out of the corner of your eye? These can be a manifestation of the angels' presence around you.

When divine intervention takes place in a life-threatening situation, the angels can render assistance by superimposing their celestial energy upon another human being. The person chosen may be totally unaware that this is taking place and they may act instinctively. So if you witness a person saving a life and being "in the right place at the right time," you may actually be witnessing an angel performing a miracle.

Who can see the angels? Anyone can open their awareness to see the angels. It takes an open mind and heart and a desire to see beyond the veil.

Are Our Loved Ones Angels?

Many people feel and experience their loved ones who have passed as their guardian angels. Their presence and love never leaves you and, yes, it can feel as if they are still around you acting as your guardian angel. As mentioned before, the angels have never been in a physical form. They are celestial beings of pure light, love, and energy.

ALERT

There are many people who claim to be mediums. You want to invest wisely and choose someone with experience and expertise. Ask around for referrals or do your research on the Internet. You can also look for a Spiritualist Church in your area. This is a spiritual community where the congregation gathers for healing and experienced mediums bring messages through from spirits.

Those that have passed and are now living in the spirit world are better referred to as spirit guides. Some loved ones may choose as part of their soul plan and evolution to be a spirit to help you along your life's journey. It is said that those relatives you were named after at the time of birth have a soul contract to watch over you as spirit guides after their transition to the other side.

If you feel a loss or miss a loved one who is not with you anymore, open the channels of communication with them just like you would contact the angels. They are still with you in spirit and if you choose to, you can attune to their ever-present love and guidance.

If you are interested in communicating with your loved ones in spirit, do your research and seek out an experienced medium. They have natural abilities or they have developed their skills to communicate with this world. Their job is to deliver evidential information and messages of love proving the continuity of life after death. This information can be very healing and it can bring peace to those who are missing their loved ones.

How Can the Angels Help You?

Legions of angels are all around you and wait in assistance to serve you in countless ways. A prayer is a request to God for help, and in truth, there is no request that goes unheard. The angels assist in any way they can to help answer your prayers.

Angels are here to help with healing of all kinds—physical, emotional, and even healing of relationships and pets. If it's physical or emotional healing you need, they will surround you with loving, healing energy and empower you to connect with your own inner healer. If you need outside support from others, they will connect you with the right people or resources you need to help you achieve health and wholeness. If you are in pain they will provide comfort and peace to help ease the pain.

If there is need for healing in your relationships with others, you can call on the angels for help. They may ask you to practice forgiveness, they may encourage you to communicate and express your feelings, or they can even give you peace if you need to let go of the relationship that is causing you pain.

The angels are there to assist all of God's creations, including animals. So if you need guidance or healing for your pets, please remember to ask for whatever you need.

QUESTION

How do I ask the angels for help?
There is no formal way to ask. You can simply call out to the angels by name or you can say, "Angels, gather around me and surround me in your love." Then ask for whatever you need. No prayer is too small or too large. Surrender your prayer to divine resolution and trust that your prayer has been heard and will be answered in divine timing.

There is help from God for all aspects of your life. If you are seeking a soul mate or looking for new friends, ask the angels for divine intervention so you connect with each other at the perfect place and time. If it's time to look for a new place to live or buy a car, make a wish list of what you want. Give it to the angels, then pay attention and expect miracles. If you want help finding a new job or you need courage to live your life purpose, know the angels will be honored to assist you in any way they can. They know that it is possible for you to find the perfect job where you can experience happiness, success, and fulfillment. There are also angels who act as financial advisers in spirit. They can assist you in finding resources or opportunities to increase your income. They can help you heal debt and create financial balance. If you are looking to invest your money wisely, ask them to guide you to the resources that will help you create financial abundance.

Later on in the book you will discover more ways in which the angels can help you in all aspects of your life. You will learn which specific angels to call upon and their prayer of invocation to create miracles.

Do You Need to be "Gifted" to Connect with the Angels?

You don't have to be special or gifted to connect with the angels and receive messages of divine guidance. It simply requires an open mind and heart and a desire to learn.

Contemplate this thought for a moment: When you decided as a soul to birth into a physical life experience, the veil dropped between heaven and earth. Gradually you forgot the truth of who you are and where you came from. If you were to consciously lift the veil again, you would begin to remember that you are not separate from God and the angels. This is why many travel down the spiritual path seeking to reconnect with heaven and earth, so they can re-remember the truth of who they are. So if you believe this to be true, it's perfectly natural and a part of your divine heritage to be one with the angels and God.

Another concept to reflect upon comes from the theory of quantum physics. It states that the universe is energy, you are energy, your thoughts are energy, and everything is energy. Everyone has energy centers called the *chakras*. They run throughout the body and they act as transmitters of energy. When your chakras are flowing and balanced your intuitive senses are heightened, attuning you to the energy of God and the angels. In this flow of consciousness you can gain clarity and receive messages of divine guidance. So if everyone has energy centers and God and the angels are energy, then everyone has the capability to make that connection.

Hopefully you can understand that God did not bless some with a special gift to communicate with the divine. We are all blessed in the oneness of God. Through the eyes of God and the angels there is no one more special than the other. It is a choice, and everyone has the ability to connect with the angels. It takes curiosity and a willingness to expand your consciousness beyond what you can see and touch. Choose to travel down the path of spiritual growth. Be open and willing to learn all you can. Learn to meditate, open your chakras, and attune your senses to the oneness of energy all around you. As you take this journey, you will witness the miracles of heaven and earth as one.

Be Open to Angels

It's very natural to be a skeptic before a believer. You have your own personal history of religion and what's been ingrained in your belief system since childhood. You may have had a negative experience and you are uncertain what to believe. If this is true for you, you can ask the angels to help you heal any old wounds so you can accept the love and peace of God and the angels.

Be a student and a curious seeker on the path of spirituality. Remember, the angels work only in the vibration of love, and this is their pure intention. If you experience fear, it resonates within you. This fear may come from a variety of sources: your parents' beliefs, what you were taught in school, society, religion, television, and possibly fears from past life experiences. No matter what the source may be, you can change your belief system and decide what's true for you.

Your truth will unfold with experience. As you open up to the angels, pay attention to your feelings and only do what feels right to you. The angels want you to feel safe and protected. They will walk side by side with you as you learn and grow. If you need to rebuild your trust in God, know that the angels are honored to assist you. They will give you everything you need to do this.

When you invite the angels into your life, expect positive changes to occur. One of the greatest gifts you will receive is knowing that you are never alone. The fear of being alone is a deep, unconscious fear that many deal with. When the angels are a part of your life this fear no longer exists. As you give your prayers and requests to the angels you begin to trust you have a team working behind the scenes. You experience a sense of peace and relief that you are not alone in your worries. You begin to witness your prayers being answered through synchronistic events and coincidences, and you experience a feeling of inner joy and magic. Life becomes exciting, and you look forward to playing with the angels every day.

It's important to know that the angels feel honored to assist humanity. They recognize how brave you are to journey through your life experiences and they have compassion for every difficulty you go through. They will wrap you in their wings of love and help you in any way they can. They know you have soul lessons to learn and these challenges may be an opportunity for growth. During these difficult times ask the angels for strength, courage, and understanding. They will surround you in loving support and encouragement.

Lastly, the angels see you and your life experiences through the eyes of unconditional love. You are never judged for your choices or actions. There is nothing you could ever have said or done that would compromise the angels' love for you. They want you to embrace yourself in unconditional love the way you are embraced by God and the angels. If you learn to accept their love it will be easier for you to love yourself, and when you love yourself it is easier to love another. The angels celebrate each and every time a human being remembers to love him or herself, and in turn, to love each other. As they witness this taking place, their purpose as messengers between heaven and earth is fulfilled.

CHAPTER 2

History of Angels

It is unknown if the idea of angels arose in different cultures independently, if the idea traveled from culture to culture, or which cultural ideas seeded the beliefs of others. For thousands of years, merchants and mercenaries, wise men and priests, prophets and pagans, and those uprooted by famine or war have wandered and intermingled. Thus it is that you can find the concept of angels in the mythologies of nearly every known ancient culture.

Ancient Angels

Angels have been recorded in history by many different cultures throughout the world. Some scholars say that the earliest religious representation of the angels dates back to the city of Ur, in the Euphrates Valley, c. 4000–2500 B.C.E. A stele, which is a stone slab, showed a winged figure descended from one of the seven heavens to pour the water of life from an overflowing jar into the cup held by the king. Other records show that in Mesopotamia, there were giant winged creatures, part human, part animal, known as griffins. And in Egypt, Nepthys, the twin sister of the goddess Isis, is shown in paintings and reliefs enfolding the dead in her beautiful wings. Her image is found carved on the inner right-hand door of Shrine III in the tomb of Tutankhamen, c. fourteenth century B.C.E. Her angelic representation encompasses the dead pharaoh and protects him from all harm.

FACT

The ancient Egyptians believed that each person born into the world had a supernatural double, called her *ka*, who was born alongside the person and stayed as a part of her life ever after. The ka was, in one sense, what we now call a guardian angel.

Without doubt, based upon archeological evidence and other prehistoric information, there were angels long before Christianity appeared on the religious stage. Angels are most ancient, predating even early Judaism. Images of angels appear all over Asia Minor, in different cultures in the ancient civilized world, and westward into Greece and Italy. Iris, "the rainbow of Zeus," and Hermes, messenger of the gods and guide of souls, both wear wings and serve angelic functions, carrying messages and bringing aid to humans. The famous Greek sculpture Winged Victory (Nike) served as a model for the Renaissance angels that proliferated into the Middle Ages, firmly establishing the concept of angels in that period.

Angels are also found in the Asian cultures represented by Buddhism and Taoism. Without question, the idea of angels appears everywhere in Asia Minor; from there it extended into the Mediterranean basin of Greece and Italy, where it would be transformed.

Angels in the Old Testament

Several angels appear in stories throughout the Hebrew Bible (The Old Testament). In the earlier books the angels are described as heavenly beings created by God. As religious beliefs transformed throughout the ages so did the view of the angels. There were angels who brought news of death and destruction and others who killed thousands. There were also stories in the Bible about ministering angels who provided protection, comfort, and delivered words of wisdom from God.

ESSENTIAL

It is said that there were angels who stood with flaming swords at the gates of the Garden of Eden. These guardians wanted to prevent Adam and Eve from returning to eat the fruit from the Tree of Immortal Life after they were expelled from the garden.

As you read the following stories from the Old Testament, allow your own truth to unfold as you learn more about the angels and their roles in history.

Abraham and Sarah

In Genesis 21:14–20, A young woman, Hagar, finds herself pregnant by an important man, Abraham, who has a powerful wife, Sarah. Sarah was not pleased, and when the poor girl Hagar could take no more abuse, she ran away. During her flight, she found a spring on the road to Shur and stopped there to rest and refresh herself. Here she had her first of two encounters with angelic presences, who told her to return home and that she would bear a son named Ishmael. After her son was born, they were cast into the desert. Dying of thirst, Hagar prayed as she had been taught to do. As she did, she heard the voice she had heard earlier: "What is the matter with you, Hagar? Do not fear, for God has heard the voice of the lad where he is," said the voice of the angel of God, and Hagar took heart hearing this call from heaven. "Then God opened her eyes and she saw a well of water; and she went and filled the skin with water, and gave the lad a drink. And God was with the lad."

Jacob

Abraham's grandson, Jacob, had a difficult experience with an angel. Jacob had a shaded history of bad choices: he cheated his brother Esau out of his inheritance, he tricked his uncle Laban out of all his wealth and possessions, he married twice, and he had illegitimate children. Later in his life Jacob returned home wanting peace and forgiveness with his brother, but he was afraid his brother would kill him. One night, an angel came and Jacob wrestled with the angel all night long. In the end, Jacob prevailed. He then demanded a boon (blessing) from the angel, who gave it without ever identifying itself. But Jacob figured out that his struggle had been with a supernatural being, and since he had won, he concluded that all would be well with his brother. Jacob remained deeply involved with angelic presences all through his life, and when he reached the end of it, reviewing his experiences with the holy ones, he in wonder exclaimed, "God . . . has been my shepherd all my life to this day, the angel who has redeemed me from all evil."

ESSENTIAL

This same Jacob is the one famous for "Jacob's ladder." He saw in a vision the multitude of angels ascending and descending a ladder that reached up to heaven. The Bible does not report whether or not the angels on the ladder in Jacob's vision had wings, but one would presume not, since they were climbing up and down the ladder.

Abraham and Isaac

One of the most famous biblical stories of angels has to do with Abraham and his son Isaac. One day, Abraham heard the voice of God spoken through an angel calling out to him. Genesis 22:11 states, "And the angel of the Lord called unto him out of heaven, and said, 'Abraham, Abraham' and he said, 'Here am I.'" The voice instructed him to sacrifice his son Isaac. It ordered him to take the boy to the top of a remote mountain and slit his throat in the manner of the usual sacrificial lamb, and to let his blood run out as an offering to prove to God that he would surrender to his will. Without question, Abraham took his son to the top of a mountain, laid him across an altar, and when he was ready to sacrifice his beloved son an angel appeared. The angel's voice stopped him and commanded, "Lay not thy hand upon the lad." Abraham obeyed, no doubt thankfully, and at that moment he spotted a sheep with its woolly fleece entangled in the thorns of a bush. He caught it and sacrificed it, offering it up to God in place of his son.

FACT

The only angel mentioned by name in the history books of the Old Testament is the Angel of Death. This angel was an agent of destruction, presumably acting under direct orders from God. At the time of David, the Angel of Death destroyed 90,000 people and on another occasion, in the Assyrian army camp, it killed 185,000 soldiers.

Moses

For forty years the Israelites were in bondage in Egypt, and the all-powerful Pharaoh refused to free them from their slavery. Moses, desperate for his people to achieve their freedom, declared, "But when we cried out to the Lord, He heard our voice and sent an angel and brought us out of Egypt" (Numbers 20:16). After having delivered the people of Israel from Egypt and overseen their emancipation from the Pharaoh, the angel did not forsake them. The angel divided the waters of the Red Sea so they could pass through without getting wet. Then when the powerful army of Egypt was in hot pursuit, the "angel of God who had been going before the camp of Israel, moved and went behind them; and the pillar of cloud moved from before them and stood behind them. So it came between the camp of Egypt and the camp of Israel and there was the cloud along with the darkness, yet it gave light at night. Thus the one did not come near the other all night" (Exodus 14:19–20)

Angels in the New Testament

The view and roles of the angels change dramatically in the New Testament. Gone are the Angels of Death and Vengeance, and also gone are the heroic deeds of angels. No longer do angels bring death and destruction, nor do they go about killing the firstborn of unbelievers. They are also no longer depicted as bland creatures without personalities. In the New Testament, the images of the angels are portrayed as being more personalized. From being purely abstract extensions of God, angels became friends to human beings, powers that could be called upon in times of stress or need.

See for yourself and draw your own conclusion as you now read and reflect upon the stories from the New Testament.

Annunciation

One of the most important angelic visitations in the view of the early Christians is the Annunciation, the speaking of those famous words: *Ave Maria, gratia plena, Dominus tecum: Hail Mary, full of grace, the Lord is with thee*. The angel came to Mary and said, "Do not be afraid, Mary; for you have found favor with God. And behold, you will conceive in your womb, and bear a son, and you shall name him Jesus. He will be great, and will be called the Son of the Most High; and the Lord God will give Him the throne of His Father David; and He will reign over the house of Jacob forever; and His kingdom will have no end" (Luke 1:30-33). When Mary's pregnancy became obvious, Joseph, her husband, was embarrassed by this situation. But an angel appeared to him in a dream, saying, "Joseph, son of David, do not be afraid . . . for that which has been conceived in her is of the Holy Spirit. And she will bear a Son; and you shall call His name Jesus, for it is He who will save His people from their sins" (Matthew 1:20-21). After the birth of the Savior, the angel continued to look after the family and appeared twice to Joseph, giving him instructions on where to go so he could keep his family safe.

Angels after the Crucifixion of Christ

The Gospel of Matthew does mention that two angels, without wings but with "a countenance like lightning" and "garments white as snow," were found sitting inside the cave in which Christ had been laid in burial. Mary Magdalene and Mary went to the tomb to care for the dead body, but when they arrived there was no body to be seen anywhere; It had disappeared. One of the angels informed them that the reason there wasn't a corpse was because Christ had "risen up from the dead." Not knowing what to think about this extraordinary occurrence, the women rushed to get the men to take a look for themselves, and they too, found the tomb empty. This story is told in many different versions by different Gospel writers, but the basic elements are the same.

Paul's Angel

In Vision of Paul, in *New Testament Apocrypha*, Paul is guided by an angel on a complicated and confusing journey through the territory of heaven and hell. The narrative shifts back and forth between beauty and horror. He has visions of utter bliss and visions of terrible punishments. Finally, the angel leads Paul to the door of the third heaven. Paul says, "And I looked at it and saw that it was a golden gate and that there were two golden tables above the pillars full of letters. (These letters are the names of the righteous, already inscribed in heaven while they still live on earth.) And again the angel turned to me and said: "Blessed are you if you enter in by these gates." After entering the gates of paradise, Paul encounters the ancient prophet Enoch, who issues a warning to Paul not to reveal what he has seen in the third heaven. Then, the angel descends, with Paul, to the second heaven and thence to the earthly paradise, where the souls of those deemed righteous await the resurrection.

FACT

It was absolutely crucial for the new early church to draw a firm line of distinction between Christ and angels, who were considered to be the lesser intermediaries between God and his people. No doubt angels had their work to do delivering messages from God, but it had to be Christ who was the closest communicator to God.

Then the angel puts Paul in a golden boat and the narrative continues: "And about three thousand angels were singing a hymn before me until I reached the City of Christ." When he reaches the City of Christ he says, "I saw in the midst of this city a great altar, very high, and there was David standing near the altar, whose countenance shone as the sun, and he held in his hands a psaltery and harp, and he sang psalms, saying Alleluia. And all in the city replied Alleluia till the very foundations of the city were shaken. . . .Turning round I saw golden thrones placed in each gate, and on them men having golden diadems and gems: and I looked carefully and saw inside between the twelve men thrones in glorious rank . . . so that no one is able to recount their praise. . . . Those thrones belong to those who had goodness and understanding of heart and made themselves fools for the sake of the Lord God." It ends with Paul seeing 200 angels preceding Mary and singing hymns, and Mary informs him that he has been granted the unusual favor of coming to this place before he dies.

Isaiah's Angel

The story of the Ascension of Isaiah (in *New Testament Apocrypha*) is far less complex. The prophet is taken out of his body and led by an angel to the first heaven above the sky: "And I saw a throne in the midst, and on the right and on the left of it were angels singing praises." He asks whom they praise and is told by the angels, "It is for the praise of him who is in the seventh heaven, for him who rests in eternity among his saints, and for his Beloved, whence I have been sent unto you."

FACT

Angels were a difficult matter for the early church, especially concerning whether they had bodies or were incorporeal or pure spirit. While Scripture clearly states that angels appear as men, it also states plainly that angels are *spiritus* (Hebrews 1:14).

The "heaven above the sky" is the first heaven of seven, and the angel then takes Isaiah to the second heaven, where once more he sees a throne and angels to the right and to the left. Awed by the situation, the holy prophet prostrates himself to worship the angel on the throne, but is told not to do that; angels are not to be worshiped.

Ascending further, each of the succeeding heavens is filled with more glory than the one before, and the sixth heaven is of such glorious brightness that it makes the previous five dark by comparison. Isaiah wants to remain in this place of wonder, but the angel explains that Isaiah's time on earth isn't finished, but Jesus himself allows Isaiah to enter the seventh heaven. The vision ends with Christ escorting Isaiah down through all the heavens to earth to witness the Annunciation and the Incarnation.

The Church's View on Angels

Constantine the Great (306–337), who was the emperor of Byzantium, converted to Christianity after having a powerful vision of a cross in the sky. It was profound enough to cause him to convert to Christianity even though it was still a minority religion at this time. This conversion convinced many others to follow. During this time period he also declared that angels have wings.

No doubt Constantine had a lot to do with the renewed interest in angels. At that time most people were used to stories of fairies and it was a small stretch from a winged fairy to an angel with wings.

What concerned the church fathers was that the common people were worshiping angels, and they believed that only God and His Son could be worshiped. This dilemma was settled by St. Paul when he attacked and denied the worship angels, with his usual "I know what's best here" attitude. Nevertheless, the First Council of Nicea in 325 decided that belief in angels was to be church dogma. Apparently, this decision unleashed a rampant renewal of the angel worship that St. Paul had so detested. It was proclaimed idolatry in 343, less than twenty years after Nicea, by another council.

Finally, in 787, to end the controversy, the second Council of Nicea, called the Seventh Ecumenical Synod, was held. It declared a limited dogma of the archangels, which included their names, their specific functions, and also formally legitimated the depiction of angels in art.

The Jewish Tradition

While all the debate about angels was going on in the predominantly Christian world in Europe, a Jewish population lived side by side with their Christian neighbors, yet remained totally isolated from them. It's hard to see just how any metaphysical or theological ideas might have been exchanged between the two communities, one clearly superior in number and political clout. Thus separated, and trying to maintain their own identity as a people through their language and traditional culture, medieval Jews lived in a religious vacuum.

Their great book and the term *Kabbalah* (also *Kabala, Kabbala, Cabala, Cabalah*) is derived from the Hebrew root *kbl*, which means "to receive." It refers to matters that are occult (meaning "hidden") or mystical knowledge so secret that it is rarely written down. It is transmitted from master to neophyte, or student, orally, in order to protect the secrets from being revealed to those not prepared to receive them or unworthy to do so.

All of the books of the Kabbalah constitute a system of guidance to the path to God, on which the believer is taken through a series of heavenly halls guided by angels. It is replete with long descriptions of how to make the journey safely up through a tree of angels, and it gives the secret passwords to bypass demons encountered along the path.

FACT

When the Jews were exiled from Babylon, Zoroastrianism was the primary religion, and with it came the concept of good angels on one side and bad angels, or demons, opposite, in an eternal tug of war. This notion of bad, or fallen angels, quite possibly influenced the Jewish tradition and later worked its way into Christianity.

In the Kabbalah are ten sefirot, or angels, considered to be the fundamental channels of divine energy. Their names are Foundation, Splendor, Eternity, Beauty, Power, Grace, Knowledge, Wisdom, Understanding, and Crown. They are arranged in the shape of a tree and called the Tree of Life. The top of this tree is occupied by the singular angel Metatron, and beyond all of this is the mystical contemplation of God. It is so distant and removed that it makes it incomprehensible to ever know God directly, but only experience Him through His angels. As you can see, the angels play an important role in the teachings of the Kabbalah. They once again act as intermediaries between heaven and earth and oversee what occurs on earth.

Shamanism

Even the world's oldest religious practice, shamanism, practiced by Native Americans, incorporates interaction with winged beings. These often come in the form of eagles or ravens or spirits and are not usually associated with the later angelic iconography.

Among Native Americans, great birds Raven and Eagle were believed to help humans, to heal or bring fire, or to carry messages from God. In this tradition, too, friendly spirits, or familiars, walk among the people and guard them from harm. These winged creatures are considered to be of great help to the tribal shaman in his work.

Angels in Art

Angels have been portrayed in art and literature throughout history. However, depictions of them in stone are the first forms of known angel art. In early recorded history one can find images of angels in many cultures around the world.

In Christian art from the twelfth century onward, angels almost always wear halos, though halos are not mentioned in Scripture as being part of standard angel gear. Artists painted halos to float over the heads of Jesus, angels, and saints, presumably to indicate that these were supernatural beings, different from humans.

Gothic Design

As Europe emerged from the Dark Ages and the great Gothic cathedrals began to rise during the twelfth through fifteenth centuries, the Gothic form dominated art and architecture. Sculpture and stained glass windows were part of the Gothic design, and these magnificent cathedrals that seem to rise up into the very heavens were graced with beautiful depictions of the entire Christian story and included a plenitude of angels and angelic hosts. For example, the angels surrounding the main portal of the cathedral at Chartres, France, are there to express the sense of perfection of God's creation as well as the sense humans had developed of angels being their protectors and guides or guardians.

Rembrandt and Leonardo da Vinci

Rembrandt was continually inspired to paint angels, many of which appear in his larger canvases; there are also glimpses of angels in his multitude of sketches. His brilliant use of bold light illuminates the figures in his paintings, especially in his piece *The Sacrifice of Isaac*, where an angel is stopping Abraham from sacrificing his son. He passionately illustrates the angels' existence, and he dramatically depicts the angels' role in protecting and guiding humanity even in desperate times.

QUESTION

Do angels really have wings?
This has been a debate throughout history. The image of the winged angel has been burned into our consciousness by centuries of beautiful and compelling art, much of it painted or sculpted by great masters, who represented angels with wings most magnificent. However, even though Scripture speaks of angels flying, there is no specific mention of *wings* per se.

One of the great Renaissance painters of all time was Leonardo da Vinci. When you view his famous works of art, you would imagine he had very clear visions of the angels' beauty and grace. You can clearly see this when you witness his painting of a young angel holding Jesus's robe in the *Baptism of Christ* and also when he shows the close relationship Tobias had with Archangel Michael in *Tobias and the Angel*. He also made copious notes regarding wings and flight in his notebooks, accompanied by many drawings speculating on how flight was accomplished by the nonsupernatural winged beings.

Russian and Greek Orthodox Icons

Not only Christian Europe, but also the Russian and Greek orthodox forms of Christianity contributed to great artistic renditions of angels (and saints). These brilliantly executed paintings, mostly on wood instead of canvas, are called icons. Their jewel-like mystical quality is riveting to the beholder's eye, and they are intended to be visual meditations for the purpose of direct contact with the image portrayed.

CHAPTER 3

Who's Who in the Angelic Realm

There are an infinite number of angelic beings in God's kingdom and they all have different roles to serve and help humanity. The more you can understand who they are and how they can aid you, the more useful they become in your life. God created these messengers of light to bridge the communication between heaven and earth. Learn about the different hierarchies of the angelic realm and discover how many divine helpers are ready to assist you on your journey.

Historic Hierarchy of the Angels

The angels do not rank themselves or see themselves as a hierarchy. It was by human design and the churches that the angels were ordered in this way. The various religions found this hierarchical arrangement necessary for several reasons. The Jewish patriarchs were producing angels swiftly and the Catholic Church was naming more and more angels. Even the great St. Augustine complained that angels "breed like flies." There were so many angels, and in order to clear the confusion and arrange them in some kind of sequential order, a hierarchy system was formed. In the Old Testament there were only two orders of angels, the Seraphim and Cherubim. Then it is said that Dionysius the Areopagite, a disciple of St. Paul, added seven more in the New Testament: Thrones, Dominions, Virtues, Powers, Principalities, Archangels, and Angels.

FACT

When researched, there are hundreds of angels' names recorded, but there are also variations of these names. For example, the archangel Raziel is also known as Akraziel, Saraqael, Suriel, Galisur, N'Zuriel, and Uriel. The seraph Semyaza's variations are Samiaza, Shemhazai, Amezyarak, Azael, Azaziel, and Uzza. Metatron had a mystery name, Bizbul, but he had over a 100 other names as well.

The following are the nine orders of angels from the New Testament. They are arranged according to their importance.

THE FIRST TRIAD (THE HIGHEST TRIAD)

- **Seraphim** are the highest order of God's angelic servants and sit closest to the throne of God. They are of pure light and because they are so bright they may be hard for humans to see. Angels in the Seraphim choir are Michael, Seraphiel, Jehoel, Kemuel, Metatron, Uriel, and Nathanael.
- **Cherubim** are the guardians of the fixed stars, keepers of the heavenly records, and bestowers of knowledge. They are the angels of harmony, protection, and wisdom and they channel positive energy from

the divine. The Cherubim choir consists of Gabriel, Cherubiel, Ophaniel, Raphael, and Zophiel.

- **Thrones** are the angels who bring God's justice to earth. They create and send positive energy to the earth and all its inhabitants. Orifiel, Zaphkiel, Zabkiel, Jolhiel (or Zophiel), and Raziel are in the Thrones choir.

THE SECOND TRIAD (MIDDLE TRIAD)

- **Dominions** are the divine leaders who regulate the angels' duties. They are the angels of intuition and wisdom and the majesty of God is manifested through them. The Dominions choir angels are Zadkiel, Hashmal, Zacharael, and Muriel.
- **Virtues** are known as "the miracle angels." They are sent to earth to help those that want to make the impossible into the possible. They are here to help those that feel called to serve and bring harmony and peace into the world. The Virtues choir angels are Uzziel, Gabriel, Michael, Peliel, Barbiel, Sabriel, Haniel, Hamaliel, and Tarshish.
- **Powers** are the defenders and protectors of the world. They keep track of human history and they are the organizers of world religions. The Powers choir includes Camael, Raphael, and Verchiel.

THE THIRD TRIAD (LOWEST TRIAD)

- **Principalities** are the protectors of politics and religion. You can call on them to help with leadership problems and human rights. Angels in the Principalities choir are Nisroc, Naniel, Requel, Cerviel, and Amael.
- **Archangels** rule over all the angels. They enjoy human contact and they can be there simultaneously for all of humanity. So even if everyone is praying for Archangel Michael's help at the same time, he can be there for all. The Archangels are Ariel, Azrael, Chamuel, Gabriel, Haniel, Jeremiel, Jophiel, Metatron, Michael, Raguel, Raphael, Raziel, Sandalphon, Ureil, and Zadkiel.
- **Angels** are placed at the bottom of the hierarchy. They are the messengers of God working the closest with humanity. There are many different kinds of angels in this choir, including the guardian angels.

Their names are numerous and varied and you will find more information about these angels and their roles later on in the book.

ESSENTIAL

It is inferred from various sources that the higher orders of angels—Seraphim, Cherubim, Thrones, Dominions—are the ones who constantly praise God and do not leave heaven to perform His chores on earth.

Remember the hierarchy system is arranged by human design, not by the angels. If you look throughout scripture it gives very little support to the angels, let alone hierarchical arrangements of them. Some modern religionists have taken issue with the very idea of angelic hierarchies. One, philosopher Mortimer Adler, finds such speculation "highly entertaining." And Christian evangelist writer Timothy Jones, in *Celebration of Angels*, states flatly:

Dionysius simply had no way to determine if his nine-fold ordering was literally true. Nor do we. Even Paul the apostle, who claimed to have been caught up into the "third heaven" (2 Corinthians 12:2), hinted that such things are not to be told. . . . Indeed, in Scripture, we gain only glimpses and fragments of how the angels might be organized. . . . However tantalizing the recorded glimpses of angels in Scripture are, they are ultimately just that: glimpses. We can take great comfort, however, in knowing that populating the heavenly spheres are creatures so great they boggle and frustrate our every attempt to pin them down.

Choose to use the hierarchy system as a guide and a tool to better understand who the angels are and what their different roles are in helping out humanity.

Guardian Angels

Guardian angels are among the angels in the lowest triad and they are the divine helpers closest to all living beings. Everyone has at least two guardian angels that were gifted by God. They will be with you from the time of birth to the time you pass from this earth plane. Your guardian angels are your personal angels and they are not assigned to anyone but you.

A poll published in *Time* magazine revealed that 69 percent of Americans believe in angels and 46 percent of that group believe they have a personal guardian angel.

Your guardian angel is here to assist you in every aspect of your life. They can make your life easier if you let them. Remember, your guardian angels love you with the same unconditional love as God, and there is nothing you could ever do or say that would change this love. Take time out of your busy schedule to pray with your guardian angels. Ask them for the help you need. Then listen, feel, and pay attention to how they answer your prayers. They know you very well and they know exactly how to get your attention.

Ascended Masters

Even though the ascended masters are not mentioned in the hierarchy, it is important to point them out. They are God's divine helpers and they play their role in helping humanity evolve. These beings of light walked before you on this earth. During their lifetimes they were great teachers. They have now ascended into heaven and their role is to help all those that need them.

Among these great beings and teachers are the Blessed Mother Mary, Jesus, Quan Yin, Buddha, Moses, Mohammed, Serapis Bey, Saint Theresa, and Saint Francis.

The ascended masters are well aware of your prayers and concerns. They have compassion and understanding of what you go through as human beings because they walked the journey themselves. Just like the angels, they honor your free will and free choice, so you need to ask for their help. Trust that they will be by your side, instantaneously, ready to assist you in unconditional love. They are very powerful enlightened beings and they have the ability to manifest healing and miracles into your life. Invite them into your life and witness the magic that begins to unfold.

Nature Angels

The fairies are also not mentioned in the hierarchy, but they have their importance as well because they are the angels of nature. Their vibration is very connected to the earth and their place in the hierarchy is in between the angels and humans.

FACT

The fairies are most prominently found in nature and among flower gardens. If you wish to connect with them and ask for their help, spend time outdoors. Talk to them and share your requests. Ask the fairies to clear your energy and raise your vibration so you can attract only good into your life. Then listen and connect with their playful wisdom and allow them to guide you.

Fairies are very playful and creative and they love to hang around children. Because of this children are more likely to see them, but they also like to assist adults, too. They will nudge you to invite more play into your life, especially if your time is overloaded with work and family responsibilities. They love to play the role of matchmaker, and if you are looking for a soul mate they will help you find one. They love creativity and will provide inspiration to help you with any project: designing your gardens, your home, or any other creative endeavor. The fairies can play a powerful role in helping you manifest your dreams into reality. Ask them to gather around you and give them a wish list of what you want. Then ask them to show you that the impossible is possible. Be open to their miracles of manifestation and trust that they will joyfully help you. Then pay attention and watch the magic unfold.

The fairies ask you to be conscious of taking care of the earth. They will team with you even more when they see you picking up trash that others have left behind. They ask you to use products that are environmentally conscious and to do what you can to save the earth. Just as you need help from the angels, the fairies ask for your help to take care of Mother Earth.

Loved Ones in Spirit

When discussing vibration, those that have died and transitioned into the spirit world resonate somewhere between the fairies and human beings. This is important to mention when reflecting on vibration and the hierarchy of the angels. When you raise your vibration and connect your energy with the angelic realm, you will receive loving, supportive guidance that's directed from God. When you communicate with loved ones who have passed you may still be communicating with certain aspects of their personalities. For example, let's say that you want guidance from a particular relative in spirit about buying a new home. If he or she had been conservative in life and liked to save money, that personality trait would still be there. It might influence the guidance given.

Angels of Birth and Death

There are special "birth angels" who helped you birth into this life experience, and there are also "death angels" that help you journey back home when it's time.

FACT

The ascended masters' vibration and their place on the hierarchy is right below the archangels and above the angels. Just like the archangels, they have the ability to be with everyone simultaneously so they can serve all humans with great love and care.

Many people believe that the just-born infant is born with an "angel twin," the guardian angel that accompanies it throughout life. Others believe that there are special birth angels, that attend the birth to make sure that all is well and then they depart for other birthings. The author of *Angels in Action*, Robert H. Kirven, asserts that "spiritual protection of infants is typical of angelic occupations in that it is a kind of service [and that] angels have a special affection for newborn children." Kirven goes on to say that other angels and spirits replace these earliest guardians when infants grow out of infancy and into childhood. The question as to whether the *first* angel assigned to a child is the lifetime guardian angel has never been definitively answered. Kirven bases his opinion on his extensive study of the works of the eighteenth-century scientist-turned-mystic Emanuel Swedenborg.

Angels also attend death. Emanuel Swedenborg, who wrote prolifically about angels, gives an account of how he first encountered "some of the kindest and most profoundly loving of all angels," in what we would today call a near-death experience. He explains that people "wake up" after dying, gradually becoming aware of angels at their heads. These "death angels" are apparently able to communicate with persons who have just died and make them feel peaceful, safe, and happily welcomed to their new state. The transition period, whether it is easy for the person that has passed or difficult (for some resist believing they are dead), is supervised by these special angels.

ESSENTIAL

Laylah is an angel of the night, and his name comes from the Hebrew word meaning sleep. Laylah watches over newborns and helps them move through the adjustment of being in a physical body.

How comforting is it to know that God sends these angels of birth and death to help you transition during these challenging times. It once again confirms how loved you are and that you will never, ever be alone.

Fallen Angels

There are many questions asked about the concept of fallen angels. Angels glow in the energy of pure light and love. They communicate only messages of love and encouragement. They always act and guide from a place of unconditional love.

Fallen angels are not a creation of God's love. They are a manifestation of man's fear. When someone is entangled in the energy of fear they are more likely to experience these dark beings. They are usually reflections of what has been programmed in their mind as evil, maybe the devil, Satan, and any other scary apparition.

There is also another form of fallen angels to be aware of called earth-bound spirits. These are deceased humans who are hanging around the earth plane. This can happen for a variety of reasons, but most often people refer to them as ghosts. Again, if you are bothered by these earthbound spirits call upon Archangel Michael and ask him to escort them back home.

If you would like to avoid these fear-based manifestations, keep your thoughts focused on love and continually surround yourself with the presence of the angels.

CHAPTER 4

Raising Your Vibration to Connect with the Angels

Heaven and earth may seem like two different places, but in truth they are one. To lift the veil and experience heaven you need to understand the concept of vibration. To better explain this, think about a radio and how you can change the channel and tune into different stations to listen to various expressions of music. The same is true for the angelic realm. You simply need to attune your energy and raise your vibration to connect with the different hierarchies of angels. As you use the tools given in this book to help you raise your vibration, you will realize that the kingdom of heaven is found from going within.

Energy and Vibration

It's important to understand the concept of energy and vibration so you can experience the angels with all your senses. As discussed before, you are energy and the angels are energy. If this is true, then why can't you see the angels like you can see other human beings? It has to do with the concept of vibration. The meaning of vibration from the *Merriam-Webster Dictionary* is, "a characteristic emanation, aura, or spirit that infuses or vitalizes someone or something and that can be instinctively sensed or experienced." Here is the key: In order to see or feel the energy of the angels, you need to raise your vibration to be in tune with their energy. The angels vibrate in the energy of pure divine love and humans resonate between the energy of fear and love.

ESSENTIAL

If you're ever having a bad day and want to feel better, simply smile. Fake it if you need to. Try it right now; smile and see how you feel. Notice how your energy changes. This is a simple technique to raise your vibration. You can change any situation, no matter where you are or who you are with, by just smiling.

The energy of fear resonates at a lower vibration, while the energy of love resonates at a higher vibration. Think about the last time you were around someone who was angry, depressed, or confused. What "vibe" did you get from that person? Did they lift you up or bring you down? Now think of an occasion when you were with someone who was fun, who made you laugh, and you had a really good time. What vibe did you get from this person? Did her energy lift your spirits or bring you down?

If you would like to hear, feel, and see the angels, you need to raise your vibration to become one with their energy. Your next question might be, "How do I raise my vibration?" The following are ways to raise your vibration, but the keys are patience and practice.

Following are different methods you can use to raise your vibration so you can attune yourself to the angels and receive messages of divine guidance. Play with them and discover which ones feel comfortable to you and your lifestyle. It's important to find a method that you enjoy and you feel connected to. When this happens, you are more likely to stick with it and use it to bond with the angels.

Silence

When sitting in stillness and silence, the mind and the body relax. By becoming still you can seek to find your center, where the ego mind quiets and the gateway to the divine opens. The angels want to get your attention and communicate with you, and it's easier when you can find this place to connect.

Silence is the pathway to follow on your journey to the center of the self. In this silence you begin to experience a unity and you recognize you are one with the divine. Almost everyone has had this experience at some time, perhaps while sitting by a lake in silence and solitude, gazing at a sleeping child, or caught alone and awestruck by a magnificent sunset on a country road. These are mystical moments that connect you to the larger totality of which you are a part. You are transfixed and transformed for the moment. It's difficult to describe the feeling, and you have no adequate words for that sense of having stepped outside your normal boundaries into something grand and inspiring. It happens in the silence, and this is where you can sense, feel, and experience the angels.

FACT

In order to experience the presence of angels, you must dare to turn off the electronic sounds around you. In order to come to your spiritual center, listen instead to the simpler sounds around you. You might hear a bird chirping, rain dripping, or the simple sound of your own breath or perhaps the flutter of an angel's wings or an angel singing.

Silence is a great spiritual teacher who guides you and illuminates your way when it is dark. In the silence of the inner self, you reach truth, and in so doing, you find your angels there, guiding and gracing you and delivering the messages you need to hear. The angels want to help you and they want you to be able to recognize their presence in your life.

Fortunately, you do not have to retire to a monastery or become a hermit to experience the contemplative silence that is at the heart of experiencing the angelic world. You can achieve your own silence and recognize the presence of angels by practicing silence on a daily basis.

Guided Meditation

Some people have a difficult time sitting in silence because their mind is too busy. If this sounds familiar to you, then try guided meditation. In guided meditation you listen to the voice of someone who guides you through the process.

Most guided meditations combine soothing music with the use of visualization. Both techniques are used to help you relax and to enhance the experience. You can sit back and relax as you are soothed by the music and all you need to do is follow the guide's soothing voice as they bring you into meditation. Your thoughts are focused on following the direction of the guide and it's easier to let go as you allow your experiences to unfold.

Most guided mediations start with a deep relaxation of the body and the mind. After you slow down your breath and release the tension in your body, you will physically and mentally relax. When this happens you naturally open up the pathway to other states of consciousness. In this altered state you can enhance your spiritual growth and development and you can communicate with the angels. Ask the angels to work with you in meditation to help you better understand who they are and how they can help you. Try guided meditation and see if it's right for you. It can be one of the most powerful ways to attune to the vibration of the angels.

ESSENTIAL

There are many forms of meditation. It's best to experiment with different types of meditation to discover what works best for you. If you have a hard time quieting your mind or if you are just getting started, you might want to seek out a meditation class in your area or purchase a guided meditation CD.

The following guided meditation will help you raise your vibration so you can attune to the angels and receive their loving guidance. During this attunement you can release your fears and ask the angels for the help you need. They will work with you during the attunement, and they will help you raise your vibration so you can feel them, hear them, and possibly see them.

It would be helpful if you could record the words beforehand so you can simply relax and listen during meditation. Remember to speak slowly and with a soothing voice when you record the meditation. Try playing soothing music in the background during your recording.

Take some nice deep breaths and just close your eyes. Set the intention with your angels to attune to their energy and raise your vibration so you can easily see, feel, hear, and sense their loving presence. (Pause)

Now ask the angels to surround you in a beautiful circle of divine light, love, and protection. Take a moment and breathe with them and feel their unconditional love flow into every cell of your being. As you do this, your body begins to relax. Feel this soothing and healing divine light flow into the top of your head, relaxing your scalp; all the muscles in your scalp relax. Now, feel it flow into your forehead and then your eyes, cheeks, jaw, and your mouth. All the muscles in your face relax. (Pause) Feel the light and relaxation flow into your neck, relaxing your neck. Feel it flow into your shoulders, down your arms, and to the tips of your fingers. It feels so good to relax and let go. (Pause) Now, breathe in the divine light into your chest and feel all your muscles relax in your chest. Then feel it flow into your stomach and all the muscles in your stomach relax. (Pause) Now, bring awareness to your back, and feel the divine light flow down your back relaxing your upper back, your middle back, all the way down to your lower back. Your entire back relaxes in this beautiful soothing light. (Pause) Feel as the light and relaxation flows down into your hips, your knees, your calves, and all the way down to the soles of your feet, the tips of your toes. (Pause) Your entire body is filled with relaxation and the divine light. Every cell of your being is illuminated with this divine light. Notice how good it feels to relax and let go. (Pause)

Imagine the angels give you this beautiful cloud chair and they ask you to sit in it and relax. This cloud chair was made just for you and it fits you perfectly. You melt into the cloud chair and relax even deeper. (Pause) Feel and imagine 10,000 angels surrounding you. Welcome them, breathe with them, and know they are there to help you. (Pause) They slowly begin to lift your cloud chair into the higher octaves of the angelic realm. Imagine your cloud chair being carried upward into the higher vibration of the angelic realm where only love exists. They know exactly what they are doing, so just trust and allow them to attune your energy to this higher vibration of love and light. (Pause) As you relax and attune to the higher vibrations of light, notice what you feel, what you hear, what you see, and what you sense. (Pause) Take a moment and release your fears to them. They have the ability to dissolve them so you can receive healing and clarity. (Pause) Now, share with them your prayers and desires. Ask for the help you need. (Pause) Trust that your prayers have been heard and they will be answered.

This attunement has transformed you. From this moment forward, you will be more in tune with the angels that surround you. You will sense their energy around you. You will hear more clearly their messages of divine guidance. You will understand how they are trying to get your attention. Know that because of this attunement, you will experience more joy, peace, fulfillment, and happiness in your life. You deserve it and the angels are there to help you create it. Just remember to ask for their help when you need it. You are never, ever alone, and you are loved unconditionally by God and the angels.

Take a moment and thank the angels. (Pause) Ask that they continue to guide you in every way.

Now feel or imagine as they bring your cloud chair slowly back into the present moment. Take some nice deep breaths and feel as you ground yourself in the moment of now. Feel light, free, and grateful, and filled with light and love. (Pause) Expect peace. Expect miracles. Expect better than you could ever imagine.

Use this guided meditation whenever you desire relaxation or if you want to let go and ask the angels for help and guidance. They are always there for you and guided meditation can be a powerful tool to help you make that connection.

Working with the Breath

Angels are pure spirit, and you can raise your vibration and enhance your connection to their world simply by using breath techniques (*breath* is synonymous with *spirit*). By becoming aware of your breathing, you become aware of your spiritual nature, for breath is life. Thus, you can use your breath, as a yogi does, to elevate your consciousness to the realm where the angels dwell. In other words, the breath is the gateway to the sacred angelic dimension.

The breath is something you take for granted. Without the breath there is no life. Most times you are unaware of the breath until you experience a shortness of breath or panic sets in and your breath speeds up. When you become aware of your breathing you connect to your spiritual self. Awareness and control of breath allows you to consciously raise your vibration and connect to the sacred realm.

When you enhance the breath and use it to open up to different realms, your natural abilities begin to unfold—mental, physical, emotional, and spiritual. It unblocks energy and channels of communication open up; information can flow into your consciousness. The breath is a powerful tool for raising your vibration so you can bring forth sacred information from other dimensions. Conscious breathing develops a communications link between body and mind, between conscious and unconscious, between spirit and angels.

Here is a rhythmic breathing technique that you can use at any time to raise your vibration. You can do it almost anywhere, whether sitting quietly at home, in your car, or when walking. It's simple and it can help you connect with your inner power.

Relax and close your eyes. Observe your breath pattern, but do not make any attempt to alter it. Just pay attention to the breath going in and coming out. Now, begin to breathe slowly and deeply. Feel the warmth of used air leave your body and breathe in fresh clean air. Imagine yourself being cleansed and energized by each breath.

Now listen to any sounds you make while breathing. Don't judge it, just listen. Also notice whether you breathe in shallow or deep breaths and where the air goes— into the diaphragm or the belly. Does your chest rise or fall or does your abdomen rise or fall?

As you inhale and exhale— allow the breath to become one continuous movement (with no separation or gaps between the inhale and the exhale). Continue doing this for several minutes and notice how you feel.

Affirmations

Another way to raise your vibration is to empower yourself by changing your thoughts from the negative to the positive. You can do this by writing or saying an affirmation. An affirmation is declaring the truth through a positive statement. For example, if you are continuously saying, "There must not be angels because I cannot see or feel them," change that statement and affirm, "I know there are plenty of angels here for me. I am willing to see and feel their loving presence." In essence, you are raising your vibration to experience the possibilities of the angelic realm. If your thoughts are filled with fear and doubt you will continue to experience the same. As you think, so shall you be. In essence, you need to fake it until you make it through the use and power of affirmations. When you practice using affirmations, you shift your thoughts to experience what you want versus what you don't want. It creates a power that opens the gateways to experience miracles.

ALERT

When you write or say an affirmation, always state your affirmation in the positive and in the present tense. For example, you don't want to say, "I will see the angels someday;" this statement keeps it in the future tense. You want to affirm having it now, for example by saying, "I am seeing the angels."

Chanting

Chanting is an ancient ritual, and it's been used in different religious and ritual ceremonies to access the divine. Through the power of chanting you can reach altered states of consciousness and raise your vibration to connect with the divine. Chanting can transform negative energy into positive energy, which immediately raises your vibration. When you chant certain phrases over and over again, it shifts the vibration and causes change in mind, body, and spirit. You quiet the mind, you open the heart, and you lift your spirit to a higher state of consciousness.

There are no hard-set rules for chanting. You can chant anywhere— in the shower, at work, in the car, or while you're walking outdoors.

Here are some different forms of chanting you can check into and practice.

- The OM chant is a universally recognized chant. Take in a breath and on the out breath, draw out the sound of OM like this: "oooooommmm-mmmmmmmm," putting the emphasis on the last part.
- Gregorian chanting is a beautiful form of music and chanting. You can buy Gregorian chanting CDs online. Play them during meditation or listen to them in the car. You can also seek out a local church that sings this medieval form of music.
- Use a mala, a string of beads used to count mantras or Sanskrit prayers. A mantra can be a word or series of words chanted out loud. As you touch each bead, repeat your mantra. You can use a Sanskrit mantra meaning peace—"Shanti, Shanti, Shanti," or you can repeat English words like "I am" or "love."
- Use rosary beads and say one of the following prayers: Our Father, Hail Mary, or Glory Be.

The most important thing about chanting is finding the method that feels right for you. Experiment and see what form of chanting creates a connection between you and the divine. When you make that connection, you will feel it in every cell of your being.

Surround Yourself with Positive People

Reflect for a moment on how you feel when you are surrounded by people who are positive, encouraging, and uplifting. You may feel lighter, happier, or even empowered. If the opposite is true and there is negativity around you, you possibly feel drained, frustrated, and unmotivated.

This is important to recognize when you are on the path of spiritual growth. To raise your vibration, seek out like-minded people who are interested in spirituality and the angels. You will learn from each other and together you will expand your awareness.

Release Fear and Remember Love

Fear can clog your energy centers or chakras. It lowers your vibration and blocks the flow of divine guidance. It's important to become conscious of when you are focusing on fear. Choose to recognize it, stop it, and focus on the positive. Fear comes in many forms: worry, stress, confusion, anger, and the list goes on. Feel the low vibration of these energies and imagine how it can weigh you down. In each and every moment, you can make a choice to let go of fear and focus your thoughts on faith. Ask the angels to lift your fears and help you remember your choices based on love.

Here is an exercise to try called Snap Out of It. Wear a rubber band on your wrist for a week. Be conscious of your thoughts, and every time you recognize a negative or fearful thought, snap it. Immediately change the thought to a positive one or focus on gratitude and love. This is a powerful exercise to raise your vibration and create positive experiences in your life.

The angels vibrate in the energy of pure love. So as you work to clear your blocks of fear and replace them with love, faith, and trust, you naturally raise your vibration to experience the angels. You can hear their loving guidance. You can see them in their loving presence and you can sense them all around you. Isn't it worth taking the time to change your thoughts from fear to love?

Gratitude

To be grateful is to recognize the blessings in your life. Gratitude is a wonderful way to open up the energy of your heart chakra. Each and every time you have thoughts of gratitude or you express gratitude, you raise your vibration and heighten your awareness to recognize the miracles all around you.

ESSENTIAL

A way to practice gratitude is to buy a journal you love and either start your day or end your day by writing ten things you are grateful for. It is so simple and it can transform your life. If you choose, you can multiply the blessings in your life and open your awareness to experience the graces of the angels all around you.

Practice recognizing the small things in life you are grateful for: a thank you or a smile from a stranger, a good cup of coffee, a sunny day, or finding time to read a good book. To raise your vibration during difficult times, choose to focus on the blessings in your life. For example, if you are going through financial difficulties, be grateful for having the money to pay the essentials, food and shelter. If you are challenged with a physical illness, be grateful for those that are there to help you in your time of need. If you are grieving a loss or separation with a family member or close friend, focus on the love and support from those that are still in your life. You have the power and the choice to change any situation in your life. Choose to start today and focus on the positive, focus on the love in your life, and expect life to change for the better.

CHAPTER 5

Opening Up to Connect with the Angels

Take a moment and think about the peace you would feel if you had a direct line of communication with God and the angels. You could release your worries and ask for help. You could ask questions to be answered by higher guidance. You could feel a team of angels surrounding you in love and support so you would never feel alone again. Feel the desire in your heart and open the lines of communication to invite the angels into your life. Be open to receive the gifts, blessings, and miracles that are waiting for you.

What Drew You to This Book?

As you journey down the path of spiritual growth you realize that nothing happens by mistake and everything happens for a reason. This book is in your hands because it was meant to be. You might have purchased it because you were curious and wanted to learn more about the angels. Maybe you are going through a challenging time and you need help from the angels. Perhaps a friend gave you this book and said, "You have to read this!" Or maybe it's possible that the angels drew you to this book because they want to communicate with you.

It doesn't matter what consciously or unconsciously brought you to this book—now is the perfect time. There is no such thing as a coincidence on the spiritual path; it's called a God-incidence. The angels want to work with you, and this book is in your hands for a reason. This is an exciting time and this is only the beginning. Open your heart, open your mind, and be curious as you open up to the possibilities of experiencing heaven on earth.

Belief

Believing something to be possible opens the door to experience. So are you ready to take your first step? Invite the angels into your life and choose to believe in their existence. Ask them to plant a seed of faith into your heart so you can trust and believe the angels are there for you in unconditional love. Take a moment and breathe with the angels and ask them to help you believe.

ESSENTIAL

Here's a prayer you can say to the angels: "Dearest angels, please help me believe in your presence and show me that you are there for me in all ways, always. Help me believe that anything is possible when you have faith and trust in God and the angels. Thank you."

To enhance your belief in the angels, read more about them, learn all that you can, and surround yourself with others who believe. As you expand your awareness to the possibilities that exist, you increase your opportunities to experience it for yourself. Trust that the angels want you to believe in them so they can make your life better.

Believing in God and the angels requires patience. You want certain things to happen now and sometimes it's just a matter of time. During these restless moments, pray for patience, keep the faith, and believe the angels are working behind the scenes. Ask the angels to empower you with patience and perseverance and trust that your desire is coming to fruition.

Learning Opens Awareness

Learning something new provides you with the opportunity to experience something different. This is especially important when opening up to the angels. The angels' world is not tangible; you cannot touch it and you cannot see it with the human eye. Therefore, you must expand your awareness to think outside of the box.

ALERT

As you walk your spiritual path and you learn more about the angels, you may release some of your old religious beliefs. What you learned as a child may no longer be true and it might not feel right anymore. Trust and be patient with yourself if you are going through these changes.

If you want to increase your intuitive abilities so you can communicate with the angelic realm, study and learn as much as you can. Your desire and motivation creates the energy of enthusiasm that is like a magnet, drawing to you everything that you need to develop your skills.

It's important to understand that the angels communicate with you through your database of information and knowledge. So as you expand your knowledge and you enhance your intuition, they have more ways to communicate with you. For example, if the angels see that you are paying attention to coincidences and synchronicities, then they will use this method of communication to get your attention.

Be open and excited to learn something new. Experiment with the exercises throughout this book. Check into your feelings and discover what feels right for you. Then store those thoughts in your spiritual toolbox, a place in your mind where you hold all your spiritual teachings. These tools will become very valuable as you learn to communicate with the angels and receive messages of divine guidance. They can also come in very handy when you need the spiritual support to get through life's difficulties and challenges.

Here is a prayer you can say for learning and growth:

"I am open and willing to expand my awareness to the possibilities of working with the angels by my side. Show me, angels, what's in my highest and best, better than I could ever imagine. I trust that you will guide me down the path that God wants me to follow."

Desire

Your focused desire to create a deeper connection with God and the angels will make things happen. Start by having a heart-to-heart dialog with your angels to open the lines of communication. Talk to the angels as if you were talking to your best friend and share with them your deepest desires and wishes. Remember, they already know who you are and everything there is to know about you. They are excited to make the connection with you and to help you in any way they can.

ESSENTIAL

There is no right or wrong way to state your desires to the angels. You can express them to your angels in your thoughts or you can focus on them during meditation. You can write your desires in a letter or you can call out to the angels and simply say, "Show me peace." It's not about the way you do it, it is important to just do it.

One way you can do this is to write a letter to the angels. Put your desires on paper and share with them why you are ready to connect with them at this time. Speak from your heart. Share your fears, worries, and concerns and ask them to help you manifest your true desires.

Take some quiet time for yourself and find a peaceful place to sit. You can start your letter by saying, "Dearest angels" . . . and then allow your thoughts to flow on to paper. Try not to think, just write. When you're finished, put your letter away and release your desires to the angels with love. Say thank you in advance for all the help and guidance coming your way. The angels stand by your side waiting for you to ask for their help. As you give them your desires they become your team in spirit, working behind the scenes to make things happen.

The Power of Intention

After you share your desires and wishes with the angels, take another step and get clear about your intentions. An intention declares your determination and effort to obtain a goal. When you state your intentions to the angels you set a powerful energy into motion. Your intentions are an invisible force of energy that makes things happen. Get clear about what you want and the rewards will be well worth the effort.

Remember, when working with the law of free will and free choice, you need to ask the angels for help. Get clear about what you want and why you need help. Then express or write your intentions and ask the angels for help. When you claim your intentions and put them into action, you ignite the divine power within you to make things happen. Imagine what the results can be when you combine your power with the team of angels waiting to assist you. Miracles happen, and you realize the possibilities are endless as you open up to help, guidance, and clear communication with God and the angels.

Here are some examples of stating your intentions:

- Help me release my fears that block clear communication with God and the angels.
- Heal my wounds from any past experiences that may block clear communication with God and the angels.
- Build my faith and trust so I can believe in the existence of God and the angels.
- Help me hear, see, and feel your presence around me.
- Help me notice the ways in which the angels are trying to get my attention to answer my prayers.
- Show me the books and guide me to the people that will help me communicate with God and the angels.

Notice which intentions feel right for you and declare them to your angels. You can repeat them in your thoughts, you can write them down on paper, or you can speak them out loud. The way you choose to express your intentions each carries a different vibration of energy. Notice what the energy feels like when you repeat your intentions in your thoughts. Then feel the energy increase when you write them. Then feel the energy expand once again when you say them out loud. The more energy you put into your intentions the more powerful they become.

Focus on What You Want

You are a powerful person and you can manifest what you desire with the help of the angels. It's important to take responsibility and own your individual power. One way you can do this is to choose your thoughts and words wisely. Have you ever heard the saying, "As you think, so shall you be"? Your thoughts and words influence what you experience in your life. To clarify this, imagine you are surrounded by a magnetic field. Your words and thoughts become the magnetic force that attracts to you what you experience in your everyday life. To phrase it another way, your life becomes a mirror reflection of your thoughts.

FACT

A quote by William James: "The greatest discovery of our generation is that human beings can alter their lives by altering their attitudes of mind. As you think, so shall you be."

There is a key factor to remember as you become this powerful magnetic attraction. Be clear with your intentions and focus on what you want, not what you don't want. The universe does not know the difference between your wants and your don't wants, it just magnetizes to you what you are focused on.

If you ask for what you *want* to happen but your thoughts and words are focused on what you *don't* want, you are sending out a mixed message to the universe. For example, if your intention is, "Help me hear, see, and feel the presence of the angels around me" but your thoughts and words are focused on, "I can't see anything. I don't feel anything," you are counteracting your intention and blocking your ability to receive what you want.

QUESTION

What if my prayer has not been answered? Does it mean that God did not hear my prayer?
All prayers are heard. Sometimes the answer comes quickly, at other times there's a delay. Trust that when there is a delay, your prayer will be answered in divine time. God looks at the big picture and He takes all things into consideration. Your prayers are always heard and they will be answered.

Pay attention to your words and thoughts and notice what energy you are sending out. If you find yourself focusing on what you *don't* want, stop and change it to what you *do* want. As you do this, you will be surprised at what happens. Just by changing your thoughts and words, the magic unfolds and what seemed impossible becomes possible .The following are examples of how you can transform and redirect your intention to create what you desire.

Don't Want	Do Want
"I don't know what to believe."	"I believe in angels and miracles."
"I am unworthy of God's love."	"I am worthy of God's love and guidance."
"I am not good enough."	"I am good enough. I deserve the best."
"I don't have time to meditate."	"I listen to my angels in the shower and in the car."
"My prayers are not being answered."	"My prayers are answered in divine time."

Surrender to the Angels

By now you have learned that the number one priority in working with the angels is to ask for help. Once you do this and your request is made, you need to trust and surrender your prayer to God and the angels. This can be hard for some people who have a hard time letting go of control. If this applies to you, contemplate this thought: Do you trust that God and the angels have your best interest in mind? If so, it's time to surrender.

A wonderful way to surrender is to find or create a surrender box. Another name for it can be your let go and let God box. Place all your desires, wishes, and intentions into this box and then affirm, "I am letting go and letting God. I am open to my highest and best, better than I could ever imagine." By doing this ritual, you release it from your control and you give it to God and the angels for miracles to occur. You break free from your human limited thinking and you open up to the unlimited possibilities of divine resolution to occur. Once you surrender, it's your job to trust. Release your expectations and trust that everything is in divine order. God will take care of all the details.

Your Divine Heritage

It is your natural birthright to connect with God and the angels. When the veil is lifted between heaven and earth there is no separation between you, the angels, and God. You are a child of God and because of your heritage you always have access to the divine. You can receive clear communication with God and the angels and you can tap into the divine wisdom where all knowledge is found.

ESSENTIAL

When looking for background music for meditation, it's important to find music that enhances relaxation in mind, body, and spirit. Find a bookstore or an online resource where you can listen to the music. Some recommendations are music designed for relaxation, Reiki, massage, or yoga. You can also find some beautiful meditation music with angelic tones in the background. (See Appendix A for recommendations.)

Meditation is a wonderful way to rediscover this connection between you and the divine. It is a powerful tool to raise your vibration so you can tap into the higher consciousness of the divine mind. In this place of meditation, you can receive helpful insight and guidance from the angels to empower you along your journey.

A Meditation to Reconnect with the Divine

When doing any of the meditations throughout this book, it's a good idea to record the session on a tape or CD. Then you can easily let go to experience the meditation versus opening and closing your eyes to read the next step. It will enhance your meditation and allow you to go deeper into the experience. Take your time recording and remember to pause in between each step.

Find a quiet place to sit where you will not be disturbed. You can do this meditation in silence or play soft meditative music in the background.

Get as comfortable as you can and take a deep breath and close your eyes.

Take another deep breath and let go of everything that happened before you closed your eyes.

Take another deep breath and let go of everything that is going to happen after you open your eyes. Now breathe into the present moment and just let go.

With intention, fill the room with divine white light and energy and begin to breathe one with that divine light.

Ask your angels to surround you in a beautiful circle of love, light, and protection.

Remember you are never alone and you are very loved.

Now, imagine a beautiful spiritual sun in front of you. This sun is the energy of the divine, God, all that is, including the angels.

To become one with this energy and divine light, imagine that you have a plug (just like a lamp has a plug to plug into electricity) coming from your solar plexus and, using your imagination, plug into the spiritual sun.

Now breathe in the energy and light from this sun into your body as if every cell in your physical body illuminates with this light.

Imagine that you can then breathe into your mind the divine wisdom and guidance you are searching for. Your mind and thoughts illuminate in this light.

You feel lighter and more peaceful with every breath that you take.

Now your body and your mind are illuminated in this light. You are no longer separate from this divine source. You are one with God, the angels, and all that is.

Breathe the light in, be one, feel the peace, feel the love. It is yours and it always has been. (Pause)

Before you come back, think of a question you would like answered by divine guidance. Ask the angels for divine guidance and then listen for your answer.

Say thank you. To return, just take some nice deep breaths and begin to feel your body, feel yourself back in the room.

Remember, you can plug in any time you choose. Each and every time you do, you reconnect with the divine wisdom and healing that's rightfully yours.

CHAPTER 6

Developing Your Intuition

You use your intuition on a daily basis, sometimes on a conscious level and many times on an unconscious level. When you consciously use your intuition, you pay attention to your inner senses. They act as a guide to help you make decisions, take action, and put forth inspiration. Everyone has some natural intuition and can choose to develop it. The angels use your intuition to communicate messages of divine guidance, so the more you enhance your abilities the easier it is to receive clear communication from God and the angels.

What Is Intuition?

Intuition is the instinctual knowing you get when you listen to your inner senses. Everyone is intuitive, and you can train yourself to become more attuned to your senses. Some people may be more sensitive to what they feel; their intuition speaks to them through sensations in their body. Others may be more sensitive to what they hear, and their intuition speaks to them through their inner thoughts or ideas. Seek to discover which senses you use the most and which ones stand out more distinctly. This helps you focus on your strongest senses to receive intuitive information.

Your intuition is a direct link to the angels. As you develop your intuition, your senses heighten and you learn to trust what you hear, feel, and sense from the angels.

You are more intuitive than you realize. The more you can understand and listen to your intuition the better it can guide you. Below is a list of expressions that people use when they are connected to their intuition. Check and see if you use any of these phrases.

- *I had a feeling.* Have you ever had a feeling that something was going to happen and then it did? Did you ever have the feeling you needed to call someone and when you did they needed your help?
- *Something told me.* Did you ever hear an inner voice guide you, telling you what to do?
- *I had a dream.* Did you ever get a direct message from someone in a dream or did you ever have a dream that later had significant meaning?
- *I had a gut feeling.* Did you ever not trust your gut feeling and disaster followed? Now think about a time when you did follow your gut feeling and everything worked out.
- *I just knew.* Did you ever have that inner understanding and you knew you were right and nobody could change your mind?

As you pay attention to your senses and you learn to interpret their messages, your intuition can become very valuable. It can direct you to the answers you are seeking.

Try this intuitive exercise. Close your eyes and place your hand on your heart. Take a couple of nice deep breaths. Ask which friend or family member needs to receive a phone call from you. Notice how you feel when you hear that name and ask if there is anything you need to know. Then call that person and see how accurate your intuition was. Don't be surprised if that person picks up the phone and calls you first.

Direct and Indirect Intuition

Your intuition can communicate in two different ways. Direct intuition is literal and you know exactly what your intuition is saying to you. For example, you are putting an addition onto your house and you have asked the angels to help you find the perfect people to help you build it. You go to the gym and during a break you talk to one of the members. As you are talking, he mentions he's a builder looking for work. There is no interpretation to be made—this is a direct answer to your prayers.

ESSENTIAL

Sometimes angelic guidance is very direct and you know exactly what they are trying to tell you, but sometimes it's symbolic and you need to ask for their help to interpret the message. When you are confused and you have trouble interpreting the messages, ask the angels to be more literal or direct with their guidance.

Then there is indirect intuition, which is more symbolic, and you need to contemplate its interpretation. Let's say you are meditating and you've invited your angels into your meditation to give you guidance. You have been looking for a new space to rent for your business. You ask the angels in meditation, "Is the place I looked at today the right space for me to rent?" In your meditation your inner vision shows you a stop sign, but up ahead in the road is a green light. This is a symbolic, indirect way your intuition is communicating with you. When you ask your angels to help you interpret the vision, you realize this place for your business is not the right one (stop sign symbol) but further down the road there is a better choice coming (light is green symbol).

What Are the Clair Senses?

Communication from the angels flows through your psychic senses called "clair" senses. These correspond with the senses you use: seeing, feeling, hearing, knowing, tasting, and smelling. It's important to become familiar with these different clairs. By learning more about them you can pay attention to your senses and use them to receive clear communication from God and the angels.

- *Clairvoyance* is clear vision. This is when you have visions, images, or symbols presented to you through your inner vision.
- *Clairsentience* is clear feeling. This is when you receive information as a feeling in your body.
- *Clairaudience* is clear hearing. This is when you experience or hear clear thoughts or words flowing through your mind and no one is physically talking to you.
- *Claircognizance* is clear knowing. When you have an inner knowing you feel very strong that something is true or you know beyond any doubt that you need to take action.
- *Clairgustance* is clear taste. When you experience this you have a clear taste of something in your mouth without any explanation of why it's happening.
- *Clairolfactory* is clear smell. When you use this ability you can smell something even though it's not physically in your presence.

If you choose to become more intuitive or psychic, learn the different clairs and practice using them. Everyone is psychic and everyone can develop his or her abilities. The more you learn to trust the information you receive, the more you can use its valuable information in everyday life.

Clairvoyance: "Clear Seeing"

Many people want to see the angels with their physical eye, but it's easier to perceive them with your inner vision or your third eye. The third eye is located in the center of your forehead right between your eyebrows. It is the energy center where spiritual visions are transmitted and received. When your third eye is open and clear, you have the ability to receive impressions, visions, and symbols about past, present, and future events.

FACT

Precognition is when you receive visions or information about a future event. Most people have precognitive dreams, but it can also happen during meditation or just walking down the street. These visions can be positive or they can be upsetting when the vision pertains to an upcoming death or disaster. If you have precognitive experiences, ask the angels to help you feel comfortable with your ability. It can be a gift, not a burden.

There are so many blessings to receive by opening your third eye and becoming clairvoyant. You can ask for answers and insight to come to you during your dream state. You can ask for clarity from the angels about relationships, health, finances, or even making a decision in order to move forward. Another blessing of being clairvoyant is seeing images of your angels through your third eye or with your physical eyes open.

The best way to receive clairvoyant insight is to put some time aside for meditation during your day. As you sit in silence, allow the visions or symbols to flow through your consciousness. You can ask the angels for guidance on a specific question and then witness what goes through your thoughts. If an image or symbol flashes across your consciousness, go back and ask the angels to clarify what it means.

Meditation for Clairvoyance: Opening Your Third Eye

Find a quiet place to sit where you will not be disturbed.

Ask the angels to surround you with divine love, light, and protection. Share with the angels your desire to become more clairvoyant and ask them to help you open your third eye so you can receive clear visions, symbols, and insight. Then surrender, allow them to help you and breathe into the divine light surrounding you.

With your eyes closed, imagine a beautiful spiritual sun in front of you, the source of God's love, wisdom, and guidance. Breathe and become one with its light. (Pause) Remind yourself that it's your natural divine birthright to see clearly into this divine wisdom and to receive the answers you are seeking.

Now, bring awareness to your third eye in the middle of your forehead. Imagine that you can open its lid so you can see more clearly. Remember, you can ask the angels to open it for you. When your third eye is open, ask for the veil to be lifted between heaven and earth. Then breathe in as much light as you can from the divine spiritual sun into your third eye. Imagine the light coming through clearing all darkness. (Pause) Now, allow the wisdom and guidance of the divine to flow into your third eye so you can see clearly all that you need to know. Take a moment and think of a question you would like answered by divine guidance. (Pause) Then ask the angels to communicate the answer through your inner visions or by symbolic understanding. Be patient and know it will come. If you do not understand what they are trying to show you, ask for clarity. (Pause) Now thank the angels and ask them to help you keep your third eye open when it's appropriate.

Then slowly come back through your breath into the present moment, feeling clear, grateful, and at peace.

Clairaudience: "Clear Hearing"

It's not uncommon when you first start connecting with the angels and you hear the voice of divine guidance that your first thought is, "It's just my imagination and I am making it up." It is important to remember that the voice of the angels isn't necessarily an audio voice heard from outside of you. It can be a loving, supportive thought communicated through your mind. Sometimes it might feel like a whisper and other times it's loud and clear.

Here are some of the possible experiences of clairaudience:

- You hear someone calling your name but no one's there.
- You hear songs in your head and the words communicate a message to you.
- You are driving and you're lost and you hear a clear voice in your thoughts telling you where to go.
- You hear inspirational messages of love and guidance communicated through your thoughts.
- You hear a ringing or different tones playing in your inner ear.

Messages from your angels are always positive, uplifting, and encouraging. If you find the words you hear come from negativity or a place of fear, know that these are not messages from your angels. Most likely they come from your ego. If this happens, ask your ego to sit on the sidelines during meditation and spend some time raising your vibration so you can attune to the higher frequencies of divine guidance.

Exercise to Practice Clairaudience

Bring your journal or some paper and a pen to your quiet place. Set your intention that you are going to receive guidance from the angel about a specific question. Keep your writing materials on your lap and get comfortable. Close your eyes and take some nice deep breaths. Ask the angels to surround you in the protection and love of the divine white light of God. Breathe into this light and imagine that your mind, body, and spirit blend and become one with its magnificence. Then write on your piece of paper, "Dearest angels please help me hear your words of wisdom and guidance to answer the following question." Then write your question and sit and listen to the words or messages that flow through your mind and thoughts. Even if you think you're making it up, write it down. Try not to think about it and just let your pen flow and allow it to record the thoughts and words that come to you. After your mind becomes quiet, stop and thank your angels. Read your message and notice how it feels.

Clairsentience: "Clear Feeling"

When you are clairsentient, your intuition speaks to you through your emotions and the physical sensations in your body. Many people who are empathetic (meaning if you are sensitive to the feelings of others around you) are naturally clairsentient. A typical comment from someone who is clairsentient is, "I just had feeling" or, "I had a hunch."

Remember, the angels use your intuition to communicate their messages of guidance. So they can use your body and its sensations to get your attention. Set your intention that you are going to become more conscious of your feelings and the sensations in your body. Ask your angels to help you know the difference between a good feeling and a bad feeling. This information becomes very valuable. Your angels can then use your body as a messenger to guide you to your highest and best, better than you could ever imagine.

ALERT

You can tap into your intuition through your sense of feeling and use it to get clarity on making a decision. Place your hand on your heart or on your solar plexus. Think about making your decision, and if you feel peace, most likely there's going to be a positive outcome. If you feel sick to your stomach, it could lead to a negative outcome.

Here are some possible experiences of clairsentience:

- You feel a chill down your spine.
- You get a gut feeling about someone you just met.
- You have a strong feeling to call a friend and when you do, she needs to talk to you.
- You feel someone standing over your shoulder and no one is there.
- Without explanation, you are overcome with emotion.
- You experience a sudden change in room temperature.

Have you had any of these experiences and did you ever think it might be your angels trying to get your attention? Start turning inward to your senses and notice if your strongest clair is clairsentience. If you recognize this to be true, learn to trust your feelings and allow your intuition to guide you.

ALERT

If you are empathetic and sensitive to other people's feelings and emotions, it's important for you to learn to protect yourself. When you are stressed and your energy is low you are more vulnerable to other people's feelings and emotions. Ask your angels to replenish your energy and surround you with a shield of divine white light. This will increase your energy level and protect you from other people's negativity.

Fun Practice with Clairsentience

Look at the following scenarios and ask yourself, "Is this a good feeling leading to a positive experience or is this a negative feeling, which yields caution?"

1. You are contemplating taking a new job. You ask for guidance and you feel confusion and nausea.
2. You think or hear an inspirational idea and you feel a chill down your spine.
3. You're shopping for a new home and you enter a house which feels cold, uncomfortable, and you can't wait to leave.
4. You meet someone new at an event. You immediately feel comfortable and you talk for hours.
5. You pull your car into a parking spot at the plaza and you feel very vulnerable.
6. You go on a first date and you feel relaxed, comfortable, and you have butterflies in your stomach.

Your feelings are your inner compass. They can guide you in any situation so you can experience a positive outcome. Your job is to pay attention and learn to understand what your feelings are saying. If it's a not-so-good feeling, think again. If the feeling is peaceful or positive, go for it.

Claircognizance: "Clear Knowing"

Claircognizance is when you have an inner knowing about something or someone. When you use this sense of intuition you know what you are thinking or saying is true beyond any doubt. Many speakers, writers, artists, and inventors naturally use their gifts of claircognizance. They consciously or unconsciously tap into the divine mind for inspiration, creativity, and innovation. When you experience claircognizance, it feels as if your idea or inspiration comes from a higher source and you feel compelled to put it into action.

Here are some possible experiences of claircognizance:

- You are talking to someone and you know exactly what she is going to say.
- You receive an idea or inspiration about writing a book and you know you have to do it.
- You know something about someone but you don't know how you know it.
- You know beyond any doubt that you need to move to a particular place.
- You knew all your life, since a very young age, that you were going to be a teacher, mother, doctor, or any other specific profession.

Have you had any of these experiences or would you like to? If so, pay attention to your ideas, inspirations, or your inner knowing. Learn to trust it and have the courage to act upon it. Know that everyone has the ability to become one with the divine mind. When you choose to, you access the unlimited resource of divine wisdom and knowledge.

Meditation and Prayer for Claircognizance

This is a meditation to open your crown chakra, the energy center at the top of your head. When it is open and clear, you can receive higher wisdom and knowledge from God and the angels. Before you start your meditation, share the following prayer with the angels:

"Dearest angels, please assist me in meditation to open and clear my crown chakra. My desire and intention is to open the channel of communication between myself and the divine so I may easily receive claircognizance information. I want to know beyond any doubt that this information is from a higher source of wisdom. Help me trust what I receive and give me the courage to act upon it for the highest and greatest good of all."

Now, in your sacred peaceful place for meditation, call upon God and the angels. Close your eyes and breathe one with their loving presence. Feel their desire to assist you. They have heard your prayer and they are working behind the scenes to help you in any way they can. As you breathe, imagine yourself lifting into the higher vibrations of light. Imagine yourself going right into the spiritual sun, where you connect to the oneness of God and the angels. (Pause) Take a few moments and give yourself permission to relax into this beautiful energy. Feel yourself merging with the one breath of God, the one heartbeat of God. (Pause) Now imagine the top of your head opening and allow the light in. Ask for the divine mind to fill your thoughts with the knowing and inspiration of God and the angels. There is nothing for you to do; just breathe in the light. Sit in quiet, relax and allow yourself to just receive. You are one with the divine mind. Trust that you will easily and effortlessly receive divine inspiration and knowing to assist you in all aspects of your life. (Pause and receive) Thank God and the angels for opening your crown chakra to receive divine wisdom. Share with them your desire to continue to receive clear knowing in your everyday life. Slowly, breathe back into the present moment with gratitude and clarity.

Clairgustance: "Clear Taste" and Clairolfactory: "Clear Smell"

These are two clairs that need to be mentioned, but the experiences of these psychic senses are not as common as the others. The reasoning for this can be that most people don't pay attention to smell and taste and so they might go unnoticed.

Clairolfactory is the ability to smell something even though it's not physically there. The most common experience of clairolfactory is when your deceased relatives are around you and you smell something familiar that reminds you of them. For example, the perfume your grandmother wore or the cookies that your mother always baked or the smell of Grandfather's cigars. Another good example of clairolfactory is the reported phenomenon of smelling roses when people claim the Blessed Mother Mary is around them.

Clairgustance is the ability to taste something when there's nothing physically in your mouth to create that taste. Again, it's more common to experience this when your deceased loved ones are around you. Instead of smelling something you actually taste it. If all of a sudden you taste tobacco and you don't smoke and there is no one around you smoking, most likely you're sensing someone around you who smoked while he was alive but has now passed. Another experience of clairgustance is you suddenly taste salt water and you are nowhere near the ocean. Your angels might be trying to tell you it's time to go to the beach or take a vacation.

You can develop both of these senses just by paying attention and taking notice. If you taste or smell something that's not physically present, ask the angels to help you understand what it's connected to. There are so many gifts to receive when you choose to develop and enhance your intuition by using your clairs. Remember, be patient with yourself and practice by using the meditations and exercises throughout this book.

CHAPTER 7

Angels Speaking or Your Imagination?

Did you ever question, "Is this message coming from my angels or am I just making it up?" This experience is very natural. The first step in discernment is to learn to distinguish between your ego's (or your personality's) voice versus the voice of divine guidance. As you discover the distinct difference between the two, you can choose to follow the voice of divine guidance, which will always lead you to the best possible outcome.

The Ego

The ego is that part of your personality that sees itself separate from God. The ego self reacts and makes decisions based on your history: past experiences, beliefs gathered over time, and your emotions. It usually wants to be in control and it focuses on fear. Some people refer to the ego as "easing God out."

When you start listening and noticing the difference between the ego's voice and the voice of divine guidance, you will realize that one comes from a place of fear and the other comes from love. The best thing you can do is learn the difference between the two. Your angels will remind you over and over again that your ego is separate from your divine self. Yet you live in your human body, which has an ego and a history from all your past experiences. Make the choice now to become a witness to your ego. Notice when your ego is focusing on fear or making decisions based on fear. Then turn to the loving guidance of the angels and ask them to help you transform the effects of fear in your life.

ALERT

A simple way to discern your ego from God is to ask yourself, "Are my thoughts coming from a place of fear or love?" God and the angels only communicate with love.

Your ego, or some call it "the lower self," does not focus on love. It sees a fearful world and it does not want to admit that it's afraid. The ego sends messages of worry, confusion, insecurity, and it certainly doesn't want you to trust yourself. It doesn't want you to feel confident, self-assured, or strong because it can no longer control your actions.

Remember, the ego is not bad, it's just afraid. You can gain some valuable wisdom by paying attention to this lower voice. Don't judge yourself for any past mistakes you've made from following the voice of your ego, just grow from it. Once you can discern and understand the messages coming from your ego, you have the power to choose differently. Consider this information your gems of wisdom to use in the future to live a better life.

The best thing you can do is learn the difference between the thoughts and feelings coming from your ego versus divine guidance. Begin practicing by learning some of the characteristics of your ego:

- Your ego is judgmental.
- Your ego is critical.
- Your ego is indecisive.
- Your ego procrastinates.
- Your ego is impatient.
- Your ego likes to control.
- Your ego is fearful.
- Your ego says you're unworthy and undeserving.
- Your ego is competitive.

As you witness your thoughts, notice if they hold any of these characteristics. Then choose to recognize your ego and turn your attention to focus on the positive, loving thoughts of the angels. Don't beat yourself up for having these thoughts. Simply say, "Here my ego goes again," and choose to take your power back.

The Angels' Guidance

The voice of divine guidance always comes from a place of love. It will never lead you down a path of pain or chaos. The voice of divine guidance will ask you to follow your heart and to believe in your dreams and desires. Messages from the angels are always positive, helpful, healing, and supportive. The angels will always encourage you and provide you with the trust and confidence you need to follow your heart. In simple terms, the voice of divine guidance is always the voice of love.

When you hear the voice of your angels it sounds like this:

- You are good enough right now.
- Follow your heart.
- Believe in yourself.
- You can do anything if you believe.
- You are never alone and you are so loved.

- You are right where you are meant to be.
- You deserve the best.
- Be patient; all is well.
- There is more than enough to go around.

Just notice how it feels when you read these words. Imagine if you listened to that voice more often. Your confidence and self-esteem would increase, you would trust yourself more, and you would believe in yourself so you could follow your heart and live your dreams. Isn't it worth taking the time out of your busy schedule to listen to your angels' guidance?

The Ego's Guidance

You are probably more used to following the guidance of your ego versus the angels. It is only natural that this would happen because your ego makes choices and takes action based on your past memories and the feelings that were experienced from those memories. For example, if you are looking to invest in a course that will guide you further down your spiritual path but you're tight in finances, your ego's voice might mirror what your mother used to say: "Don't waste your money on silly stuff like that!" Then fear sets in and you might hold yourself back from an opportunity.

Here are some sample questions from someone asking for guidance. Pay attention to the voice of the ego and notice how you feel after you read the response.

- I just got a great idea about writing a book and I am curious what my next step is? **Ego's response:** Who do you think you are? You can't do that, you're not an expert.
- I just met this new guy. Is he the right one for me? **Ego's response:** He might be like the rest. Be careful because you might get hurt.
- I want to leave my job and start my own business. What should I do? **Ego's response:** What is everyone going to think? You should stay right where you are; it's safe.

- I am so mad at my sister. How can I make peace with her? **Ego's response:** It's her fault. Wait till she apologizes.
- I have been so stressed out at work. What can I do? **Ego's response:** Just remember, if you don't work hard you might not succeed.

Notice how the ego can be critical, judgmental, afraid, cautious, and blaming. Do you want this voice influencing your choices and decisions? If this voice feels familiar to you, choose to recognize it and then tune into a different channel so you can hear the voice of the angels.

Following Divine Guidance

The more you can practice discernment when listening to the voice of your ego versus the voice of your angels, the more you can trust yourself and the messages you are receiving. Building trust with the angels is like taking a journey back home to God where you can experience peace, ease, and grace.

ESSENTIAL

Awareness is a wonderful gift. Once you realize your ego is controlling your thoughts and actions, you have the power to choose differently. Recognize it and then turn your attention to the angels so they can give you guidance and direction from a higher place of love.

Now review below the same questions that the ego answered and notice how the angels respond.

Pay attention to how you feel as you read the answer.

- I just got a great idea about writing a book and I am curious what my next step is? **Angels' response:** Believe in yourself. Let your ideas flow onto the paper and see how it unfolds.
- I just met this new guy. Is he the right one for me? **Angels' response:** Notice how you feel when you are with him and take one day at a time. We are with you.

- I want to leave my job and start my own business. What should I do? **Angels' response:** Follow your heart. You will have everything you need as long as you believe.
- I am so mad at my sister. How can I make peace with her? **Angels' response:** Practice forgiveness and pray for peace.
- I have been so stressed out at work. What can I do? **Angels' response:** Take some deep breaths during the day. Know you are doing the best job you can and give us your worries.

When you read the answer to these questions you possibly feel comforted, reassured, encouraged, and peaceful, and you may even experience a feeling that you are not alone in your challenges. This is the love of the angels and this is how they would guide you if you asked for help.

When the Ego Interferes with the Voice of Divine Guidance

You are becoming more knowledgeable and you are learning to discern the difference between the lower self's voice and the voice of divine guidance. With practice, you will begin to trust yourself and your angels. With this renewed trust you will follow the voice of divine guidance and you will take action accordingly. When this happens, don't be surprised if your ego's voice gets stronger. It will want to interfere and hold you back from further joy, happiness, and confidence.

A great example of this would be you've consulted with your angels about changing careers and you feel confident about following your passion and pursing a job in photography. You have received validation from your angels and you've experienced synchronistic events confirming your decision. You start the process of looking for possible job opportunities and, right then, the ego's voice kicks in and gets stronger. It says, "Who do you think you are?" "You don't have enough experience." "You'll never make enough money to support yourself."

The question is, now what do you do? Take a time-out. Sit in contemplation and ask yourself, "Where is this voice coming from, a place of love or fear?" Then sit with your angels and ask for divine guidance and the support and courage to follow it. Divine guidance will always be consistent, it will never waiver from the truth and the best possible outcome. Ask the angels for continued confirmation that you are on the right path and practice ignoring the voice of the ego.

Simplified Fear Versus Love

It's easier than you think. When simplified, the ego is fear and the angels are love. An easy way to discern where your guidance is coming from is to reflect on this question: "Is what I am hearing or feeling coming from a place of love or fear?" The angels only answer your prayers from love.

In Karen Paolino's first book *What Would Love Do? Live a Life Guided by the Miracles of Love,* the participant spends forty days asking the simple question: "What would love do?" She discovered that this simple, yet powerful, question can empower her to make choices and decisions based on love versus fear. It can create transformation and positive change in every aspect of her life. Throughout the book there are miraculous stories of people who received answers of divine guidance by asking this simple question. It proves that anyone can receive messages of divine guidance if they only ask, listen, and discern.

ESSENTIAL

Another way to understand the ego is to look at the word "fear" in the following way: F.E.A.R, False Evidence Appearing Real. Think about it. Many times you are feeling fear in a given moment and you can't justify where the feeling of fear is coming from. The next time you are afraid, ask yourself, "Is this real?"

When you want to hear the answer of divine guidance for yourself, ask the simple questions, "What would love do?" or "What would love say?" If you want to understand how the ego would answer your question, ask the simple question, "What would fear do?" or "What would fear say?"

Exercise

Here is an exercise to practice discerning the voice of fear versus love:

1. On a piece of paper, write two questions you would like the angels to answer. Leave enough space between the questions so you can write your answers.
2. Now look at your first question and ask yourself and respond to the questions, "What would fear do?" or "What would fear say?" Write your answer down.
3. Now take a deep breath and let that go. Read the same question again and ask yourself and respond to the questions, "What would love do?" or "What would love say?" Write the answer down.
4. Repeat the same steps for your other question.
5. Look at your answers and ask yourself, "Which answer feels better and which do I choose to follow?"

The more you can practice this simple question, the more you will discover that you can find the divine answer to any question. It is that simple.

Reflection Time

To continue learning about the difference between the voice of your ego (fear) and the voice of divine guidance (love), take some time for reflection. Get your journal or a piece of paper and first, write down a time in your life when you listened and acted upon the voice of your ego (fear). You might have felt confused about making your decision or maybe you felt a tightness, or knot, in the pit of your stomach. You didn't have a good feeling about it, you ignored your feelings and you acted against your intuition. What was the outcome of your decision and how did it feel?

Next, reflect on a situation in your life when you listened to your intuition and it came from the higher voice of love or divine guidance. In this circumstance, your decision was based on following your heart or maybe you just had a good feeling about something or someone and you acted on it. Everything fell into place with this decision. What was the outcome and how did it feel?

When you follow the ego's path you will experience indecision, confusion, and sometimes chaos. It may feel like a rollercoaster ride. You might experience resistance from others or your actions along the way may feel blocked, as if you keep hitting detours in the road. Pay attention to your thoughts and if you feel stress, procrastination, or any other uneasy feelings, you are on the path of your ego.

ALERT

Your ego is smart and sly like a fox. When you start listening to the angels and you follow their guidance, the ego will try to step in and change your mind with thoughts of fear, doubt, and insecurity. When this happens, recognize it and ask the angels for reassurance. Ask them to help you tune into the messages of love versus the messages of fear.

When you follow the path of divine guidance everything falls into place. You experience magic, synchronicity, and everything you need appears with ease. You feel peaceful, excited, and inspired. You have this inner knowing to keep moving forward, you trust you're not alone, and you know everything's going to work out.

The key is to recognize and feel the difference between the two paths. Once you have this discernment, you feel empowered with wisdom to choose the path of least resistance. The path of love and divine guidance will always lead you to a better place.

Surrender Your Fears

Do you now understand how powerful the ego is and how long fear has been controlling you and playing havoc in your life? Are you ready to release yourself from its control? If you are, ask the angels to help you. You don't have to figure out how they're going to do it, just surrender your fears to them. Simply say, "I release and surrender my fears to the angels. Show me the path of love."

Every time you release fear and replace it with love, the pathways of divine guidance become clear and open. A great analogy to better understand this is: you turn on the radio and you want to listen to your favorite station. You experience static as you turn the dial to find your station, this is fear. When you ask the angels to release your conscious or unconscious fears, the static clears and you can easily "tune in" to your favorite station, where you can enjoy hearing the voices of the angels.

ESSENTIAL

Everyone has conscious and unconscious fear. It's important to surrender both to the angels. The fear in your unconscious mind also has control over you. You unconsciously make decisions and take action from this part of your mind. The angels know you inside and out and they can heal all fears if you ask them.

Exercise

Bring some paper and a pen to a quiet peaceful place where you can commune with your angels. Share with them that you would like their help and you are open to healing. Then on the top of one piece of paper write, "Please, angels, release me from the following fears. I surrender these and any unconscious fears to be healed by God." Then just list all your fears both small and big. Take your time and just keep writing until you feel complete.

Then take out a second sheet of paper and write at the top, "Help me to feel and experience the following:" On this sheet of paper you want to transform and list all the experiences and feelings you desire instead of the fear. For example, instead of fear you want trust, instead of confusion you want clarity, and instead of insecurity you desire confidence. Note that everything on your new sheet should reflect the positive nature of what you want to experience.

When this list feels complete, surrender it to the angels and continue to ask for their loving support and assistance. If you choose, you can also do a ritual releasement. This is a powerful technique where you burn your piece of paper in a pan or in a barbecue outdoors. Or you can simply drown your piece of paper in a bowl. Both of these rituals symbolize a powerful clear intention that you are ready to let it go.

Keep your piece of paper with your new desires and intentions for transformation in a sacred place. Every once in a while look at them and ask the angels to help you. Imagine the angels surrounding you and empowering you with their unconditional love. Then imagine your desired outcome and focus on the feeling you will experience when your new intentions have come to fruition.

ALERT

Remember, it doesn't matter how you surrender your fears. Just affirm that you are ready to let them go. The angels know who you are and what you need. Your job is to believe and to trust with faith that they can heal and transform your fears into miracles of love.

The lessons in this chapter are very important. As you learn and practice this valuable information, you will clearly know the difference between the voice of divine guidance and the voice of the ego. With this knowledge comes power. You will be open to hear and receive messages of divine guidance and you will have the confidence to act upon them with faith and trust.

CHAPTER 8

Communicating with the Angels

The foundation is laid and it's time to start your communication with your angels. The angels are just as excited to connect with you, and it is an honor for them to serve you and guide you along your journey. Be open and experiment with the different suggestions. Discover what feels right for you and which method provides you with a direct link to experience heaven on earth.

Creating a Sacred Space

Your sacred space is a place of retreat where you can step away from your busy everyday life. It's a quiet, peaceful place where you can connect with the loving presence and assistance of the angels. You don't need to wait until you have a whole room available. You can pick a favorite chair, a small corner of your home or apartment, a bench outdoors, or even the shower can be a perfect place to retreat where no one can bother you.

ESSENTIAL

A wonderful way to start your day is to enter your sacred space and ask the angels to fill your day with blessings. Ask them to show you what you need to know throughout the day. Enter again at night and release your worries and fears to the angels. Complete your day with gratitude and thank the angels for all that they do.

How do you create your sacred space? It's very personal and must be meaningful to you. Picture your sacred space as a little getaway where you can experience safety, peace, and clarity.

Here are some suggestions for creating your sacred space:

- Play peaceful music.
- Display pictures of your favorite religious deities.
- Display pictures of your loved ones living or deceased.
- Light candles to create the energy.
- Place crystals or rocks collected from meaningful places.
- Place pictures or statues of angels.
- Find a special journal to write in.
- Have a fountain with the soothing sound of water.
- Turn the ringer off on your phone.

After your sacred space is created, set your intention that this is your special place to come where you can let go, pray, and be open to the gifts and miracles of the angels. Each and every time you enter your space, invite the angels to gather and ask them to surround you in their loving light and protection. Ask them to fill your space with the highest vibration of divine white light and energy and know that with every breath that you take, you will become one with this sacred healing light.

Meditation

Meditation is one of the most powerful ways to connect and communicate with the angelic realm. Your body relaxes and the chatter in your mind slows down so you can connect with the higher vibration of the angels that surround you. The sensations in your body are more attuned to feel the love and warmth of the angels. Your mind quiets and the pathways open so you can listen and hear messages of divine guidance. Meditation will also create a space where it's easier for the angels to communicate with you because the outside distractions of the world are silenced.

ALERT

After you meditate or do intuitive exercises, ask the angels to "zip up" your energy field. You don't want to walk around wide open to receive psychic information from everyone. Ask the angels to protect you and request that they keep your clairs open only when it's in your highest and best to receive this information.

If you are curious to learn more and you are ready to open your heart to the angels, then make a point to schedule some quality time for meditation. You can start with ten minutes. Spend some time in prayer and share with the angels your concerns and requests. As you discover the benefits from taking this time for yourself, you might want to experiment with listening to a guided meditation CD or spend some time writing your thoughts to the angels.

Another option is to seek out a meditation class or retreat. Some people benefit from the group energy atmosphere. It may help you to connect with other like-minded people and a facilitator who can give you some guidance and answer your questions. Trust and know that there is no right or wrong way to meditate; it's a matter of experimenting and discovering the best method for you.

Meeting Your Guardian Angel

Can you imagine what it would feel like to know that you are never alone and you have an angel watching over you and protecting you at all times? God assigned you at least two guardian angels at the time of your birth and they will be with you until the time that you leave this earth plane. Remember, you have to ask your guardian angels to be a part of your life.

QUESTION

How can I know for sure that my guardian angel is there?
Ask for a sign from them to know beyond any doubt that they are there to guide you along your journey. You can ask for a specific sign like a rose or you can ask for something that is significant to you.

There are different ways to connect with your guardian angels. First, share your desires with them. If you want to meet them in your meditation or dream state, ask them to make their presence known to you. If you want to feel comforted by their love or you want to know that you are safe and protected, then ask your guardian angels to help you feel this. If you want to receive messages of guidance, ask them to help you hear their loving voices through your thoughts.

Meditation to Connect with Your Guardian Angel

Would you like to meet your guardian angel? Go to your sacred space and set the intention that you will meet your guardian angel.

Get comfortable and close your eyes and take a couple of deep breaths. (Pause) Let go of whatever happened before your meditation and do the same for whatever is going to take place after your meditation. This is your special time and you are going to meet your guardian angel. Now in your mind's eye, imagine yourself in a beautiful meadow: the sun's shining, it's a beautiful day, and nature is singing all around you. The beautiful soothing light from the sun relaxes you and comforts you. You can really let go and just be there. (Pause)

As you look ahead, you see a beautiful path and you go toward the path, intrigued by where it may lead. As you follow the path you feel lighter and lighter. (Pause) It leads you into the most beautiful garden you have ever seen. This is your soul's garden. You can see, feel, and create all the beauty you desire in your garden. If you want waterfalls, there are waterfalls. If you desire animals, beautiful flowers and colors, it's all there. You create the garden of your wishes. Know that it's peaceful, it's sacred, and there is so much love in this garden. (Pause) Now, look for that perfect place to sit and rest. It could be a bench, a hammock, or you may just lie on the ground. (Pause) Know that as you sit in this beautiful place, your desire is to meet your guardian angel. Call out and ask your guardian angel to come close so you can feel or see her presence and know beyond any doubt that this is your guardian angel. Sit in silence, breathe, and receive. (Pause) When you're ready, ask your guardian angel if she has a message for you. (Pause) Ask that your guardian angel continue to guide you to the answers to your prayers. Share if there is anything you need help with. Thank your guardian angel and express your desire that you would like your guardian angel to continue to make her presence known to you.

Your guardian angels' mission is to serve and guide you. If you allow them, they can be your best friends, your teachers, and your bodyguards in spirit.

Writing with Your Angels

Journaling with your angels can be both healing and enlightening. Some people do very well with this technique of communication. Writing the messages might make it easier for you to bypass your intellectual mind so you can allow the pen to record the angelic thoughts flowing through your consciousness.

One way to start is to clear your mind. You can do this by writing on paper all the thoughts that go through your mind. They can be mundane like, "I loved my cup of coffee this morning" or they can be filled with stress and fear like, "I don't know how I am going to pay my mortgage this month." Just write and fill the pages until the pen stops or your mind quiets.

ESSENTIAL

The more you practice, the easier it gets and the more the words just flow onto the paper. A wonderful time to do this is early in the morning before you start your day. The mind is clearer, and what a beautiful way to start the day, with a message from your angels.

After your mind is clear, turn to a blank page and write at the top of the page, "My dearest angels, what would you like to say to me today?" Then breathe in the love of the angels all around you, listen, feel, and write down whatever comes to you. If you get images or colors, write them down. If you just get words, write them down. If you receive feelings, record the feeling. Trust that as you put your pen to the paper and you start writing, the words will come. Try not to think about what you are writing and certainly don't concern yourself with spelling, just write and let it flow.

Asking a Specific Question

You can also use writing to ask your angels to answer a specific question. Again, clear your mind through meditation or release your thoughts by writing them on paper. Then ask your angels to guide you during your writing session and ask them to lead you to your highest and best. On a blank piece of paper, write at the top, "Dearest angels, please give me your guidance on the following question (then write your question)." Breathe with the angels, listen, feel, and write down anything that comes to you. When you read your message, notice how it feels. If it is loving, encouraging, and supportive then this is a message from your angels. Then ask for guidance, ask for peace and allow yourself to receive the answers you are searching for. Trust that these messages can flow easily through the clarity of your thoughts onto the paper.

Angel Mail

This is a very powerful yet playful way to communicate with your angels. The angels want you to surrender your worries and prayers to them so they can help you.

Have you ever heard of the statement, "Let go and let God"? When you hold on so tight to your issues or when you want to control the outcome of your life, you get in your own way and it's harder for the angels to help you. Sending angel mail is a wonderful way to let go and ask for help. Write a letter to your angels and share your prayers, worries, and concerns, both for yourself and others. Then put it in an envelope and symbolically or literally mail it to God and the angels. As you mail it, surrender it and trust that it will be read and heard. Ask for divine resolution to occur and then let it go.

QUESTION

I am only getting words and not sentences. Am I doing something wrong?
No, there is no right or wrong way to communicate with the angels. Words can be very powerful. Listen and pay attention to the words you received. If you practice, words will eventually flow into sentences.

This is also a wonderful technique for children to use. They can color or write their prayers or fears on paper and together you can mail it to God. Imagine if you can teach a child from a very young age that she can let go of what's bothering her. Remind her that she can go to God and the angels for help. After you share this gift with your child, watch the peace on her face as she puts the letter in the mailbox.

Spend Time in Nature

Nature is God's sacred space and by spending time in its beauty you can easily connect to the oneness of all that is. In nature you can let go of the outside world and you can take time to breathe. You can distance yourself from the distractions that clog your mind and your emotions. Nature can be a very healing place if you allow yourself to receive its gifts.

No matter what time of year it is, you can commune with the angels and the energy of God in nature. Leave your headphones at home and walk in silence, listen and breathe. Ask the angels to clear your energy and your mind. Imagine the wind taking away all your cares and worries. As you breathe with nature, imagine breathing with the one breath of God. Then ask for guidance, ask for peace, and allow yourself to receive the answers you are searching for. The message might come from the sounds of nature or through the clarity of your thoughts. Nature is also just a wonderful place to just be with nothing to do. Take time out of your busy schedule to receive the blessings of God's beautiful creation.

Talking to Your Angels in the Car

Life can be crazy, running from one thing to the other. If you can relate to this and your day is filled with responsibilities and an endless to-do list, then this method of connecting with the angels is perfect for you.

ESSENTIAL

If you are running late and rushing to get somewhere on time, ask the angels to clear the traffic and give you green lights until you reach your destination. Also ask them to stretch time so you can get there on time.

God and the angels are everywhere and they are even present while you are driving in your car. So make the car your sacred space. Turn off the radio and invite your angels into your car. Ask your guardian angel to sit in the passenger seat and ask your other angels to fill the back seat. Then breathe with the comfort and support of knowing they are there with you. The angels are great listeners, so share with them your worries, fears, and concerns. Ask for the help you need so you can experience peace, balance, and joy.

It sounds so simple, but this time can be precious for those on the go. You will find that spending this time in silence and communion with your angels will create blessings throughout your entire day.

Dream with the Angels

Dream encounters with the angels have been described both in the Bible and in other sacred texts. Their visitations are also experienced by the everyday person. It's also noted that some people who have had near-death experiences or have been in a coma state have had very detailed and emotional encounters with the angels and God.

The average person spends eight hours a day sleeping, so this time can be used very wisely when working with the angels. During your time of sleep your conscious mind steps back, and because of this, you can get out of your own way so you can open up to other realms of consciousness. Before you go to sleep at night, ask the angels to enter your dream state. Ask them to help you remember what you dreamed the night before.

ALERT

If you tend to have scary dreams or you are afraid of opening up in your dreamtime, before you go to sleep ask the angels to keep you safe and protected. If you are experiencing precognitive dreams (dreaming about future events), ask the angels to help you remember only what you need to know.

You can ask for help with the following in your dream state:

- Ask the angels for any healing you need, physical, emotional, or mental.
- Ask the angels to help you connect with your loved ones in spirit so you can receive a message that they are okay.
- Ask the angels for guidance about anything in your life.
- Ask the angels for spiritual teaching or help in learning what you need to know to further your development.
- Ask the angels to help you travel to other places and other times.
- Ask the angels to help you connect with them and any other guides or divine helpers that want to work with you.

Choose to open up to the angels during this powerful time of sleep. Affirm before you go to bed, "Dearest angels, please enter my dreamtime tonight and help me with healing and share with me your clear messages of divine guidance (ask a specific question if you like). Please help me remember whatever I need to know when I awaken. Thank you." Keep a dream journal by your bed and when you wake up, record all your thoughts and impressions from the night before. You may be able to interpret some dreams immediately, while other dreams may be more symbolic and you might not understand them in that moment. Continue to record your dreams and in time your symbolism will transform into meaningful insight.

As you can see, there are many fun and different ways to explore and experiment with as you learn to communicate and connect with your angels. Play with them and enjoy each one. Discover which methods work best for you and continue your practice as you create a beautiful relationship and channel of communication between yourself and the angels.

CHAPTER 9

Doing an Angel Card Reading

Are you ready to have some fun and learn how to use the angel cards so you can do a reading for yourself? You will discover a playful way to receive powerful messages of divine guidance. The cards can be useful when you want clarity and messages of divine guidance about your past, present, and future. They can also help you get answers of divine guidance concerning your relationships, career, finances, health, and well-being. It's easier than you think, so open your heart and believe that you can do it.

Why Use Angel Cards?

Angel cards are tools. You can have some fun with the cards and, at the same time, you can enhance your relationship with the angels as you learn more about them. Use the cards as educational tools to help you learn more about the different roles the angels play and how they can help you in your life. For those of you who have a hard time hearing messages of divine guidance on your own, the cards can provide the clarity you need.

Most of the cards on the marketplace have helpful words and images. Each deck usually comes with a book that gives a description and detailed information about each card along with a message of divine guidance.

FACT

Another term used for the angel decks is oracle cards. The common theme of oracle cards is the power of positive thought. They are similar to divinity tarot cards, but they do not portray any of the darker images like the traditional tarot deck.

Angel cards are very different than tarot cards. They can act as a guide just like tarot cards, but angel cards have no negativity and there is nothing to fear. Angel cards reflect the positive, loving, and encouraging messages of the angels. They are a wonderful tool and they can help you gain clarity about anything and everything in your life.

Choosing Your Angel Cards

Take time to shop for your angel cards. It's very important to feel connected with your deck just as you want to feel connected with your angels. You can find angel decks at major bookstores, most new age shops, or shop online (in Appendix A you will find some specific recommendations of highly respected decks). Most stores will have open boxes so you can actually look at the decks. Pay attention to the images, the messages, and the feelings you get when you look at the cards. Trust that you will know and find the perfect deck for you.

You can also find some sites online where you have the option to choose an individual angel card or a series of angel cards by simply clicking on the featured deck. This is a great tool to get an idea of which decks resonate with you before you go out and purchase one.

ESSENTIAL

The dream state can be a wonderful time in which you can go to school with the angels. While in this altered state of consciousness, the time is ideal to journey into different dimensions where the angels can guide you and teach you all that you need to know.

Finding the perfect deck of cards for you is an adventure. Be curious and explore your options. Once you've found your perfect deck you will be pleasantly surprised. You will have a valuable tool in your spiritual toolbox that enhances your ability to connect with the angelic realm so you can receive loving messages of divine guidance.

Getting to Know Your Deck

Once you've selected your deck, take some time to get familiar with the cards. They each have their own significance and meaning. The more you know and understand about the meaning of the cards, the easier they are to work with.

There are several ways you can get to know your deck. Here are some suggestions you can try:

- Read the entire booklet that comes with your deck describing each card and its significant meaning.
- Pick one card at a time and learn the meaning of that card.
- Pick a card and before you read the booklet, write to the angels and ask them for the message and meaning of each card. (After you've finished writing, you can always go back and see what the book says.)
- Pick a card and place it by your bedside or under your pillow. Ask the angels to teach you the meaning of the card during your dream state.

The more you play with your cards and discover the meaning of their messages, the clearer the lines of communication become. The angels can use the cards to get your attention and to provide you with the answers to your prayers. The results will be well worth the time you spent getting to know your deck.

Gaining Insight from the Cards

The angel cards can become a helpful tool to communicate with the angels. You can use the cards to receive insight and to ask questions about all aspects of your life: relationships, finances, health, emotional well-being, life purpose, career, and other everyday questions. When you pick your cards you may understand immediately what the cards are trying to tell you. At other times you may need to pause for reflection to gain a full perspective on the messages. The following are some of the possible insights that you may receive from your reading:

- The reading may reveal an immediate answer to a prayer.
- The reading may suggest that you need to make some changes in your life.
- The reading might initiate healing: physical, emotional, mental, or spiritual.
- The reading might open your awareness so you can pay attention to the angels.
- The reading might provide you with the help and guidance you are seeking.
- The reading may give you direction or reveal steps to take that will lead you to the answer to your prayers.
- The reading may provide you with a feeling of peace, that you are right where you are meant to be and all is well.

Everyone has questions they would like answered. That's why psychics are so popular and so many people go to see them. But what if you could go to the angels and receive their loving guidance through the use of the cards? You could ask your questions and you would feel a sense of peace that the cards were guiding you with supportive insight. Experiment with the cards and see for yourself how it feels. Seek to discover if this is a good tool for you to communicate with the angels.

Preparing for an Angel Reading

Any time you pick cards or do an angel reading you want to create your sacred space and set your intention. Invite the angels into your sacred space and ask them to help you through the use of the cards. They are happy to assist you in any way they can. You can use the following steps to prepare for your angel reading:

1. Bring your journal or some paper to your sacred space.
2. Play some peaceful or angelic music in the background.
3. Close your eyes and always surround yourself with divine white light and protection.
4. Invoke your angels and ask them to surround you in a beautiful circle of love, light, and healing. Take a few moments and breathe as one with the angels and their loving presence.
5. Do a meditation that will raise your vibration so you can attune to their energy. (It does not have to be a long meditation; it's all about intention.)
6. When you are ready to do your reading, ask the angels to help you through the use of the cards. Ask them to guide you to the answers you are looking for.

Preparing for your angel reading sets intention and it clears your energy so you easily receive messages of divine guidance. Be open to receive your highest and best and know that the angels are right there with you, guiding you to the answers you are seeking.

Picking Angel Cards

Picking an angel card is a fun and insightful way to connect with your angels and to receive a message of divine guidance. You can pick an angel card to answer a specific question or you can just ask for guidance on what you need to know in that moment.

For example, "Dearest angels, what do I need to know today?" or you can ask a specific question. For example, "What do I need to know about_____?"

Take the follow steps to do a one-card reading:

1. Remember, always ask your angels to surround you in divine white light and energy before you pick a card.
2. Hold your deck of cards in your hands and say a prayer to receive a message that will guide you to your highest and best, better than you could ever imagine. (If you are asking a specific question, then state the question and ask that you be guided to the best card that will answer your question.)
3. Spread your cards out on the table. Then breathe and ask your angels to help you pick the perfect card. You can always look at the cards and see which card jumps out at you or you can pass your hand slowly across the cards. Feel through the energy in your hands and notice where your hand is drawn to and then pick that card.
4. After you select your card, you might have a clear meaning of what the card is telling you. If not, read the book that comes with the deck or ask the angels to help you understand what it means.
5. Thank your angels and ask that they continue to guide you.

Enjoy your journey while working with your angel deck. Witness your connections deepen between yourself, God, and the angels, and allow the cards to guide you to the answer to your prayers.

It may seem as if the card you selected doesn't have any significant meaning. If this happens, write down the card that you picked in your journal and stay in tune to the angels. Pay attention during the upcoming week. Most likely the card's meaning will be revealed in the next couple of days or by the end of the week.

Reading for Past, Present, and Future

Now that you've learned how to pick an angel card and receive a message of divine guidance, you are ready to move on to experience a three-card angel reading. The intention of this reading is to receive insight and guidance about your past, present, and future. Most people want to know what their future holds, but it's also important to realize how your past may still influence your present and the future. The greatest gift you can give yourself from this reading is to learn from the cards and allow them to give you the direction you need to live your best life in the present moment. Take these steps to do a reading to receive insight about your past, present, and future:

1. Ask your angels to surround you in divine white light and energy before picking your cards.

2. Hold your deck of cards in your hands and say a prayer asking to receive insight and guidance about your past, present, and future so you can be guided to your highest and best, better than you could ever imagine.

3. Spread your cards out on the table. Then breathe and ask your angels to help you pick the perfect cards. The first card is about the past. Choose your card and place it face-side up. The second card is about something significant or something you need to know about your present life. Choose your card and place it to the right (it will be your middle card). The last card is about your future and this card gets placed to the right of your present card. All cards can be faced right-side up.

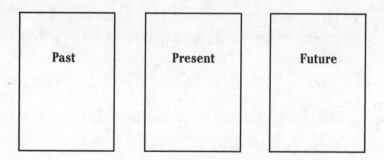

4. Take a few minutes and look at your spread of cards and ask the angels for guidance. Listen, feel, and ask for the clarity you need. If it is helpful, use the book enclosed with your deck of cards for further insight.

5. Close the reading by thanking your angels and asking them to continue to guide you so you may fully understand the significance of your reading.

6. If some of your cards don't make sense at the time of your reading, record your cards and review them at a later time. Trust that you will receive exactly what you need from your reading.

Each card shares a message or a story about what you need to know. The past card is very important. It shares information from your past that could help you heal or better your life in the present and the future. Your present card asks you to pay attention to what's happening in your life right now. Your future card is sending you a message about an opportunity or a healing that might take place down the road.

ALERT

It is always important to use discernment when doing a card reading. If the cards you pick don't feel right or you really don't understand the meaning of the cards, then reshuffle the cards and pray with the angels and ask for help in picking new cards.

Use this reading when you want to receive clarity or you need help understanding a current life situation. It will provide you with the insight you need to make better decisions, to take appropriate action or to just pay attention. Most often, you will finish your reading with a sense of peace and understanding.

Reading for Different Aspects of Your Life

Most people who come for an angel reading are looking for answers about certain areas of their lives. The most common questions asked are about relationships, career or life purpose, health and well-being, and finances. The following angel card reading will help you answer these questions, and it will also give you the opportunity to ask a specific question to be answered by divine guidance. Take the following steps to gain insight on these different aspects of your life:

1. Take the steps you've learned for preparing for an angel reading. Always ask your angels to surround you in divine white light and energy before picking your cards.

2. Hold your deck of cards in your hands and say a prayer asking to receive insight and guidance about your life so you can be guided to your highest and best, better than you could ever imagine.

3. Spread your cards out on the table. Breathe and ask your angels to help you choose the perfect cards as you pick with the following intentions.

4 The first card you choose is about relationships. You can ask about a specific relationship or you can ask for guidance about your relationships in general. Choose your card and face it right-side up.

5. The second card is about career or life purpose. Choose your card and place it to the right of the first card you picked.

6. The third card is about health or emotional well-being and this card gets placed to the right of your career and life purpose card.

7. The fourth card you choose is about a question of your choice and this card is placed at the end of the other cards. All cards can be faced right- side up.

Relationships	Career	Health	Question of Choice

8. Take a few minutes and look at your spread of cards and ask the angels for guidance. Listen, feel, and ask for the clarity you need. If it is helpful, use the book enclosed with your deck of cards for further insight.

9. Close the reading by thanking your angels and asking them to continue to guide you so you may fully understand the significance of your reading.

After you finish your reading take some time for reflection. See if the guidance you received can empower you to make some decisions or choices that will help you create the life you desire. God and the angels want you to live a life filled with peace, joy, happiness, health, and fulfillment. Allow this reading to be your compass guiding you in this direction.

Can You Do a Reading for Someone Else?

You can absolutely do an angel reading for someone else. It's recommended that you do readings for yourself first and really get to know your cards. Practice is the key. Each time you do a reading for yourself you expand your knowledge about the angels and their messages. With experience you gain confidence. This is exactly what you need to best facilitate an angel reading for another. Take the following steps when facilitating a reading for another person:

1. Explain what an angel reading is and how it can help them. Be sure to mention that the messages from the angels are always filled with positive thoughts, unconditional love, and encouragement.
2. Ask for permission to hold her hands. Your hands are faced palms up, because you are facilitating the reading. Ask both of your angels to create a beautiful circle of love, light, healing, and protection around you. Then breathe one with the angels' loving presence and relax and trust that they will guide you.
3. Ask the person you are reading for to take a deep breath and as she exhales, ask her to let go of everything that happened before the reading (you do the same). Then ask her to take another breath and as she exhales, ask her to let go of everything that's going to happen after her reading. Then together breathe in the present moment.
4. Set the following intention either silently or with your partner: "Dearest angels, guide me so I can give a reading for (say the person's name). Allow me to receive the guidance I need for her highest and best, better than she could ever imagine."
5. Release your hands. Then decide or ask her if she wants a one-card reading: a reading about past, present, and future; or a reading for the different aspects of her life.

6. Have her shuffle the deck or you can shuffle it for her. Spread out the cards and guide her to choose the number of cards needed to do the reading.

7. Take a few minutes and look at the cards. Ask the angels for help so you can share in their wisdom and guidance for the person you are doing a reading for. Listen, feel, and ask for the clarity you need. If it is helpful, use the book enclosed with your deck of cards for further insight.

8. After you complete the reading ask the other person if she understands the messages shared. If she seems confused about certain cards or messages shared, ask her to be open to her angels' guidance. Explain that she might not understand the meaning of the message now, but it is very possible that the clarity will come in the next couple of days or near future.

9. Give thanks to the angels and ask them to continue to help and guide the person you did a reading for. Share and encourage her to be open to the miracles ahead of her and to pay attention to how the angels might be trying to get her attention.

It is important to remember that after you facilitate the reading you need to disconnect from the energy of the other person. Your intention was to help her during the angel reading and now you need to release her to the angels. Imagine yourself "unplugging" from her energy just like unplugging a lamp from electricity. Trust it's in the highest and best of both of you to release and let go.

ESSENTIAL

Another way to receive guidance from the cards is to look at the illustrations expressed on the card. It can provide you with some valuable insight that you might not find in the words written on the cards or in the book enclosed with the deck.

It can be very rewarding when you share the angels' messages of love with another. Many people say that their life has been touched in a positive way after an angel reading. You will witness the other person experiencing a sense of peace and a knowing that she is never alone. The reading will reassure her that the angels are watching over her and are there to help her in any way they can.

You can use an angel reading to gain insight into all aspects of your life. The cards can be a fun and empowering tool to help you to receive messages of divine guidance. These messages can enlighten your life with more healing, joy, peace, and protection. Be open and practice using the angel cards so you can receive your personal miracles of divine inspiration.

CHAPTER 10

Synchronicity, Signs, and Coincidences

When you invite the angels into your life the world around you becomes a magical place. You enter into a flow of life where coincidences and synchronicities become your clues, leading you to the answer to your prayers. The angels know exactly how to get your attention. So get ready for some fun! The angels love to play and they want you to know beyond any doubt that they are here to guide you and assist in any and every way they can.

Angels' Nudges

Have you been asking the angels to help you? If so, it's time to start learning how they might be trying to get your attention so they can guide you to the answers you are seeking. The angels are always working behind the scenes in your favor. Sometimes it's through gentle nudges. For example, you're stuck and you need a sitter for the kids. You pray to the angels for help and minutes later your friend calls and offers to take your kids. Think about it: Maybe the angels planted your name in her thoughts so she would call you.

ESSENTIAL

An affirmation that will help you notice the angels' nudges: "Dearest angels, please get my attention and show me what I need to know. Help me see, hear, and experience the miracles of your love and guidance throughout my day. Thank you."

Other times the nudge might bonk you over the head. For example, you know the next step in your career is to get certified in a certain specialty and you ask your angels for help because you need the finances to pay for the course. Within the next week, you receive an unexpected check in the mail that covers the expense of the entire course.

The angels love to help and they are always working behind the scenes in your favor. Sometimes it's in small ways and other times it seems like a miracle. Be open to all their loving nudges and get ready to experience the magic of heaven on earth unfolding before your very eyes.

What Is Synchronicity?

Synchronicity is a coincidental occurrence of two or more events that have no relevance to one another, yet when it takes place it has great meaning to the person who is witnessing or experiencing it. The person who experiences a synchronistic event has previously said a prayer or they had a thought or a dream that later comes to fruition. They witness something that confirms what once was only an image or thought in their psyche. When this happens to you, you need to pay attention. This may be a form of divine communication where the angels are trying to give you a message or they want your attention.

ESSENTIAL

When you walk the spiritual path and you become more conscious, you realize everything happens for a reason. So a synchronicity is no accident. The angels use synchronicity to awaken you to their presence and guidance.

Carl Jung coined the term synchronicity and defined it as a meaningful coincidence. In his memoirs, he described a dream he had when he met his inner mentor archetype. He described him as a wise old man named Philemon. Philemon appeared as Hellenistic Gnostic and he wore a robe, had a long grey beard and colorful wings of a kingfisher. After his dream, Jung tried to illustrate the image of Philemon into a painting. The following quote describes what happened a few days after the dream took place:

During the days when I was occupied with the painting, I found in my garden, by the lakeshore, a dead kingfisher! I was thunderstruck, for kingfishers are quite rare in the vicinity of Zurich and I have never since found a dead one. The body was recently dead—at the most, two or three days—and showed no external injuries.

Carl Jung's experience is a perfect example of a how a dream can later manifest into a physical experience. Do you imagine that when Jung had this profound moment that he was being asked to pay attention to his wise inner guide? Make the choice from this moment forward to pay attention to those synchronistic events and if it's not as clear as Jung's experience, ask the angels to help you discern what it means.

What Is a Coincidence?

The word "coincidence" is actually two words, "co" and "incidence," which means when two things happen at the same time for no apparent reason. The meaning of coincidence is very similar to that of synchronicity, except when you experience a synchronicity, it is coincidence with meaning or significance. Here are some ways the angels work through coincidences.

- **The angels are trying to get your attention.** Example: You keep finding dropped dimes all around the house in the most obscure places.
- **The angels are reassuring you that you are not alone.** Example: You have asked the angels to make their presence known to you and you see angel pictures and statues wherever you go.
- **The angels are trying to point you in the direction that will lead you to your highest and best.** Example: You have asked the angels if it's in your best interest to go back to school and get your degree and that same week you receive a brochure in the mail from the college you were considering.
- **The angels are answering a prayer.** Example: You ask the angels to send you the perfect lawyer to help you through your divorce; you meet someone at an event and she shares that her husband is a divorce lawyer.
- **The angels are encouraging you to move forward toward your dreams.** Example: Your family has grown and you are looking for a bigger house but you're nervous about making the changes. You have been looking at this particular neighborhood and a "For Sale" sign goes up and the realtor's name is Maria Angell.

ESSENTIAL

Pay attention to how you feel after experiencing a coincidence or synchronicity. It's a natural high filled with excitement, wonder, and gratitude. Some people refer to coincidence as a God-incidence because it is a moment touched by the divine.

Experiencing coincidences can be magical and they can also validate that there is someone guiding you from the other side. Start noticing them and allow the angels to guide you through their gentle nudges so you can experience more peace, fulfillment, joy, and prosperity. It's all there waiting for you. Imagine that coincidences are gifts from the angels so you can manifest your dreams into reality.

What Is a Sign?

A sign is a confirmation from your angels. You can ask for a sign when you want the angels to validate their presence in your life. A good example of asking for a sign is that you did the meditation in this book to meet your guardian angel, but after you finished, you weren't quite sure if it was real. Then you ask your guardian angel to give you a sign that would confirm her presence. Watch for and pay attention to some of the following signs:

- Dropped dimes and pennies from heaven
- White feathers
- Angel trinkets or religious medals found in spontaneous places
- Strange animals appearing out of nowhere
- Smelling roses or flowers when none are present
- Hearing a song on the radio about angels or one that has significant meaning
- A street sign or a billboard with a message
- The phone ringing but no one is there
- Blinking lights or electrical items turning on and off
- Angel lights or forms appearing in your pictures

It's an amazing experience to witness any of these signs. They are all around you if you only notice and the more you notice, the more signs you experience. Allow the angels to get your attention and feel their loving presence through these magical moments.

Asking for a Sign

How do you ask for a sign? First, you need to decide if you want a specific sign from the angels, such as a rose or a butterfly, or if you want to leave it up to the angels to decide. Either way, tell the angels you want your sign to be recognizable beyond any doubt. It's important that you know for sure that the sign you receive is from your angels.

Second, tell your angels that you want your sign delivered by a certain day or time. This is especially important for those of you who are impatient or if you need to make a decision within a certain period of time.

Lastly, surrender your request to your angels and pay attention. Keep your eyes, ears, and heart open so you can expand your awareness to receive your sign. When you have received your sign, thank the angels. Feel the peace and joy in your heart knowing that you are not alone and that you have a council in spirit watching over you.

Another time you can ask the angels for a sign is when you need a specific question answered or you need confirmation to make a decision about something. Share your situation with the angels and tell them you want your question answered or confirmed with a specific sign. For example, you want to invest a large sum of money in a new stock that someone has recommended. You ask the angels for an undeniable sign of a star to confirm this particular stock and to validate that it's a good decision. The very next day your son brings home a picture from preschool and says, "Mom, look what I made" and there it is, a big yellow star, with the word "STAR" written on it and glitter splashed all over it. Do you think the sign was received and it's a good investment to make?

QUESTION

What if I didn't get a sign from my angels?
The angels might want you to look again at the decision or question you asked about. There might be a better direction they want you to contemplate or explore. If you have any more questions, go into meditation and ask the angels for clarity.

You will come to realize that a sign is a gift from God. It is a message from the divine saying you are not alone and we are here to help you. Take a moment and ask for your sign from the angels. Then open your awareness and expect the miracle of receiving your sign.

Angel Numbers

The angels can also use numbers and the sequence of numbers to get your attention. Most people have a favorite number and the angels know your number. If they are trying to get your attention, you might notice your favorite number on a license plate or it could be the address of the house you pass.

There are two well-known, specific angelic numbers to pay attention to, and when you see them, it could be a sign from your angels. The numbers are 1111 and 444. So when you see these numbers on a clock, in a phone number, or even on a check, feel reassured that the angels are all around you.

Angel messages for number sequences from *Angel Numbers* by Doreen Virtue, PhD and Lynnette Brown:

- **111:** An energetic gateway has opened for you rapidly manifesting your thoughts into reality. Choose your thoughts wisely at this time, ensuring that they match your desires. Don't put any energy into thinking about fears at all, lest you manifest them."
- **222:** Have faith, everything's going to be all right. Don't worry about anything as this situation is resolving itself beautifully for everyone involved.
- **333:** You're with the ascended masters, and they're working with you day and night—on many levels. They love, guide, and protect you in all ways.
- **444:** Thousands of angels surround you at this moment, loving and supporting you. You have a strong and clear connection with the angelic realm, and are an earth angel yourself. You have nothing to fear—all is well.
- **555:** Major changes and significant transformations are here for you. You have an opportunity to break out of the chrysalis and uncover the amazing life you truly desire.
- **666:** It's time to focus on Spirit to balance and heal your life. Tell heaven about any fears you have concerning material supply. Be open to receiving help and love from both humans and the angels.
- **777:** Congratulations! You've listened well to your divine guidance and have put that wisdom into fruitful action. You're now reaping the rewards. Your success is inspiring and helping others, so please keep up the good work.

- **888:** The universe is abundant and generous, and you have learned how to step into the shower of its ever-present flow. Great financial success is yours, now and in the future.
- **999:** Get to work, Lightworker! The world needs your divine life purpose right now. Fully embark upon your sacred mission without delay or hesitation.

From this moment forward be conscious of the numbers that grab your attention. They could be a sign from your angels trying to get your attention or maybe they just want to send their love and reassure you that you are not alone.

Pay Attention

Once you ask the angels to guide you through signs, synchronicities, and coincidences, you need to play your part, and that is, to open your awareness and pay attention. The answers are already there for you to discover.

ESSENTIAL

Affirmation to expand your awareness: "Dearest angels, please help me to be open so I can clearly recognize and notice the gifts of divine guidance all around me."

Here is a great analogy to contemplate that will help you understand this concept. Think about the last time you went shopping for a car. You went to the car dealership looking to test drive some cars that intrigued you. Let's say you really fell in love with the Toyota Camry, especially the silver-colored one. You leave the dealership with the intention that you're going home to think about it. The entire ride home all you see on the road are Toyota Camrys, especially in silver. Were those cars always on the road? Yes, but your awareness wasn't focused on noticing them. Now your awareness has expanded and you consistently see what you're focused on and what you desire.

The same is true about the angels. They have always been there. Now, you are choosing to see and experience them. You are opening up to different ways in which they can help you. You are expanding your awareness and you're noticing how they try to get your attention so they can communicate with you. Just like the cars, all of a sudden you begin to witness the angels working their miracles all around you. What a gift you give yourself every time you choose to pay attention and notice.

Notice Repetition

When you are not paying attention and the angels are trying to get their message across, they might use a little humor to help you take notice; it's called repetition. Have you ever heard the saying, "Pay attention when things happen in threes"? For example, within a matter of days three different people mention the same person. Maybe this is a sign to get in touch with that person.

The angels don't give up on you. So if you hear the same thing repeated over and over again in your head, listen to it and act upon it. When you experience repeated coincidences, synchronicities, or dreams around the same theme, pay attention because the angels are trying to tell you that it's important. Once you have noticed the repetition and you've acted accordingly or healed the situation, it will stop.

ESSENTIAL

If you are experiencing repetitive dreams, ask the angels to help you understand what the dream is trying to tell you. Some dreams are there to help you heal. So if there is healing that needs to take place, ask the angels to help you heal the root cause of the dream.

You can also ask the angels to reassure you with repetition when you don't trust the answers you are getting. For example, you have a major decision to make and you received a sign that affirmed your answer but you are still afraid of moving forward. Ask the angels to give you more confirmation so you can be reassured about making your decision.

Record the Magical Moments

When you walk your spiritual path and you open up to the angels, the world around you transforms into a magical place. Just imagine entering a fairytale where heaven and earth coexist.

No matter where you are along your journey, there is so much more for you to experience. The magic will continue to unfold and multiply if you choose. If you would like to initiate this energy, start a Magical Moments journal and record all the signs, coincidences, synchronicities, and miracles that occur around you. This practice will not only expand your awareness, but will also multiply your experience of the magic.

Remember the analogy of buying a new car. Once you bring your attention to what you want to see, the more you notice it's already there. As you record your magical moments in your journal, you begin to see how the angels are guiding you to the answer to your prayers. You gain clarity and confidence and you allow these magical moments to be signposts from heaven guiding you to your highest and best, better than you could ever imagine.

CHAPTER 11

How the Angels Want to Help You

The angels have a mission to serve and assist you along your journey. It is important to know that it is an honor for them to do so. In the following chapters you will discover how the angels can help you in all aspects of your life: career, finances, manifesting your dreams, relationships, and so much more. You will learn about the specific angels, their roles, and how they can help you in your everyday life. You will discover the power of prayer and how you can use it to invoke the angels into your life so you can be touched and blessed by their miracles.

Angel Assignments

God blessed you with the angels who act as messengers between heaven and earth. He knew that you would be challenged throughout your life experience and He did not want you to feel alone or separate from His love. The angels are here to help you. Just as you have roles here on earth—being a mother, a brother, a student, a teacher—the angels have roles, too.

Because God loves you so much, He assigned you at least two personal guardian angels. They are here to help you in any way they can and they watch over you twenty-four hours a day until you leave this lifetime.

If you are working in any type of healing or helping profession, you have a team of angels assigned to help you. There are also money angels, weather angels, prosperity angels, healing angels, and angels for everything you could imagine.

The archangels, who oversee the angels, also have specific roles to assist humanity in both subtle and profound ways. They are very powerful and even if a large number of people are praying for their help at the same time, they can be with each person simultaneously.

ALERT

Don't worry about memorizing the specific angel names and their roles; just call out and ask for the help. For example, you've lost your sense of direction and you don't know where you are. Call out, "Direction angels, please help me find my way or connect me with someone who can show me the way."

There are legions of divine helpers here on earth and there is no task too small or unimaginable that they cannot handle. Just remember, your assignment is to ask for their help; otherwise, they will not intervene unless it's a life-threatening situation.

Praying for Help

Many people who have experienced a strong religious upbringing struggle with guilt. Are you one of those people who feel guilty when you have a long list of prayers? Have you been taught that it's selfish to pray for yourself and you should only be praying for the needs of others? It's time to change your beliefs about the power of prayer. Here is what your angels want you to know when praying for help:

- Ask for help with anything and everything you need.
- There is no prayer too small or too big.
- You don't need to pray in any certain way. Discover what feels right for you.
- There is no special place for prayer. Pray everywhere and anywhere.
- Prayers are never counted. Ask in abundance.
- The angels would never see a prayer as selfish. Ask for yourself as much as you do for others.
- God knows exactly which angels to assign to the task.
- Trust and know there are more than enough angels.

God and the angels want you to be at peace when you communicate with them. They love you unconditionally, so there is nothing you could do or say that would take away from this love. They want you to feel comfortable asking for what you need. As you discover the power of prayer, you will understand how loved you really are.

Once You Pray, Then What?

You have sat in prayer with the angels and you've shared your desires and what you need help with. A powerful way to end your prayers and requests is with the following statement: "I am open to my highest and best, better than I could ever imagine, and the highest and best of all."

Think about the powerful intention of this affirmation.

"I am open to my highest and best, better than I could ever imagine."

You are surrendering your prayer to God, asking for divine will, and trusting that He knows what's in your highest and best. You are also affirming that you are allowing the best possible outcome to occur. This is significant if you have any issues around fear, guilt, or unworthiness. Can you imagine if your prayers were answered and the outcome was beyond your wildest expectations?

The last part of the affirmation, "and the highest and best of all," is very important. You want to affirm to yourself and the angels that the desired outcome of your prayer will benefit all concerned. For example, if you are praying for guidance about a new job that involves moving your family, you want God and the angels to show you an answer that will benefit all concerned. So if for some reason things do not work out, you would know based on your prayer that it did not manifest because it was not in everyone's highest and best to make the move. This can bring you great peace even in the midst of disappointment.

Once you pray to God and the angels and you ask for the help you need, your job is to surrender and then affirm that you are open to receive more than you can imagine. This gives the angels permission to intervene and it affirms your worthiness to receive.

Have Faith and Trust

Trusting in God and believing in something greater, especially when you can't see it or touch it, is a challenge. It requires patience and determination. As you open your heart to the divine, you begin to experience these beautiful manifestations of love and naturally your faith and trust builds over time.

FACT

Faith means a firm belief in something for which there is no proof. Another meaning is belief and trust in God. Maybe that's why in Matthew 17:20 Jesus says, "I tell you the truth, if you have faith as small as a mustard seed, you can say to this mountain, 'Move from here to there' and it will move. Nothing will be impossible for you."

Isn't it true that your faith deepens every time you witness your prayers being answered and fulfilled? But what happens when you feel your prayers are left unanswered? Have you ever gone through a time in your life when you questioned, "Is there really a God out there watching over me?" The truth is, your prayers are heard and answered, but not always in the way you expect. It could be a matter of timing, where everything needs to fall into place before the answer is shown. Some people call this divine timing, which means that your prayers are being answered in God's time. It's important to understand that you also have soul lessons to learn. You need to go through certain life experiences so you can learn valuable lessons. Instead of having them healed immediately by God and the angels, you might need to go through the experience so you can accept its gifts and the lessons it has to teach you. This is important to understand so you can keep the faith and truly believe that you have spiritual helpers assisting you along the journey.

ESSENTIAL

If you want to enhance your faith in God and the angels, use the following affirmation: "I choose to deepen my faith and believe. I trust that all my prayers are heard and answered for my highest and best and the highest and best of all."

Another reason your prayers may not be answered in the way you expect is because God and the angels know what's best for you. Think about it: Have you ever looked back on your journey and realized that an unanswered prayer was a blessing in disguise? For example, you were ready to sign a purchase and sale agreement on a new home and it fell through, leaving you feeling disappointed and discouraged. Because of this situation, you found a house that was better and less expensive than the first one. Later on you found out that the first house had water issues. You can believe that your angels are working behind the scenes and they do know what's in your best interest.

Feeling Worthy and Deserving

Many people struggle with the issue of feeling unworthy and undeserving. They have trouble receiving what's rightfully theirs as a child of God. The angels will remind you that you deserve the best and it's your divine right to be happy, joyful, fulfilled, and prosperous.

If you deal with these issues, then it's your job to shift your thinking. You need to change your beliefs so they match your worth as a child of God. This is so important when you think about the angels answering your prayers. Let's say you asked the angels to help you fulfill your dream of going to Italy, but deep down inside you feel unworthy of receiving such an expensive and luxurious trip. Believe it or not, you are very powerful, and because of your inner beliefs, you could block that trip from happening, even though the angels have everything worked out to make it possible.

ESSENTIAL

Ask the angels, "Dearest angels, help me change my thinking so I can believe and know beyond any doubt that I am worthy and deserving of the best. I am a child of God and I am open to receive the kingdom of heaven here on earth."

Another question to ask yourself is, "Can you accept help and do you deserve it?" Take a couple of moments and reflect on this thought. Are you willing to let others help you so you can experience more peace, health, fulfillment, or prosperity, and if they do, do you deserve it? This is significant because the angels might send people into your life that act as earth angels. They come as an answer to your prayers and it's your job to let them in, allowing them to help you in any way they can. This may be hard for you, so get ready to be humbled by the help of others. Did you ever stop to think that when you allow others to help you, you might be helping them?

When you ask the angels for help with certain aspects of your life— relationships, finances, health, home, or career— make sure you check in and affirm to yourself that you are worthy and deserving of receiving the best. This will clear the way so you can easily receive what you've asked for and more.

Believe

Now that you have planted the mustard seed of faith in your heart and you feel worthy and deserving of the best, your next step is to believe that anything is possible with the help of God and the angels. Release your prayers and requests to the angels and then let go of the specifics. You don't have to know how it's going to happen, when it's going to happen, or where it's going to take place. Your job is to hold the vision and believe that anything's possible. When it does come fruition, you need to play your part. If action is required and you need to initiate it, then do so. The manifestation of a prayer is a cocreation; the angels do their part and so do you.

ALERT

Stay away from negative people and situations when you are focused on manifesting your dreams into reality. Surround yourself with people who believe in you and support your vision.

Here is an example to help you understand the power of believing. You've asked the angels to help you find the perfect job, at the perfect place, with the perfect people, and at the perfect pay; therefore, you've set your clear intentions on what you want. You take the time to research the market and you spend time looking for that perfect job, but still there's nothing out there that matches your desires. When this happens, you need to keep the faith and stay focused on your dreams and desires. Affirm your dream, visualize it, and keep surrendering it to the angels. Ask the angels for patience and perseverance and then continue to believe that anything is possible, and most importantly, don't settle for less. You will witness your faith and belief in the angels paying off. Before you know it, you will be sharing your story with others and encouraging them to believe that anything is possible.

Take Action

Throughout this book you have learned some key steps to take when working with the angels. Here is a quick review of the basics:

1. Ask the angels for help.
2. Surrender your prayers and feel worthy to receive your highest and best.
3. Have faith and trust in God and the angels and believe anything is possible.
4. Pay attention to the signs, synchronicities, and coincidences.
5. Take action.

This last step is one of the most important steps. You need to take action on any guidance you receive. You need to follow every clue the angels give you until your prayers are answered. Here are some great examples:

- You are praying for more prosperity and someone crosses your path and recommends a book about creating more abundance in your life. Do you buy the book or do you ignore the message?
- You ask your angels to help you meet your soul partner and you unexpectedly get invited to a social event. Do you have the courage to go or do you remain in your comfort zone and stay home?
- You ask the angels to guide you toward your life purpose. An old coworker from a previous job calls you and says she's starting a new business. She wants to know if the two of you can meet. Do you respond in fear and question her motives or do you approach it with curiosity, wondering if there's an opportunity waiting for you?

ESSENTIAL

When you think of miracles you think of Jesus. He was a teacher and He was the embodiment of Spirit in human form. He performed miracles proving to everyone that when you become one God and you create from the divine power of love, miracles happen.

You play an important role in helping the angels answer your prayers. It takes courage to follow the clues and, when you take action accordingly, you will discover that you can cocreate with the angels so you can manifest what you really want in your life.

Expect Miracles

One definition of miracle is "a wonder or a wonderful thing" and another definition is "an extraordinary event of divine intervention." When you look at these two definitions, miracles occur every day. Some miracles are small, such as you think you're going to be late for work and you get a green light at every intersection and you actually get to work on time. Other miracles are extraordinary, like a man falling fifteen stories and surviving with only minor breaks and bruises.

When you work with the divine power of love, expect miracles to happen in both subtle and profound ways. A powerful affirmation you can say to invite miracles into your life is: "I am fearless. I embrace today with love in my heart. I am expecting miracles and I am accepting miracles." As you say this statement, feel your worth and believe that you deserve to receive miracles in every aspect of your life. Then begin to notice the blessings of love all around you. Say thank you to God and the angels each and every time you witness a miracle and share your miracles with others so they, too, can be open to their blessings.

CHAPTER 12

Help from the Angels in Everyday Life

What if your angels could help you with your everyday life challenges? Think how much more peaceful you would feel if you could surrender your worry, negativity, and impatience to God and the angels. They truly want to help you throughout your day so you can experience more balance, ease, and joy. Make the choice to wake up every morning and thank the angels for helping you behind the scenes so you can witness a day filled with blessings and grace.

Everyday Life Stuff

Life is a journey and every day is a new experience. Sometimes life is predictable, and you understand your responsibilities and what to expect from your day. Then there are other days, where life can be unpredictable. You experience minor challenges that cause you stress and throw you off balance. For example, your alarm clock doesn't go off, you get stuck in traffic, your boss is in a bad mood, or the kids are fighting. Other challenges may have a greater affect on your life. For example, a death or sickness in the family, a change or loss of job, a divorce, or a local or world event that may directly distress you and your family. Whatever the experience may be, the angels know you have good days and bad days and they are willing to help you in any way they can.

Here are some different ways you can ask the angels to help you throughout your day:

- Before you get out of bed in the morning, ask the angels to help you create a day filled with ease and grace.
- If you're running late, ask the angels to stretch time or ask them to intervene so you can get where you need to go and still be on time.
- If you are worried about anything that's going to take place during your day, surrender it to the angels and ask for their help.
- Ask the angels to surround you with divine white light so no negativity from others can affect you.
- On your way home from work, release your day to the angels and give all your cares and worries to them so you can go home and relax.
- If you're worried about someone during your day, pray to the angels and ask them to watch over that person.
- If you want to enjoy a peaceful night's sleep, surrender your day to the angels and ask for any help you need for anything left unresolved.

Make a point throughout your day to check in and notice how you feel. If things are flowing and you feel calm, be grateful. If you need help from the angels, stop and consciously ask for what you need. Over time you will realize you have the power to shift your experience in any given moment, no matter what's happening around you. Remember that your angels are always there to help you do this.

Gaining Patience

One of the meanings of patience is, "to suffer with strength of mind and courage." Another meaning is, "to hold steadfast in the midst of difficulty." Maybe that's why they say patience is a virtue; because it takes strength to hold back and breathe when you feel things are out of your control or you can't see the outcome of what's going to happen.

One of the most common messages of divine guidance is that of patience. The angels ask you to trust in divine timing and that everything is happening for a reason. Most people want to be in control, and when they feel things are out of their control they suffer. When this happens the angels will step in and remind you to have patience. This patience could be about your own personal growth and goals or about other people with whom you need to practice patience. You may be asked to accept them for who they are and not to judge their choices. It's important to remember that when you practice patience, you experience compassion and peace both for yourself and others.

FACT

Reflect on these famous quotes about patience: "The greatest prayer is patience." –Buddha; "I just have three things to teach: simplicity, patience, compassion. These three are your greatest treasures." —Lao Tzu; "Adopt the pace of nature: her secret is patience." —Ralph Waldo Emerson

Exercise to Practice Patience

Think of something going on in your life right now that requires patience. Take out your journal or a piece of paper. Ask your angels to surround you and breathe one with their love. Then write the following question: "Dearest angels, is there anything I can do today that will bring me more peace?" Listen, feel, and allow the answer to come. When you finish, ask the angels if there are any action steps you can take. If the angels share with you that you need to be patient and they advise you to accept what is right now, pray for patience and surrender the issue to the angels for divine resolution. Know that you have the power to choose peace in any moment. Simply affirm, "I am patient, and the angels will show me what I need to know."

Healing Guilt

The words that are associated with guilt are: remorseful, wrongdoing, blame, and sinful. The words associated with guilt are based on fear, not love. Guilt is so unnecessary and it causes heaviness in mind, body, and spirit. If and when you do experience guilt, learn from your choices and make changes if you need to, but most importantly, don't stay stuck in it. It does not serve you or anyone else involved.

To release guilt you need to practice forgiveness for yourself. Archangel Zadkiel, the archangel of mercy and benevolence, will help you with this. He will remind you to stop judging yourself and he will help you feel compassion toward yourself. As you do this, you will feel peace and freedom from the restrictions of guilt.

ESSENTIAL

Prayer for healing guilt: "Archangel Zadkiel, help me to forgive myself and free myself from guilt. Teach me about self love and compassion and help me to learn from my choices so I can be a better person and ultimately experience inner peace."

Take some time to reflect on this discussion of guilt and see how the emotion of guilt might be holding you back. If you're ready and you want to heal and transform guilt to forgiveness and compassion, then call on God and Archangel Zadkiel for help. Let them help you free yourself so you can accept the innocence of who you are.

Releasing Worry

How much time do you spend worrying about things that are out of your control? Do you ever look back and realize how much time and energy you spend on wasted worry? If you think about it, most of the time, you end up worrying about something that never happens. If you take worry to an extreme, it can mentally exhaust you and cause you physical illness.

Some worries are justified and can help you make better choices. For example, the doctor says you're overweight and because you worry you choose to eat better and exercise. There are the worries that cause needless stress such as worrying about what other people think or obsessing during the day about whether you locked the door when you left the house or worrying about the safety of your teenager who is driving in the snow. When it comes to worry, the angels can help you. Your job is to recognize it and then choose to release it to the angels.

Follow these steps to release your worry and ask for help from the angels:

1. Recognize and acknowledge your worry. Spend a couple of days being conscious and record all the things you worry about—both your minor and major worries.
2. Sit with your list and ask yourself, "How does it make me feel to worry about these things?"
3. Next, take a look at your list again and ask yourself, "How many of those things I feared or worried about actually happened?"
4. Take responsibility. Is there anything on your list that you are worried about that's within your control and you can affect? If so, list your action steps.
5. Surrender the rest of your worries to the angels. Let go and let God find the divine resolution.

You can use this powerful visualization to release worry. Imagine the angels want to help you by giving you a worry basket. They ask you to release all your worries into the basket, both big and small. Next, imagine they lift your worries and they carry the basket into the divine light. They place the basket into the hands of God for divine resolution.

Every time you let go of worry you free your mind, body, and spirit. Not only do you free yourself but you also help all those people you once worried about. Think about it: If you send fear and worry to others, what do you imagine they feel? Reflect on how they might feel after you ask the angels for help and you release them from your fear and worry. Trust that the angels will watch over them and they will feel loved and protected. What a gift you give them by choosing to surrender your worry.

Protection for Your Children

It's natural for parents to worry about their children, and the angels know that one of the toughest jobs here on earth is being a parent. Unfortunately, God didn't send each child with a manual, but he did send his angels to watch over and protect every one of them.

It's important to remember that when your thoughts are focused on worry and fear, your children will feel this energy, even if you are hundreds of miles away. When you choose to call on the angels and you ask them to surround your children in love and protection, imagine what they would feel in comparison to worry and fear. It's in the highest and best for you and your children to learn how to stop and shift your thoughts from fear into faith, and the angels can help you do this. Following are some examples of when you can invoke the angels to watch over and protect your children:

- Your child is sick and you are worried.
- You are leaving your kids with a sitter or home alone.
- Your teenager is driving or is with another teen driver.
- Your children are at school and you're concerned.
- You have older children and you're having a hard time accepting their choices.
- You have a troubled child and you don't know what to do.
- You have grandchildren and you worry about them.

It doesn't matter what the situation is, the angels know your thoughts and they can feel your concern. From the instant that you request their assistance, they will surround you and your children in love and protection.

Call on Archangel Michael

Archangel Michael is the powerful protector, and his name means "he who is like God." You might recognize him as the archangel who carries a sword, symbolizing his ability to release resistance and cut through fear. He is the archangel of protection, so when you call on him you will immediately feel his warmth, love, and protection. Ask Archangel Michael to watch over your children when you worry or if you cannot be with them. He will embrace them with love and he will shield them in his powerful protection. After you call on him, notice how you feel. Trust that your children are in God's hands and they are being well taken care of.

Call on Their Guardian Angels and Ten Thousand Angels

Not only can you call on Archangel Michael, but remember, God assigned your children at least two guardian angels to watch over them for their entire lifetime. Whenever you need help with your children, go to their guardian angels and talk to them. Tell them what your worries and fears are and ask them to help your child. Then let go and trust that they will do their job. Be open to the miracles of their assistance and welcome the peace you will feel as you let go and allow the angels to take over.

ESSENTIAL

Prayer for protection for your children: "Dearest Archangel Michael, please be with my children now. Watch over them and surround them in your powerful protection. Keep them safe. Help them feel loved and surrounded in God's love and light. I trust God and have peace that you are watching over them. Thank you."

Last but not least, in the kingdom of God there are countless numbers of angels to serve humanity. When you feel the need, you can assign 10,000 angels to watch over your children. Imagine how you and your children will feel when Archangel Michael, their guardian angels, and 10,000 angels watch over and protect them. Isn't it worth taking the time to pray to invoke their assistance?

Negative Thoughts to Positive

You are very powerful and your thoughts are very powerful. Have you heard the quote from William James, "As you think, so shall you be"? Your thoughts create your experiences and your reality. When your thoughts are positive you create happiness, joy, fulfillment, and peace. If your thoughts are focused on the negative you can create fear, sickness, and stress. This is why it's so important to stay conscious of your thoughts and when you are focused on the negative, call out to the angels for help.

ALERT

When you catch yourself focusing on the negative or thinking about something you don't want to experience, say, "Cancel, cancel." This affirms that you are stopping the energy of your thoughts from going out into the universe to take on form or to reach other people.

The angels will encourage you to raise your vibration from negative thinking to positive thinking. Here are some ways to shift your energy and thoughts to the positive:

- When you're focused on lack or what you don't have, focus on the blessings in your life.
- Change your negative thoughts into positive affirmations. Say or write them daily until you create what you do want.
- When you're feeling doubtful or afraid, spend time in meditation with the angels. Spend time visualizing and feeling what you do want to experience.
- If you have negative thoughts about another person, send love to them and pray for them.
- Be conscious of your negative self-talk and when you catch yourself, say something kind and loving to yourself.
- Keep a gratitude journal and express gratitude every day.

As Norman Vincent Peale said, "Change your thoughts and you change your world." You have the power to do this and the angels will help you in any way they can. Make a commitment to yourself that you will pay attention to your thoughts. Focus on kind and loving thoughts toward yourself, others, and the world.

Gaining Peace with the Angels

Peace is a feeling, and you experience it when you're calm in mind, body, and spirit. Choosing your thoughts carefully is a step toward peace, but making choices and taking action to create more peace in your life is equally important.

Once you realize there's a situation in your life that's causing you pain, sadness, or stress, it's time to step back and reflect. Ask this question: "What do I really want and what will bring me peace?" Sometimes peace requires change, and change can be scary. Call on the angels for courage and ask them to support and guide you as you make the necessary changes in order to move forward. The angels know you deserve serenity and it's your divine right to have peace.

Peace is a choice, and in any moment you can choose to experience peace. It doesn't matter where you are, who you are with, or what's going on, you can always choose to stop and breathe. As you take that precious breath, ask the angels to surround you in peace and then affirm, "I choose peace. I am peaceful."

Prayer for Peace

Dearest angels, I call on you now to help me find peace in this situation (share your situation with the angels). I realize peace is found in the moment, so please help me stay present in this moment, knowing that I am okay right here and right now (breathe with the angels). Help me become one with peace in my mind, body, and spirit. I surrender this situation to divine intervention and I trust that all is well. Thank you, angels, for this gift of peace and for your continued love and support.

Accepting What Is

Millions of people use the serenity prayer. Part of the passage says, "God grant me the serenity to accept the things I cannot change; courage to change the things I can; and the wisdom to know the difference." The depth of its meaning is profound, and when it's practiced, it can open up a pathway to peace. As the prayer states, serenity is experienced when you can accept the things you cannot change. Have you ever tried to change someone, expecting them to be different or wanting them to be someone you thought they should be? It can be exhausting and disappointing. Peace comes when you finally accept that person for who they are. If it works, great; if not, you find the courage to make your own choices or go your own way.

It's the same for situations in your life. You need to ask yourself, "Is this something I can change or is it out of my control and do I need to accept what is with peace?" For example, the price of gasoline, goes up and you decide that you can't control the price of gasoline but you can conserve on gas and plan your errands accordingly. You can find peace in accepting what is (the price of gasoline) and you can also feel empowered to make choices that will benefit you (conserving gasoline), and in the end you create more peace.

Serenity Prayer

It takes patience and determination to accept the things you cannot change. Call upon God and the angels and ask for the healing that you need in order to let go. If the words from the serenity prayer have meaning to you, print a copy of it and place it somewhere special. Use it and allow yourself to be blessed by its words of wisdom.

God, give us grace to accept with serenity the things that cannot be changed, Courage to change the things which should be changed, and the Wisdom to distinguish the one from the other.

Living in the Moment

When you live in the moment, the past is history and the future does not exist. There is only the now. Many on the spiritual path practice living in the moment because this is where they discover peace. It's easier said than done because you are human, and the mind wanders into the past and the future, causing your thoughts to create emotions that disturb your peace. For example, you may be thinking about someone who hurt you in the past and you feel sad or angry or your mind may wander into the future, thinking about the bills you need to pay, and this creates anxiety and worry. It takes practice and consciousness to live in the present, but the reward is peace.

ESSENTIAL

Reflect on these quotes about living in the present: "You can clutch the past so tightly to your chest that it leaves your arms too full to embrace the present." ~Jan Glidewell; "Yesterday is history. Tomorrow is a mystery. And today? Today is a gift. That's why we call it the present." ~Babatunde Olatunji

You can practice living in the moment to create peace in lots of different ways. For example:

- Be conscious of your breath. By simply breathing, you can pull yourself back into the present moment.
- You can practice being present while washing the dishes, brushing your teeth, or doing the laundry. Pay attention to the feeling, the colors, and the movement.
- Try a meditation or yoga class.
- Take a walk and notice your surroundings, the wind blowing the trees, the color of the flowers, and the animals moving in nature.
- While driving in the car, don't worry about your destination; practice paying attention to your hands on the wheel, the traffic lights, or the signs on the road.
- The next time you're with someone, really pay attention. Listen to what they say, focus on eye contact, and breathe with them.
- Watch children and learn from them. They can live fully in the present moment.

The gift of being present to the moment is inner peace. In this place of inner peace is a state of oneness, and when you experience this, you know God and the angels are present with you.

Prayer for living in the present moment

Dearest angels, I realize peace is found in the present moment. I need your help in finding peace. Help me let go and remember the past is the past. Help me surrender my worries and my what ifs about the future, knowing that there is nothing to worry about if I trust God. Remind me when I am drifting into the past or the future and please nudge me back into the present moment where peace is found. With your help, I accept the gifts and peace found in the sacredness of the present moment.

You have the opportunity in every moment to feel more peaceful just by reaching out to the angels and asking for help. Set your intentions in the morning and declare what you want to feel and experience throughout your day. Believe that the angels are with you, and if something comes up, know that they can help you transform worry into trust, impatience into patience, guilt into forgiveness, and anxiety into peace.

CHAPTER 13

Fun Help from the Angels

The angels want you to enjoy life and live it to its fullest. Every day is precious, and you have the opportunity to see it for its best or its worst. Are you ready to have some fun? Expect to smile when the angels give you the perfect parking spot and choose to celebrate when a cloudy forecast on vacation turns into the perfect sunny day. Invite the joy of the angels into your life and feel a childlike wonder as you experience the magic of heaven on earth.

Lighten Up with the Angels

Are you feeling overworked, underpaid, or unfulfilled? Are you taking life too seriously and feeling overwhelmed with responsibilities? If this is the case, then you need to invite the angels into your life and ask them to play with you. Ask them to help you lighten up so you can enjoy life, even if it's for a small amount of time, in the midst of all your responsibilities.

ALERT

Guilt can hold you back from joy. When you struggle with this emotion, ask your angels to free you from this burden. Ask them to replace it with freedom so you can take care of yourself and enjoy life.

Life is too short, and most people only discover this when they go through a serious illness or they've lost a loved one. Don't wait for this to happen to you. Give yourself permission to enjoy life and ask your angels to show you the opportunities to do this. Then pay attention. When you're invited to parties, to the theater, or any other fun activity, say yes and give yourself permission to have some fun. If you need the funds to support the things you love to do, then ask the angels for the extra money you need and trust that it will come.

Here are some different ways the angels might nudge you to play:

- Take a vacation. Ask the angels to help you find the time to go and the finances to support it. Make your plans and trust that you deserve a vacation.
- Forget the diet and enjoy your favorite ice cream or dessert.
- Take a spontaneous day and give yourself permission to do all the things you love.
- Start a hobby or take a class that you are interested in.
- Get on the floor and play with your children or grandchildren.
- Go to the movies with friends or by yourself.
- Take a walk on the beach, build a sandcastle, or read your favorite book.
- Do nothing. Stop thinking you have to do something.

Believe that God and the angels want you to be happy and they will support you with everything you need to enjoy life. Your job is to feel worthy and deserving of receiving joy and taking the time to experience it. The next time you get an idea to have some fun or an opportunity comes your way, see it as a gift from your angels. Say yes and have some fun.

ESSENTIAL

Prayer to lighten up: "Dearest angels, help me and remind me to accept joy, play, and fun into my life. Show me the opportunities and encourage me to take the time so I can enjoy life and live it to its fullest."

Parking Angels

Yes, there really are parking angels and you might not believe it until you try it out for yourself. The next time you're looking for a parking spot, call on the parking angels and ask them for the perfect spot closest to the entrance. Don't be surprised if it's either waiting for you or someone pulls out right when you get there. Invoking the angels at Christmas time is very helpful, especially if you're off to the mall and living in colder climates. Just remember, it's always a kind gesture to thank your angels after receiving your perfect spot.

FACT

One of the specific angels to call on for parking spaces is Gamliel. He is known as the gracious gift giver, and you can call on him to help you find the perfect spot in any crowded parking lot.

Calling on the parking angels is also a great way to get kids involved in asking for help from the angels. They think it's magical when the perfect spot reveals itself and it helps them believe that the angels are really listening. Sometimes with children you need to start with the small prayers so they feel more comfortable when it's time to ask for the bigger things in life.

Once they witness the miracles of asking and receiving, they are more open to the possibilities or working with the angels.

Weather Angels

Reflect on this for a moment: You've worked really hard and it's time for a vacation and it's important for you to have nice weather to experience it to its fullest. Wouldn't it be nice if you could call on the help of the weather angels so you could really enjoy your vacation? It might be hard to believe that the angels can help you with the weather, but why wouldn't they want to help you experience a fun and enjoyable vacation?

So the next time you go on vacation or when you're having an important event like a party, graduation, or barbecue, pray to the weather angels beforehand and ask them for a beautiful, clear, and sunny day (if that's important) so everyone can fully enjoy the event. You can also call on the weather angels when you desire clear weather for traveling of any kind. Simply ask, "Please, weather angels, clear the way for smooth traveling and clear weather so we can reach our destination safely with ease and timeliness."

ESSENTIAL

One of the specific angels to call on for weather is Archangel Uriel. He was the archangel who warned Noah that the floods were coming and he is the one who helps with all those affected by weather conditions and natural disasters. He will immediately come when you call him.

You can also call on the weather angels if you need help during unexpected weather conditions like snowstorms, heavy downpours, hurricanes, or thunderstorms. For example, "Archangel Uriel, please provide protection for myself and my loved ones and help us to feel safe as the effects of Mother Nature move peacefully through our surroundings."

Traveling Angels

Traveling can be very joyful, adventurous, and exciting, and other times it can be a journey into the unknown, where you experience fear, anxiety, and stress. Inviting the angels to travel with you can give you a sense of peace that you are not alone and you are being watched over, no matter what the situation might be.

There are many ways in which the angels can assist you while traveling:

- When flying, request that the angels watch over the plane and the pilot and ask that your flight be safe, smooth, and on time. You can also imagine angels resting on the wings of the plane.
- When traveling by car, ask the angels to watch over and protect your vehicle and all passengers with you. Ask for a clear path ahead so your travels are smooth and timely.
- When traveling with luggage, ask your angels to watch over it and request that it arrive at your destination when you do.
- When visiting unfamiliar places, ask for protection so you can feel safe and ask the angels to send the perfect people to help and guide you to the best places to visit, stay, and eat.
- If you are traveling on business, ask the angels for everything you need to make it a pleasurable and successful trip.
- Remember to ask for the weather you need to get to your destination and to enjoy it while you are there.
- If loved ones are traveling without you, ask for the angels to protect them and watch over them until they return safely home.
- Ask the angels to watch over your home, your job or business, or any loved ones left behind while you are traveling.
- If an issue or glitch in your travel plans emerges, ask the angels to resolve it quickly and to provide everything you need to work through it with ease and grace.

It is a gift to travel so you can connect with loved ones, experience new places, create success in business, or to just rest and relax. The angels want you to experience these opportunities with ease and joy. So call on them and discover how they can lighten the load for you when it comes to travel.

Specific Traveling Angels

The following are specific angels to invoke while traveling. Simply call them by name and ask them for what you need. Know that it is an honor for them to serve you and assist you in any way they can.

- Archangel Raphael is the patron of travelers. He watches over all those who ask for safe and smooth travel.
- Archangel Michael is the protector, and can keep you from harm in all situations. You can also call on Michael if you get lost and need directions or if you need any assistance in solving mechanical difficulties.
- Suriel is the angel named in the Kabbalah who rules over earth and is considered the angel of protection. Ask Suriel to watch over your home and possessions while traveling.
- Archangels Uriel and Zapiel work on regulating weather conditions.

You can call on these angels and archangels individually or you can call on them as a team. When you assign them to their tasks, notice how you feel. You can travel worry free and feel reassured that you have a team working behind the scenes taking care of all your needs.

Traveling prayer

Archangel Raphael, Archangel Michael, Suriel, Archangel Uriel, and Zapiel, please watch over and protect all of us as we travel to our destination. Please watch over and make sure our method of transportation is working efficiently and that it's safe and wrapped in the protective light of God. Assist Mother Nature and ensure that the weather is perfect for our travels and we arrive at our destination in a timely manner. Our travels are smooth, safe, and easy because of your loving attention and assistance. Thank you for watching over our home, pets, and children while we are away.

Mechanical Angels

Take a moment and reflect on the last time you experienced mechanical difficulties. Maybe it involved a problem with your computer, a household appliance, or even your car. When this happens you usually experience unexpected financial expenses, worry, and the excess stress of being inconvenienced. This is a perfect time to call on the angels for help, and you can specifically call upon the mechanical angels to assist you.

Archangel Michael is one of these divine helpers, and he can miraculously fix mechanical and electrical devices of all kinds. Call on him to assist you in any situation: with your car, computer, or any household appliance. Simply assign him to the task that needs fixing and trust that he will rush to the job with the intention of resolving the problem. Pathiel is another angel you can call upon specifically to help you with resolving computer problems. Allow him to assist you and watch how you receive everything you need with ease and peace.

QUESTION

What prayer can I say to the mechanical angels?
"Mechanical angels, Archangels Michael and Pathiel, please repair or restore my _____ to perfect working condition. If I need someone to fix it or I need financial payment to replace it, then show me the answer now so I may have peace. Thank you, angels, for taking care of this in a timely manner."

Trust that Archangel Michael and the angels will direct you to the perfect person or resource that you need to resolve your issue or they will provide you with the funds you need to pay for a replacement or a repair. The angels want to ease your pain in these times of difficulty, so please don't forget to ask them for the support that you need.

Finding Lost Objects

It can be very frustrating when you lose or misplace something, especially if it's of value. Remember the last time you misplaced your keys and how it set you in a tailspin or reflect back to a time when you lost something of importance like a piece of jewelry. Next time you misplace something, call out for help and ask the angels to help you find what you've lost. Then your job is to believe in the saying that nothing can be lost in the mind of God. God is everywhere; therefore, the angels know exactly where it is. Don't be surprised if your item miraculously appears out of nowhere or trust that the angels will direct you to it.

ALERT

If for some reason you do not find your lost item, trust and know that it was either time for you to let it go or it will be replaced by something better or more meaningful.

Many know Saint Anthony, the Catholic patron saint of lost items, but there are also two specific angels you can call upon to help you recover lost items. The first is Archangel Chamuel, and his name means "he who sees God." The other is Zerachiel, who is one of the seven archangels named in the Book of Enoch. Pray to these angels and then listen and pay attention to your inner guidance. The angels may communicate through your thoughts to look in certain places or you may be physically pulled to a specific location. They could ask you to retrace your steps or you might have a dream in which you are shown the specific location of your lost item.

Prayer for Finding Lost Items

The next time you lose your keys, misplace your jewelry or your credit card, or even when your pet has run away, call on angels of lost items and say the following prayer:

Dearest Archangel Chamuel or Zerachiel, I lost my _____ (state the object). Please help me find it now or direct me to its location, for I believe that nothing is lost in the mind of God and you know exactly where it is. Thank you for the miracle of it being found.

Be open to witnessing a miracle when you say this prayer. Just remember to step back and express your gratitude to the angel when it's fulfilled.

Shopping Angels

Those of you who love to shop might have a smile on your face right now, imagining all these angels surrounding you with shopping bags. If you really dislike shopping and you always have a hard time picking out the perfect gift for your loved one, then keep reading; There is heavenly help on its way. The shopping angels can save you money and ease your life. For example:

- Before you go shopping, sit in quiet and ask the angels to tell you the store where you can find exactly what you need at the best price.
- When shopping for someone else, ask their guardian angels to direct you to the perfect gift at the perfect price.
- When you're overwhelmed with a big store or too much merchandise, ask the angels to guide you in the direction and show you exactly where you need to go.
- Share with the angels how much money you have to spend. Ask them to help you spend it wisely and to guide you toward the perfect purchase.
- Check in with the angels before you make a purchase (especially if it's a major one or if you are a compulsive shopper) and notice how it feels. If you feel peaceful or warm, then it's right. If it doesn't feel right and you feel anxious or uncomfortable, then they are asking you to wait or they're trying to tell you that something better is coming.

Calling on your shopping angels can be very helpful. It can save you time and money. You don't need to go to a fancy department store to get a personal shopper because you have them all around you. Just call out and be specific about what you need and how you want them to help you. Then enjoy and have fun playing with your shopping angels.

Dropped Coins from Heaven

The angels love to play, so they might be trying to get your attention when you see a penny or a dime on the ground. Dropped coins from heaven could also be a gift from your loved ones in spirit. So the next time you see a coin on the ground, someone might be sending you one of the following messages:

- You are never alone.
- I am here and I love you very much.
- We miss you.
- Cheer up and smile.
- Everything is going to be okay.
- I am watching over you.

Notice how you feel from this moment forward when you find a penny or a series of dimes in the parking lot, in your home, or even in the most obscure places. Pay attention to that warm fuzzy feeling you have inside and the smile that appears on your face knowing that someone from heaven is saying, "I am right here and I love you."

CHAPTER 14

Enhancing Your Intuition and Psychic Abilities with the Angels

The angels and archangels are excited about your spiritual growth. They want to empower you with confidence and clarity so you can enhance your abilities to communicate with them. They understand that when the pathway of communication is clear and open, it's easier for them to connect with you. So get ready to hear, see, and feel their messages of divine guidance with more clarity and knowing. With this information, you can experience more peace, grace, and joy and hopefully, you will want to inspire others to do the same.

Spiritual Growth

There is a difference between spirituality and religion. Religion offers a specific set of beliefs and rules for people to follow and be inspired by. Spirituality is more about your own personal relationship with the divine. You develop your own belief system based on what feels comfortable to you. Neither is right or wrong, good or bad. They are all pathways leading you back home to God, where you can feel a deeper connection with the divine.

ESSENTIAL

The angels ask you not to judge what others choose as their faith or belief in God. Be willing to learn from them and honor their choices with love. The world would be a peaceful place if everyone just accepted one another and what they believed to be true.

It's important to follow the path that feels right for you. Honor your own personal belief system and be open to learning and growth. This is what spirituality is all about. The angels honor who you are and what you choose with unconditional love. They will work with you and help you enhance your abilities to communicate in your own personal way. Continue to communicate with them and tell them what you need.

Clear Communication Between You and the Divine

Because God and the angels want to communicate with you, they will assist you in clearing the different pathways so you can use your clairs to receive information. They can remove the fear and the confusion that hinders your ability to hear or see more clearly. They can help you raise your vibration so you can feel their messages of divine guidance and experience the clear knowing so you can take action accordingly.

The angels ask you to have the desire and intention to open up and receive their messages of divine guidance. This creates a powerful energy of cocreation, where together, you can create miracles.

A Prayer for Clear Communication

Dear God and the angels, I have a profound desire to feel a deeper connection with you. Please help me clear the pathways of communication so I may easily receive your loving messages of divine guidance. My desire is to hear clearly, see clearly, and feel clearly. Help me understand and have a clear knowing of what the messages mean. Thank you for all your help as I journey toward a deeper connection with the divine.

Angels Who Can Help with Intuition, Psychic Abilities, and Clear Communication

The following archangels are here to assist you and help you enhance your abilities so you can clearly receive messages of divine guidance. They want to help you release any negativity or fear that may be blocking your energy centers. Then you can use your intuition and your psychic abilities to hear with clarity, see with clarity, and feel with clarity. They will also help you interpret the information you receive so you can clearly understand and discern the messages. Read ahead and use the prayers to open the pathways of communication.

Archangel Gabriel

Gabriel's name means "God is my strength." Gabriel was the messenger who told Mary she was pregnant with Jesus. He is one of the highest-ranking angels who reside by the throne of God. You might recognize Gabriel because he is usually seen with a trumpet in his hand. He brings messages of hope to humankind and he is the archangel who helps all those who choose to be a messenger for the divine. He also assists those who choose a life purpose in communication or the arts. For example, writers, teachers, artists, and anyone involved in communicating divine messages.

Prayer to Archangel Gabriel

Archangel Gabriel, you are a strong and powerful messenger for God. Please clear the channels of communication between myself and the divine. Help me clearly hear your messages of hope, inspiration, and guidance. If it is appropriate and helpful to share these messages with others, please give me the courage and strength to speak them. Thank you, Gabriel, for continuing to watch over me.

Archangel Haniel

Haniel's name means "glory of the grace of God." Haniel is the archangel who delivers grace to all those who ask. She works with the moon energy and she is patient and mystical. She will gladly work with you so you can enhance your psychic abilities, especially the ability to see clearly. If you ask her, she will help you discover and develop your spiritual gifts.

Prayer to Archangel Haniel

Archangel Haniel, please come to me now. My true desire is to enhance and develop my intuitive and psychic abilities. Please gift me with the graces of God so I can clearly see the divine and easily interpret any messages of divine guidance. Help me discover my spiritual gifts and give me the confidence and courage to use them so I can help others. Thank you, Haniel, and please give me the patience I need as this all unfolds.

Archangel Jeremiel

Jeremiel means "mercy of God," and in Judaism is known as one of the seven core archangels. Jeremiel is known for his prophetic visions: the coming of the Messiah and taking Baruch to the different levels of heaven. He also helps those who choose to go through a life review so they can take an inventory of their existence. With this information they can heal and make better choices. He is a visionary who helps people see into their dreams and receive and interpret messages of awareness and divine guidance.

Prayer to Archangel Jeremiel

Archangel Jeremiel, you are a visionary and I have the desire to become a visionary, too. Help me receive clear guidance through my dreams and gift me with the ability to interpret their meaning. If it is in my highest and best and the highest and best of all, I am open and willing to receive information about the future to help myself or another. If it is important for me to review any aspects of my life to heal and enlighten myself, please bring this information to the fore-front with peace and ease. Thank you, Jeremiel, for sharing your visionary gift with me.

Archangel Michael

Michael is the leader of the archangels. His name means "he who is like God." His job is to rid you of fear and negativity. He has the ability to clear your chakras (the energy centers of your body) so you can receive clear communication from God and the angels. He also provides courage, strength, and self-esteem to all those who choose to use their spiritual gifts to help and heal others. He is often referred to as the leader of the lightworkers, a term referring to those who choose to bring spiritual teaching to others.

Prayer to Archangel Michael

Archangel Michael, I know you have the powerful ability to rid me of any fear, negativity, and insecurity. Please clear all my chakras and enlighten my energy centers with pure divine light so I may clearly receive divine guidance. Empower me with courage and strength so I can use all my spiritual gifts and abilities to help myself and others. Please heighten my self-esteem so I can trust what I receive and easily act upon it with confidence. Lead me, Archangel Michael, to a deeper connection with God and the divine. Thank you for all these gifts of healing and awareness.

Archangel Raziel

Raziel's name means "secret of God." He knows all the secrets of the universe and he can help you understand esoteric information and increase your psychic abilities. He will help you hear clearly, see clearly, and feel clearly and, most importantly, he will help you understand the information you received. He wants to be your spiritual teacher, guiding you along a path of spiritual growth and development.

Prayer to Archangel Raziel

Archangel Raziel, please bless me with your secrets of the universe. Release me from any negative beliefs so I may clearly understand the information I receive. Please open all my channels of communication so I may hear clearly, see clearly, feel clearly, and understand clearly. I would be honored if you would be my spiritual teacher, helping me enhance my psychic abilities and growth in spiritual development. Thank you, Raziel, for your gifts of wisdom and for healing me with your divine magic.

Archangel Sariel

In the Book of Enoch, Sariel is called the "light of God" or "the light of the moon." Sariel is the gate keeper between the waking consciousness and the consciousness of your dream state. He will help you receive information from your dreams and he will provide you with the information you need to interpret them. He is referred to as the magical angel of the night. You can best feel his presence at night and during your dream state he will always keep you safe and protected.

Prayer of Archangel Sariel

Archangel Sariel, gatekeeper of my dream state, I would be honored if you could help me receive the information I need to spiritually grow and enhance my abilities to clearly communicate with God and the angels. If I need to remember this information, help me retain it and recall it when I wake up from a peaceful night's sleep. Please provide me with everything I need to interpret these dreams with ease and clarity. Thank you, Sariel, for this valuable insight and information.

These archangels are excited to help you develop and enhance your intuitive abilities. They are your team in spirit, cheering you on so you can grow spiritually and communicate with the divine. Remember, the more they assist you in your development the easier it is for them to communicate with you. Work with their energy and invoke them by using some of these powerful prayers—then just witness the magic unfold.

Clearing and Removing the Blocks

The angels are here, right now, surrounding you in love and support. The veil of disbelief, fear, and negativity keeps you from feeling them, hearing them, seeing them, and knowing of their truth. You can lift this veil by staying committed to your desire—to know and experience the truth of the divine. Trust that the angels will also work behind the scenes to clear the disbelief, fear, and negativity. You can clear and remove the blocks in many ways. Try the following:

- Use affirmations to transform your negative thoughts into positive manifestations. For example: Instead of saying, "I can't see anything when I meditate or ask for help," affirm, "I clearly see images, symbols, and visions and I understand what these messages mean."

- Meditate, pray, and ask the angels to clear your blocks so you can receive their messages.

Prayer for clearing the blocks:
Archangel Michael, Archangel Raziel, Archangel Gabriel, Archangel Jeremiel, and Archangel Haniel, please come to me now and release all disbelief, fear, and negativity that keeps me from hearing, seeing, feeling, and knowing clear communication with God and the angels. You know exactly what's blocking me and I am willing to let it go. Please give me the courage to know the divine. Help me understand that I have the ability to receive and discern messages of divine guidance. I desire with all my heart this connection with the divine and I know you will help me. Thank you for your loving assistance.

- Ask the angels to heal your blocks during your dream state. Ask for their help before you go to sleep and then invite them to work on you while you sleep.
- Try alternative healing modalities: hypnosis, Reiki, breathwork, massage, or acupuncture.
- Clear your chakras, your energy centers that receive intuitive information. (see page 150).

Any of these techniques will release the blocks. Experiment and discover which ones work best for you. As you release and let go, the channels of communication will open and your intuition will heighten. It will be well worth the effort and the time you spend healing what no longer serves you.

Chakra Clearing Meditation

The word *chakra* is Sanskrit for "wheel" or "disk." Your chakras are the energy centers in your body. There are seven of them and they are aligned from the crown of your head to the base of your spine. These energy centers are where you receive intuitive information from the divine. Clearing the chakras is a powerful way to open up the channels of communication.

Set your intention for the following meditation. Ask Archangel Michael, Archangel Raziel, Archangel Gabriel, Archangel Jeremiel, Archangel Haniel, and Archangel Raphael to help you clear your chakras so you can enhance your intuition.

Find a quiet place to sit, and if you choose, select some peaceful meditation music to play in the background. Ask the archangels to surround you in a beautiful circle of light, love, and protection. (Pause) Sit upright and imagine a column of light connecting you to the heavenly light above to the core of the earth below. Imagine or see it running through your spinal column, grounding you from above to below. Just breathe with the divine white flowing through it. Imagine inhaling the energy up from the core of the earth and then exhaling it down from the heavens. Eventually it becomes one flowing breath. (Pause)

Now, focus on your first chakra at the base of your spine. This energy center is red, so imagine the color red spinning in your base chakra in a clockwise motion. Ask the archangels to clear any darkness in this chakra. (Pause) Then ask Archangel Raphael to bring any healing to this energy center so it flows with peace, light, and harmony. Affirm, "I am safe. All my needs are met. I am grounded to the physical plane. I am healthy and I am prosperous." (Pause)

Now, focus on your second chakra, located in the lower abdomen, and sexual organs. This energy center is orange, so imagine the color orange spinning in your second chakra in a clockwise motion. Ask the archangels to clear any darkness in this chakra. (Pause) Then ask Archangel Raphael to bring any healing to this energy center so it flows with peace, light, and harmony.

Affirm, "I am able to accept change with ease. I am creative, passionate, and sensual." (Pause)

Now, focus on your third chakra, located in solar plexus. This energy center is yellow, so imagine the color yellow spinning in your third chakra in a clockwise motion. Ask the archangels to clear any darkness in this chakra. (Pause) Then ask Archangel Raphael to bring any healing to this energy center so it flows with peace, light, and harmony.

Affirm, "I am comfortable being in my power. I am confident and I believe in myself." (Pause)

Now, focus on your fourth chakra, the heart chakra. This energy center is green, so imagine the color green spinning in your fourth chakra in a clockwise motion. Ask the archangels to clear any darkness in this chakra. (Pause) Then ask Archangel Raphael to bring any healing to this energy center so it flows with peace, light, and harmony.

Affirm, "I am loved and I love deeply. I am compassionate and I accept myself and others for who they are." (Pause)

Now, focus on your fifth chakra, the throat chakra. This energy center is blue, so imagine the color blue spinning in your fifth chakra in a clockwise motion. Ask the archangels to clear any darkness in this chakra. (Pause) Then ask Archangel Raphael to bring any healing to this energy center so it flows with peace, light, and harmony. Affirm, "I can easily express myself and my feelings from a place of love. I am open to divine will." (Pause)

Now, focus on your sixth chakra, the brow chakra or third eye chakra. This energy center is indigo, so imagine the color indigo spinning in your sixth chakra in a clockwise motion. Ask the archangels to clear any darkness in this chakra. (Pause) Then ask Archangel Raphael to bring any healing to this energy center so it flows with peace, light, and harmony. Affirm, "I easily see intuitive guidance from the divine. I am clear and open to see physically and intuitively." (Pause)

Now, focus on your seventh chakra, the crown chakra at the top of your head. This energy center is violet, so imagine the color violet spinning in your seventh chakra in a clockwise motion. Ask the archangels to clear any darkness in this chakra. (Pause) Then ask Archangel Raphael to bring any healing to this energy center so it flows with peace, light, and harmony. Affirm, "I am one with the divine. I easily receive clear knowing and wisdom from the divine." (Pause)

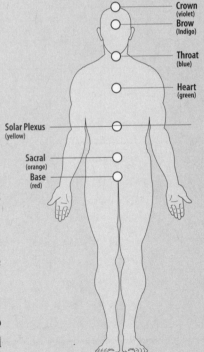

Crown
(violet)
Brow
(Indigo)
Throat
(blue)
Heart
(green)
Solar Plexus
(yellow)
Sacral
(orange)
Base
(red)

When you are finished clearing your chakras, ask if there are any messages of divine guidance for you to receive at this time. (Pause) Then slowly breathe back into the present moment. Notice how clear and peaceful you feel. Say thank you to the archangels and be open to the divine guidance you receive throughout your day.

This is a wonderful meditation to do in the morning to start your day and before you do your angel readings. If you practice this meditation regularly you will enhance your intuition to new levels. Enjoy doing this practice and consider it as another tool for your spiritual toolbox.

Enhancing Your Psychic Abilities

Everyone has psychic abilities, even if they are unaware of these abilities. The *Merriam-Webster Dictionary* defines psychic as someone who is "sensitive to nonphysical or supernatural forces and influences." In other words, you are using your psychic abilities to connect with the angels.

Using your intuition and your psychic abilities are pretty much the same, except the term "psychic" has received a bad reputation over the years. When you use your psychic abilities you receive information about the past, present, and future. You can ask the angels for this information and they will communicate the answers to you by using your different clairs.

> *Archangels Gabriel, Haniel, Jeremiel, Michael, Raziel, and Sariel, help me enhance my psychic abilities to receive information from the divine about the past, present, and future. Help me know beyond any doubt that this information is from the highest source. I am open to receive this information for myself and others and please confirm to me when it is appropriate for me to share it. Thank you for enhancing and strengthening my abilities and giving me the courage and confidence to trust it.*

Here are some possible intuitive or psychic impressions you might receive from divine guidance:

- The angels might show you a past memory from childhood as an answer to a prayer.
- You might hear the angels giving you directions in the car to avoid an accident ahead. For example, "Slow Down" or "Move over to the right."
- You might get a sick feeling in your stomach when you meet a new business associate.
- You might see your future home or future soul mate in detail during your meditation.
- You might have a dream about a past life that is giving you insight into a present situation.
- You might get a feeling that someone is going to pass into heaven very soon.

If you begin to receive these intuitive or psychic impressions and you feel nervous about getting this information, ask your angels to comfort you. They will reassure you that everything is okay. You would not be receiving this information if it wasn't meant to be. If you are unsure about the information, ask the angels to give you confirmation that this information is coming from a divine source. They will do everything in their power to make you feel comfortable and safe.

Receiving Future Insight

Have you ever wished you had a crystal ball to look into the future? Why do you think psychics are so popular? People want to know about their future because they are impatient and curious or maybe they just fear the unknown.

ALERT

Take time and do your research before you go to just any psychic. Receiving information from someone who is not centered in the highest intention can be detrimental. If they share something "bad" (which divine guidance would not do), it can make a lasting impression and cause unnecessary stress and worry.

The angels will share information about your future when it's beneficial for you to know. They will also show you the path of the highest potential, but it's important to understand there are other paths to choose from. There is no right or wrong path; it's just a different experience based on the path you chose. Remember, you live in a world of free will and free choice. So if you are shown something about your future, you always have the power to choose differently. For example, you're meditating and the angels share a vision with you about a potential new home in South Carolina and a month later your husband gets transferred to upstate New York. The course has changed, therefore the future potential has changed. Realize that when this happens, you can go back into meditation and ask the angels for information about your new location.

If you would like insight into your future, ask the angels to provide you with this information. Then pay attention. Notice your dreams and significant signs or synchronicities. Ask for guidance during your meditation or use the angel cards to see if you can get any insight. If it's in your highest and best to know, they will share this information with you. If not, trust in divine timing and stay conscious of the present moment.

Prayer to Receive Future Insight
Archangels Gabriel, Haniel, Jeremiel, Michael, Raziel, and Sariel, if it's in my highest and best, could you please share some insight into my future about _____ (state the situation). I would like confirmation and validation so I can feel reassured and peaceful that all is well. When you share this information, please make it clear to me so I can understand it beyond any doubt. Thank you, archangels, for your support and unconditional love.

Receiving Guidance in Your Dreams

Your dream time is a very sacred space for the soul to do its work. In essence, you are a spiritual being and you have the ability to return "home" and visit the angels during this time of rest. Anything is possible during your dream time: healing, learning, receiving insight into all aspects of your life, and connecting with the divine. You can utilize this valuable time and enhance your spiritual experiences during this altered state of consciousness.

ESSENTIAL

Keep a dream diary by your bed. Write down everything about your dream when you first wake up. Ask for insight if the meaning of the dream is not clear. If nothing comes, keep recording your dreams and eventually the pieces of the puzzle will come together.

There are two specific archangels you can call on for help during your dream time. Archangel Jeremiel is the visionary who can help you see into your dreams. Archangel Sariel, often referred to as the magical angel of the night, is the gatekeeper between your waking consciousness and your dream consciousness. He will always watch over and keep you safe and protected during this time of rest. Both of these divine helpers can assist you in the following ways:

- Healing, both physical and emotional, can take place in your dreams.
- Healing of your past in this lifetime and other lifetimes can take place in your dreams.
- Insight that answers your prayers can take place in your dreams.
- Seeing the future can take place in your dreams.
- Meeting angels, guides, and loved ones can take place in your dreams.
- Learning and spiritual growth can take place in your dreams.

Ask Archangels Jeremiel and Sariel to assist you in any and all of these ways. Before you go to sleep, invite them into your dream time and ask them to be your guides. Set your intention to remember your dreams and ask them to give you everything you need to know in order to interpret them. It is an honor for them to serve you. Work with them and discover how your eight hours of rest can become your magical time to visit heaven and receive some valuable insight.

Communicating with Loved Ones in Spirit

One of the most difficult things to go through is losing a loved one. The angels know this and they want to help. If you have lost a loved one, they will ease your pain so you can experience more peace and healing. One of the ways they can assist you in doing this is to help you communicate with your loved ones in heaven. It is only the veil between heaven and earth that separates you and the angels can help you hear, feel, and see beyond the veil.

Trust that the angels can be your "mediums" in spirit. They can communicate for your loved ones or they can bring you to visit them in your dream state. Ask for their help in making that connection and ask that you receive validation that they are happy and at peace.

Prayer to Communicate with a Loved One

Archangels Azrael, Gabriel, Haniel, Jeremiel, Michael, Raziel, and Sariel, please help lift the veil so I can visit and connect to _____ _____ (state your loved one's name). I am asking for undeniable validation that they are still with me. Let me know and feel that they are happy and peaceful in heaven. Please bring peace to all concerned. You know who _____ (state your loved one's name) is and you know how to bring us together. I trust that this will happen soon and I thank you in advance for this beautiful gift of peace and healing.

There are so many ways you can enhance your intuitive and psychic abilities with the help of the angels. They want to assist you in every possible way they can. Your divine birthright is to have clear communication with the divine. The angels will enhance all your intuitive abilities to receive this information, if you only ask. Have the burning desire and the committed determination to receive this divine information with clarity. Your prayers will be answered and you will develop a lasting relationship with the angels.

CHAPTER 15

Protection from the Angels

Everyone wants to feel safe and protected, especially in a world where bad things happen and life can be unpredictable. God and the angels want you to feel safe because fear can immobilize you. It can hold you back from living your life to the fullest. Open your heart and ask for protection for you and your loved ones, and learn how you can move into the unknown with more peace, trust, and adventure.

Fear Versus Faith

Fear is a strong emotion that you experience when you feel in danger or you're anticipating that something bad might happen. In both of these circumstances it triggers a feeling of being out of control, and your greatest fear becomes the fear of the unknown. The mind starts imagining all these different scenarios that might take place and your subconscious mind replays all the tapes from your past memories that are associated with fear. These memories could be your personal experiences, a friend or family member's experience, or something you witnessed through the media. No matter where the source is, the fearful memory creates an emotion that causes unnecessary stress, anxiety, and worry.

Here are some examples of fear:

- **You are listening to the news and you hear a child has been abducted.** You immediately go into fear about your own child. Your thoughts might be, "Should I pick him up at school today?" or "It's not safe, so he can't go outside and play."
- **You're on a plane, leaving for vacation.** Your thoughts are focused on the house: "Did I leave the stove on? What if there's a fire?" or "What if someone knows we're not home?"
- **Your daughter is at college.** Your thoughts are focused on fear and not on trusting your daughter: "What if she walks home alone in the dark?" or "What if she is influenced by others and gets involved in drugs or drinking?"

Take a moment and notice how you feel reading these scenarios and then reflect back to your own personal experiences and recognize when you've allowed yourself to be carried away by your fearful thoughts.

Whenever this happens it's time to call on God and the angels for protection and ask them to help you transform your fear into faith. As you do this, you will feel yourself released from the grip of fear, and in that moment you can take your power back so you can choose more peaceful and empowering thoughts.

Read the same examples used before, but now they're focused on faith:

- **You are listening to the news and you hear a child has been abducted.** You say a prayer for the child and her family. Then you ask 10,000 angels to surround your children in divine light and protection.
- **You're on a plane, leaving for vacation.** You ask the angels to watch over your house and your valuables while you're gone.
- **Your daughter is at college.** You call on Archangel Michael and her guardian angels and you ask them to watch over her and you affirm, "Only good can come to her. She is smart and she makes good decisions."

After you've read both examples, notice the difference between the two. Ask yourself which feels better and which one you would choose to practice. God and the angels want to help you transform your fear into faith. They know that it will not only help you, but it will help the lives of everyone else around you.

Exercise to Transform Fear into Faith

This is an exercise you can use when you experience fear of any kind. The first step is to recognize that you are having a physical response that's connected to the fearful thoughts that are running through your mind. You might be thinking, "What if…" and all your thoughts are focused on the bad things that could happen or the harmful circumstances that might occur. Next, get grounded in the present moment by taking a deep breath and just stop and acknowledge that you're afraid. Call on God, Archangel Michael, and as many angels as you want. Ask for help. Tell them you're afraid and you want to feel safe, protected, and calm. Then just breathe with them, imagining that they are surrounding you in a protective shield of light where no harm can come to you. Remind yourself of where you are and affirm to yourself, "I am in the present moment and the angels are surrounding me and protecting me in their loving light. Please, angels, release me from this fear and help me feel the presence of God's love." Continue breathing deeply until the physical reactions in your body subside. Focus your thoughts on the angels and the word "faith." When you feel more peaceful, continue to imagine yourself in the protective divine light, knowing that you are encircled by heavenly helpers.

Angels of Protection

The following angels and archangels have a specific role: to watch over and protect humanity. As you read about each angel, pay attention to your feelings and notice which angels you feel connected to. Then call them by name and ask for the help you need. Trust that they will immediately assist you and they will be at your side in comfort and protection.

Archangel Michael Provides Protection

Archangel Michael is the leader of the archangels. His name means "he who is like God," and he is the archangel of protection and the patron saint of policemen. He carries a sword that symbolizes his ability to cut through all fear and resistance. He lends his courage and his strength to anyone who calls on him. Michael has a fiery energy, and when you invoke him it's very possible you might feel warm or even begin to sweat. If you tap into your clairvoyance, you might see the colors purple and blue, which are associated with Archangel Michael's presence. Call on Archangel Michael, and he will help you with protection of all kinds. He will empower you with the courage you need for any situation.

Prayer to Archangel Michael

Archangel Michael, please come to me now and surround me in your protective shield of light. Please clear my energy field and release me from all negativity. Help me feel safe and protected in your loving presence and provide me with the courage I need.

Archangel Raphael Protects Travelers

Archangel Raphael's name means "God heals" or "God has healed." Raphael is not only a healer, but he protects travelers of all kinds. Call on Raphael when you want to feel safe and protected while traveling. Ask that your journey from beginning to end be experienced with ease and protection.

Prayer to Archangel Raphael

Archangel Raphael, I know you are with us at all times. I ask for your assistance during our travels. Please protect me and all concerned so we feel surrounded in God's loving presence until we reach our destination safely and with ease.

Archangel Ariel Protects the Environment and Animals

Archangel Ariel's name means "lion or lioness of God." She is committed to helping heal and protect Mother Nature, which includes all animals. She is the protector of the waters. She watches over all bodies of water and aquatic life. Ariel also protects those who travel upon the water, like fishermen. If you feel concerned about the environment and you want to do your part in protecting it, call on Ariel for support and help.

When your pets are sick or in trouble, ask both Archangel Ariel and Archangel Raphael to intervene. Ask them to watch over your pets and trust that they will receive the protection and healing they need.

Prayer to Archangel Ariel to Protect Mother Nature

Archangel Ariel, I see that Mother Nature needs some healing and balance. Please watch over all of her inhabitants and see that they are protected from all harm. Please bring healing to the earth and remind me how I can play my part in helping and healing Mother Nature.

Prayer to Archangel Ariel and Archangel Raphael for Your Pets

Archangel Ariel and Archangel Raphael, please watch over _____ (say your pet's name). Surround her in your healing and protective divine light. Comfort her and remind her she is not alone and she is loved. Help her to heal completely and feel healthy, whole, and vibrant once again. Thank you, Ariel and Raphael; with you taking care of her I trust that all is well.

Archangel Zaphiel Protects Children

Archangel Zaphiel is the leader of the choir of cherubim. He watches over children and will help them in any way he can. If they are having trouble in school, with friends, at home, or even with physical or emotional issues, ask Zaphiel to watch over and protect them. Imagine him wrapping his wings around them and protecting them in love.

Prayer to Archangel Zaphiel

Archangel Zaphiel, I know God loves my child dearly. Please help _____ (state their name or names) and bring divine resolution to the following situation_____(state the situation). Please wrap him in your wings of love and protection and help him feel safe and loved in your divine presence. I trust that he will receive exactly what he needs for his highest and best, better than I could ever imagine.

Suriel Protects Your Home and Possessions

Suriel is named in the Kabbalah as the angel who rules over the earth. He will watch over your home and possessions. Whenever you recognize that you're focused on fear, call on Suriel and ask him to keep your home and your possessions safe.

Prayer to Archangel Suriel

Archangel Suriel, please watch over our home and our possessions at all times. Surround our home with angels and keep it safe and protected. Fill it with love and light so only good can come into our home.

Laylah Protects Newborns

Laylah is an angel of the night, and his name comes from the Hebrew word meaning sleep. Laylah watches over infants and helps them move through the adjustment of being in a physical body. If you are a mother with a newborn child, call on Laylah for help. Ask him to watch over your precious child with love, compassion, and protection.

Prayer to Laylah

Please watch over my newborn _____ (share his name). Help him adjust beautifully and easily into his new life. Let him know how dearly loved he is and that we are happy he is here and that he chose us as parents. Keep him safe and protected and help me feel calm and peaceful as I adjust to being a new mother.

These angels and archangels of protection are honored to assist you along your journey. They know how vulnerable you feel when fear takes over. Call them by name and know that their role is to protect you and shield you from all harm.

Protecting Yourself from Negativity

Negative situations or people can drain your energy. When you're around someone who is very controlling or even needy, that person can deplete your energy supply, leaving you feeling drained and exhausted. The same feeling may occur when you have to participate in high-pressure situations or you have to visit someone who is going through a very stressful time. It's important to recognize these situations when they arise and call on the angels of protection for help. The following are situations where you can call on the angels of protection:

- When visiting a hospital or someone who is ill
- When attending a funeral
- When you have to go to court for any reason
- When there is a lot of negativity in your work place
- When dealing with authoritative figures
- When you need to do any kind of public speaking
- When you work as a caretaker or if you're doing any kind of healing work
- When dealing with people who can negatively affect you in any way

At one time or another, everyone has to deal with some of these circumstances. The next time one of these situations occurs, you could have the help of the angels by your side. When you ask for help, they will surround you in a protective bubble of light and immediately you will feel strong and centered. You will know beyond any doubt that you can get through any situation.

If you practice and make a conscious effort, in time you can transmute the energy of negativity. Instead of being affected by it, you can choose to send love to others who might be suffering. By protecting yourself from negativity you stay strong in your own energy; therefore, you have the ability to empower yourself and everyone around you.

Prayer for Protection from Negativity

Use the following prayer for protection when dealing with any negativity that might affect your well-being and the well-being of others.

Archangel Michael and my guardian angels, I have this situation _____ (state the situation) and I need your help. Please surround me in God's divine white light of protection (imagine a bubble of light surrounding you). Fill me with love and empower me with your strength and courage. Help me be centered in love and allow no negativity to enter my bubble. If any negativity comes my way, allow it to be transmuted into love and send it back out as waves of love to everyone involved. Thank you. I now feel safe and protected in your love.

Prayer to Release Negativity

When you are affected by negativity, you may have a physical reaction such as feeling shaky, drained, or even nauseous. You could also have an emotional reaction like anger, sadness, or distress. Mentally you might feel confused or forgetful. All these reactions to negativity can be uncomfortable. The angels want to help you be at peace. Use this prayer to remove all negativity from your energy field. Notice how much better you feel after you invoke the assistance of Archangel Michael.

Archangel Michael, please release me from all negativity and heal me right now. Release me from the negativity of others. Release my energy from anyone I am in fear with. (Imagine that everyone is unplugging from you and you are unplugging from others.) Archangel Raphael, God's healer, please restore my energy with green emerald healing light (imagine all your cells illuminating in green emerald healing light) and please send healing to all others involved. Thank you, Archangel Michael and Raphael, for your loving assistance.

Protection for Your Family

One of the most common fears people struggle with is the fear of losing someone they love. When panic sets in, the mind's imagination takes off just like a small snowball being pushed off the top of the hill and turning into a giant snowball. For example, a family member is late coming home from work, and your mind jumps to the assumption that she is dead in a car accident. Or your child didn't call when he got to his friend's house, and your mind concludes that he's been abducted.

ALERT

Remember, there is no limit to the number of angels you can call on for help. Call on 10,000 angels for protection if you feel you need them. They are waiting in multitudes ready to assist you in any way they can.

When fear begins to consume you, stop and call upon the angels of protection to help you and your loved ones. Immediately ask Archangel Michael, Archangel Zaphiel, and everyone's guardian angels to surround all those involved in love and protection. Choose to have faith and imagine them being embraced in the wings of the angels. See Michael and Zaphiel by their side. Ask the angels to release your fear and replace it with peace. Remind yourself to stay present in the moment where everything is okay. Realize that your imagination has taken over and that fear is creating all the what ifs.

Call on the angels of protection in the following situations:

- When your loved one is late in coming home
- When a loved one is sick or not feeling well
- When your children are home alone and you're worried
- When your loved one is going through a challenging time and you can't be with him
- When your loved one is going through emotional issues and you don't know what to do
- When your loved one is traveling alone and you're worried for her safety

In all of these situations you can call on God and the angels to watch over your loved ones. Recognize that your thoughts wander into the what ifs and acknowledge that you're worried and afraid. Seize the opportunity to shift your thoughts from fear into faith. Ask the angels for help and know that everyone involved will benefit when you shift your intention from fear to love.

Prayer for Protection for Your Family

Use the following prayer when you realize your thoughts are focused on fear and you need help from the angels of protection:

Guardian angels, Archangel Michael, and Archangel Zaphiel, please go to my loved ones (or say their name) right now. Surround them, protect them, and keep them safe. Help me release my fear so I can move into faith knowing that my loved ones are safe. Bless us all with peace and allow us to feel comforted and embraced in God's loving protection. Thank you.

Protection for Your Home

Your home is your sacred dwelling place. You want your home to be filled with a positive, loving, and peaceful energy. When your home is filled with love, it feels light and happy and everyone feels comfortable and safe. If there is negativity in the home, you might feel heaviness in the air or you may feel uncomfortable being in the house. When this happens, call on the angels of protection and ask them to clear the energy in your home. Request that they remove all negativity so it feels peaceful once again.

Prayer for Removing Negativity from Your Home

Archangel Michael is the divine helper to call on for removing negativity from your home. You can also use this prayer for any space that needs clearing: your office, the building you work in, or even your car.

Archangel Michael, please remove all negativity from this dwelling place. Please clear it from the foundation to the roof. When this is complete, please fill this space with love, light, and healing so all those who enter feel safe and peaceful. Archangel Michael, watch over my home and only send those who are good to its doors. Please ensure that har-mony, love, happiness, and cooperation be the essence of our home. Thank you for your help.

Protecting Your Home

Fear can easily set in when you're home alone and your mind wanders to that scary movie or that dreadful story from the news. Before you know it, you're in the grip of fear. What if you could feel more peace when you're home alone? What if you could trust that your children or pets were being watched over when you're not at home? Imagine how good you would feel if you knew there was someone watching over your home twenty-four hours a day while you were on vacation. Whenever you are faced with any of these situations, call on Archangels Michael and Suriel to watch over your home and ask them to keep it safe from harm. God sent you these divine helpers so you could have peace and enjoy life, feeling safe wherever you are.

ESSENTIAL

Denise Linn, author of *Sacred Space* and a practitioner of *feng shui*, says that there are house angels who serve to protect the home. She says: "I believe that the most powerful guardian for your home is an angel. Calling upon the angels to be your house guardians for protec-tion and spiritual rejuvenation can bring a wonderful feeling of peace, harmony, and safety to your home."

Prayer for Protecting Your Home

Use the following prayer before leaving your home and trust that the angels will do their job to watch over and protect both your home and any loved ones left behind.

I ask that four guardian angels stand watch at each corner of my home and property. I also call on Archangels Michael and Suriel to protect my home, its possessions, and all those who stay behind. Please help everyone feel safe and at peace knowing that our home is protected in the divine white light of God and the angels. Thank you.

Protection for Your Car

Your car is a place where you spend a significant amount of time, and you want to feel safe and secure no matter where you go. Think of the last time you felt vulnerable in your car. Maybe someone near you was driving recklessly. Maybe the weather conditions were poor, you got lost, or your car was experiencing mechanical difficulties.

Whenever these situations occur, it's time to call on the angels of protection. Imagine a beautiful radiant light surrounding your car. Ask the angels to keep your car and everyone in it safe. Ask that they stay with you until you arrive at your destination safely.

ALERT

Remember, it is always your job to be a responsible driver. The angels can help you if you are afraid or unsafe, but you will always need to be responsible before and after you get behind the wheel. Always follow the rules of the road.

Another time you can call on the angels of protection is when you need help driving the car itself. Let's say you've worked a long day or you're traveling a long distance and you're exhausted. Imagine the angels sitting by your side in the passenger seat and ask them to help you stay alert so you can arrive at your destination safely. Another example might be when you're driving in bad weather and you feel afraid and doubt your ability to maneuver the car. Ask the angels to help you drive the car and ask for the courage and confidence you need. Also ask them to advise you if it's safer to pull over and wait the storm out.

Know that in any circumstance where you feel unsafe or afraid, it's time to call on the angels of protection. You can feel reassured that you are not alone and they are watching over you. Remember, everyone benefits when you feel safe and confident while driving your car.

CHAPTER 16

Healing with the Angels

God sent the angels to help you in your times of need. If you require healing of any kind, reach out to the angels and ask for help. Healing means returning to a state of wholeness on every level—mind, body, and spirit. God wants this for you and all of humanity. Discover how you can use the power of prayer to initiate your healing so you can become one with your true state of health and well-being.

Asking for Healing

Healing can take place on many levels and the angels can help you with all aspects of healing. The first step you need to take in order to initiate your healing process is to simply ask, "Angels, help me heal." Then be specific. Ask for the help you need and share with the angels how you want to feel when you are restored to full health and wholeness.

Try these examples of asking the angels for help with healing:

- You are in physical pain. Ask the angels to ease your pain and ask them to guide you to the resources you need (rest, doctors, healers, or medicine) in order to heal quickly and completely.
- You are emotionally depressed. Ask the angels for peace and the help you need to heal the source of your emotional pain.
- You are struggling with relationship issues. Ask the angels for healing so all involved experience harmony, peace, and cooperation.
- You are mentally confused and forgetful. Ask the angels for clarity so you can remember.
- You feel alone and disconnected from God. Ask the angels for spiritual healing so you can feel one with God and the angels.

ESSENTIAL

A prayer to invoke healing: "Dearest angels of healing, please give me everything I need to heal completely. I am willing to heal on every level—mind, body, and spirit. I surrender and trust that you know exactly what I need and you will show me the way. I am paying attention and I commit to taking action on anything I must do in order to achieve wholeness."

After you ask the angels for help and you're specific about what you want, then you need to surrender and trust. The angels know how to help you heal as a whole person in mind, body, and spirit. This is important because it's not unusual that in order for someone to heal physically he needs to heal emotionally. For example, if Jack has a heart condition, the angels know that in order for him to heal completely he needs to release the stress in his life. Therefore, they might arrange (behind the scenes) the necessary changes that must take place in order for him to reduce his stress. This is exactly what he requires in order to heal and achieve full health and wholeness. So remember, when you ask the angels for healing, be willing to surrender and trust that you will be given exactly what you need in order to accomplish this.

The last step when asking the angels for help is your responsibility. Pay attention and take action on anything you receive intuitively or from outside resources. For example, let's say you've asked the angels to heal your depression and someone tells you about a meditation class. It's your job to pay attention and take action, knowing that your angels have sent you an opportunity to heal.

These are the steps you take to begin and complete your healing process:

1. Ask for healing.
2. Be specific about what you want to feel.
3. Surrender and trust the angels.
4. Pay attention and take action.
5. Say thank you for the healing.

Angels of Healing

The following angels and archangels have the specific role of helping humanity heal. They help with healing of all kinds: physical, emotional, mental, spiritual, and healing for both humans and animals. Read about each one and see which of these divine helpers can help you in your life right now. Then use the prayers to invoke them into your life so they can help you heal.

Archangel Raphael Provides Healing of all Kinds

Raphael's name means "God heals" or "God has healed." Raphael is the master healer and he is committed to humanity, doing healing work of all kinds for mind, body, and spirit. He is known as the doctor archangel, who brings healing both to humans and animals. If you use your clairvoyance, you might see a green emerald healing light associated with Archangel Raphael's presence. He will come to all those who call on him and because he is an archangel, he can be with everyone simultaneously. If you are a healer of any kind, ask Archangel Raphael to guide you and assist you in your healing work. He wants to be of assistance to all those passionate about healing the world.

Prayer to Archangel Raphael

Archangel Raphael, please surround me in your green emerald healing light. You are God's healer and therefore you have been given the power to heal for God. I request and accept divine healing on all levels: physical, emotional, mental, and spiritual healing. Show me and help me become one with the truth. I am healed, whole, and healthy. Thank you, Raphael, for this miracle of healing.

Archangel Zadkiel Provides Emotional Healing

Zadkiel's name means "the righteousness of God." Archangel Zadkiel helps all those who call on him for emotional healing. He is known as the archangel of mercy and benevolence, and he wants humanity to let go of judgment and to accept each other with love, compassion, and understanding. If you are struggling with emotional issues of any kind, invoke the assistance of Zadkiel and ask him to intervene. Request that he heal your heart so you can feel compassion and forgiveness. Then ask for the healing to expand into your mind, body, and spirit so you experience emotional healing on all levels of consciousness.

Prayer to Archangel Zadkiel

Archangel Zadkiel, I request your help for emotional healing. Help me release and dissolve any negative feelings toward myself and others. Help me heal and be free from the negative effects of judgment, unforgiveness, anger, and resentment. I am ready to heal with your help. Zadkiel, come into my heart and heal it so I can love myself and others and find peace once again.

Archangel Azrael Provides Healing for the Dying and Grieving

Azreal's name means "whom God heals." His role is to comfort and assist the dying as they transition into the afterlife. He also watches over and helps heal all those grieving from a loss of any kind. If you know of someone who is close to death, send Azreal to their side and ask that they be eased of their suffering. If you are still grieving from a loss, ask Azreal to help heal your heart. He can also help you if you want to communicate with your loved one who has passed; just ask him to help you make that connection.

Prayer to Archangel Azrael

Archangel Azrael, we are suffering a loss of someone we love very much. Please help _____ (state their name) have a smooth and peaceful transition back home to heaven. Please bring healing and peace to all those left behind and help them know that their loved one is at peace. If they want to communicate with their loved one, please help them connect and give them that miracle. Thank you for reminding us we are not alone and we are truly loved during these difficult times.

FACT

You can also call on your guardian angels for healing. Remember they are assigned to you and they will help you in every aspect of your life. You can also just call on the angels of healing knowing that there is an unlimited number of angels and God knows exactly who to send.

Archangel Zerachiel Provides Healing of Addictions

Zerachiel is one of the seven archangels mentioned in the Book of Enoch. He is the angel of healing who watches over and helps all those suffering from addiction. He will also help all the children affected by parents with addiction. When you call on him you might feel warmth in your chest or tingling in your body. If you want to release an addictive behavior or if you know of someone who is suffering from addiction, call on Zerachiel and ask for his assistance.

Prayer to Archangel Zerachiel

Archangel Zerachiel, please help _____ (state their name). She is struggling with this addiction and it's affecting everyone involved. I am asking for divine intervention to take place. Please bring healing to everyone, especially _____ (state their name). Help her heal and find the courage and strength to stop and get the help she needs. Help her awaken to the desire to live a peaceful, healthy, and productive life where she rediscovers her worth and how loved she really is.

These archangels of healing will lovingly guide you along your journey to wellness. They know how hard it can be when you feel less than 100 percent both physically and emotionally. Call them by name and know that their role is to ease your pain and provide you with the peace you deserve so you can heal.

Physical Healing

Your natural state of being is one of health and vitality. Do you remember the last time you were feeling sick and you had the flu or a cold? Now recall how good it felt and how grateful you were when you finally recovered.

Your body can be a wonderful messenger. If you are out of balance physically, mentally, or emotionally, disease will come knocking at your door trying to get your attention. Your body is telling you it's time to heal and take care of yourself. The angels of healing can help you do this and they want to assist you in bringing your body back into balance.

ALERT

Pay attention to the word "disease." Break it down and look at it this way: "dis-ease." The body is not at peace. When disease sets in there is something off balance and you need to listen to your body and see what it's trying to tell you.

Whenever you're in pain or you're suffering from illness, call out to Archangel Raphael and the angels and ask them for physical healing. If you are in pain, ask them to relieve your pain so you can feel more peaceful. When you are sick or suffering from illness, ask them to give you everything you need so you can return to your natural state of health and well-being. Your job is to take responsibility for your health and follow your inner guidance so you can do what's necessary to heal yourself.

The angels of healing can help if you:

- Ask for the best medical care for your highest and greatest good.
- Ask for the patience you need to rest and heal.
- Ask for the emotional and mental healing you need to physically get better.
- Ask for the earth angels who can help you and be willing to accept their help.
- Ask for any holistic or alternative approaches that will help you heal.
- Ask for any financial support you need to fund your healing process.
- Ask for a miracle.

The angels of healing can provide you with the support and resources you need to accelerate your healing process. When you are out of balance, surrender and trust that all is well. Your body and the angels are helping you remember that it's time to take care of yourself.

Prayer for Physical Healing

Use the following prayer whenever you are experiencing any kind of pain, sickness, or disease. Use it whenever you need it or until you feel healed, whole, and healthy.

Archangel Raphael and all the healing angels, please illuminate every cell in my being with green emerald healing light and restore my cells back to perfect health and wholeness. Give me everything I need to heal as a whole person: mind, body, and spirit. Provide me with the comfort, patience, and help I need so I can nurture myself back to full health. Thank you for the powerful healing and your loving support.

Emotional Healing

Most people don't realize this, but your emotional well-being is just as important as your physical health; they are interrelated. When you are peaceful and content with your life, your body feels light, you take care of yourself, and you stay healthy. When you feel unfulfilled, depressed, and confused about your life, your body feels heavy, you don't take care of yourself, and you experience more sickness.

Throughout your life you will have many experiences, and emotional highs and emotional lows. Your health depends on how you process your emotions. Ask yourself, "Do I process my emotions in a healthy way or do I stuff them and bury them within?"

ESSENTIAL

The best thing you can do when you're feeling your emotions bubbling to the surface is BREATHE! Remember this simple saying: "Feel it to heal it." Next time, instead of stuffing your emotions, let yourself feel and just breathe. This is where healing takes place.

The angels of emotional healing can help you release and heal any toxic emotions that are affecting your life in a negative way. This can free you so you can experience more peace, joy, happiness, health, and overall well-being. The angels of emotional healing can help you. Here's how you can ask for help:

- When you notice painful emotions like sadness, anger, resentment, or hurt bubbling to the surface, call on the angels and ask for healing.
- Sit with the angels in prayer or meditation and ask them to help you heal. Share with them how you feel in the moment (you can always write about it) and then tell them how you want to feel.
- If you feel you need counseling or support of some kind, ask the angels to guide you to what you require in order to heal.
- Ask the angels to guide you to the perfect books, classes, or anything else you need that can bring you healing or new awareness.
- Before bed, ask the angels to help you heal during your dream state.
- Ask for a miracle and a feeling of inner peace.

The angels know you deserve peace and they want you to be happy. Allow them to guide you along your journey of emotional healing. They will be gentle, and God never gives you more than you can handle. Share with the angels of healing that you want to heal at a peaceful pace and ask them to give you everything you need in order to do so.

Prayer for Emotional Healing

Use the following prayer whenever you are experiencing any kind of emotional pain such as sadness, depression, confusion, anger, jealousy, or resentment. Allow yourself to honor your emotions without judgment, knowing that the angels of healing are surrounding you and supporting you in unconditional love.

Archangel Raphael, Archangel Zerachiel, and all my healing angels, please surround me and help me feel safe and supported in your loving presence. I am asking for emotional healing. I am feeling _____ (state your emotions). I know it's healthy for me to feel and heal these emotions, but I need your help. Please go to the root cause of my unsettling emotions and help me heal so I can feel _____ (state the emotions you desire to feel). Thank you, and please continue to give me everything I need for my highest and greatest good.

Healing from Addictions

There are addictions of all kinds: food, drugs, alcohol, sex, and even work. Having an addictive behavior or habit can create disharmony and even destruction when it gets out of control. It can be very upsetting for the friends and family members of someone who is affected by addiction and most of the time they feel helpless. If you or someone you know is suffering from an addiction of any kind, it's time to call on the angels of healing for help. No one has to feel alone in their struggle; the angels want to assist you and all those involved.

Take the following steps with the angels to heal an addiction:

1. Admit and share with the angels what your addiction is.
2. Ask Archangel Zerachiel and the angels of healing for help.

3. Ask for healing on all levels: physical, emotional, mental, and spiritual.
4. Ask for the people and resources you need to free yourself from addiction.
5. Take action to help yourself; reach out for help if you need it.
6. Watch for the signs. Continue to pray until you reach freedom.

FACT

Jaoel is another angel who helps with those seeking to overcome addiction. He is associated with Archangel Michael and his energy is very compassionate. He will help you overcome even the strongest resistance.

Whenever you have an addictive behavior or habit, it feels like it has control over you. The angels want you to know that you can experience freedom from this feeling of control. Trust in the power of God. Feel worthy and deserving and ask to receive this miracle of freedom. God and the angels want you to be healthy, happy, and peaceful.

Prayer for Healing from a Personal Addiction

Archangel Zerakiel and the angels of healing, I am ready to receive your help and guidance so I can heal and be free of my addiction to _____ (state what it is). Please give me the courage, strength, and will to persevere until I feel free and peaceful with my choices and decisions. Please provide me with everything I need to move through this with support, love, and grace. Help me know that I am not alone and that I have a team of spiritual helpers guiding me. Thank you.

Healing for Others

You can work with the healing angels and send healing to your loved ones and others in need. It's not necessary to ask for their permission; just affirm your intention comes from a place of love and compassion. When you send healing to others it's important to surrender the outcome to God and the angels.

Only God knows what's in the highest and best for each individual and you can't control this, but you can learn to trust in a higher plan. There might be soul lessons taking place that you are unaware of. For example, maybe they have life lessons to learn through the experience of their illness or maybe they don't want to heal (everyone has free will) or maybe other people involved are meant to learn their own life lessons. This might not be easy when you're praying for the physical or emotional healing of a loved one who is not getting better. This is when you can sit with the healing angels and ask for the comfort and clarity you need. Request that they bring healing to everyone involved for their highest and greatest good. Then trust and surrender that this will be done.

ESSENTIAL

There are more and more studies being done on the power of prayer and healing and more doctors are paying attention to the results. Researchers say that prayer is the most prominent form of alternative medicine, surpassing acupuncture, herbs, and other alternative remedies.

Prayer for Healing for Others

Use the following prayer whenever you want to send healing to others. With the help of the angels you can even send healing long distance.

Archangel Raphael, Archangel Zerachiel, Archangel Zadkiel, Archangel Azrael, and all the healing angels, please send healing, comfort, and peace to _____ (state the name or names). Please surround them in your loving support and healing presence. You know exactly what they need for complete healing and I pray that they are open to receive this. Thank you for giving them the miracles of love and healing for their highest and best.

Healing for the Dying and Grieving

There are countless angel stories where the dying and their family members describe the presence of angels or a visitation from a loved one. They come to the dying and their family members in hopes of reassuring them that they are being helped from the other side. Imagine the comfort you would feel if you knew the angels were by your side helping you or your loved ones transition from this world into the next.

FACT

If you would like to connect with your loved one in spirit, ask Archangel Azrael to help you make that connection. You can ask for a visitation in your dreams or you can request to receive a clear and undeniable sign so you can be sure, beyond any doubt, that your loved one is okay and happy in heaven.

If you have a loved one who is dying, call on Archangel Azrael for help. His job is to comfort the dying and to help them when they're ready to cross over into heaven. Once they're in heaven he will stay with them, helping them make the transition as they adjust to their new surroundings. Be reassured that Azrael will make sure that there is no suffering at the time of death, whether it's a sudden death or the person has been sick. He will also lend his support and provide healing for the grieving family members. Call on Azrael if you are grieving a loss of any kind and ask him to help you heal. Know that he will stay by your side until you transition through your loss and you feel peace again.

Prayer for the Dying

Use the following prayer whenever you want to send comfort and healing to the dying. You can also say this prayer if someone recently passed or they experienced a sudden or tragic death.

Archangel Azrael and the angels of healing, please surround_____ (state the person's name) with your loving presence. Bring her comfort and peace and allow her to feel embraced and protected in God's love. Please watch over her and help her transition peacefully and smoothly into heaven.

Prayer for Grieving

Use the following prayer if you have experienced a loss of any kind or if you want to send prayers and comfort to others who are grieving:

Archangel Azrael and the angels of healing, please come to me (or state the person you are praying for) now and comfort me. Help me heal the pain and sadness in my heart. Help me focus on the goodness and the blessings we've had. Give me the strength to move forward and find peace in my heart.

As you become more spiritually conscious, your angels and your soul will nudge toward healing. They know that in order for you to receive what you are praying for—peace, prosperity, relationships, health, and overall well-being— you need to heal what no longer serves you in your life. There is an abundance of support and love available to you both on the spiritual plane and the earth plane. It's up to you to reach out and ask for help.

As you heal and accept more love, joy, and balance into your life, you will realize that you have the ability to create what you desire by healing from the inside out. The angels are elated to assist you along your healing journey. Call them by name or just call on the angels of healing and use the prayers to invoke their powerful healing abilities. Discover that you are not alone and together with the angels you can create miracles.

CHAPTER 17

Forgiveness with the Angels

Have you ever been so hurt and angry that you had a hard time forgiving what was done? Did you also realize that it didn't make you feel any better to hold on to your resentment? In the future, the angels of forgiveness can help you heal during these difficult times. God and the angels want to teach you about the power of forgiveness. They know that as you forgive, you receive back the gift of freedom. Discover how the angels can help you forgive so you can experience more love and compassion.

How Do You Forgive?

Forgiveness means letting go of any resentment, hurt, and anger you may feel because of the actions or choices of another. Self-forgiveness means letting go of any guilt or resentment you may feel toward yourself because of the choices you've made in the past. If you really think about it, you've probably had many experiences where you've had the opportunity to practice forgiveness both for yourself and others.

ESSENTIAL

The act of forgiveness comes more easily when you can have compassion, remembering that everyone is doing the best job they can with what they know in every moment. Try to understand that if they've had a rough past, their actions and choices are going to reflect this.

When you are unable to forgive the emotions consume you. The angels of forgiveness can help heal these emotions that bind you to the past. They will provide you with everything you need to transform your painful emotions and ultimately come to a place of forgiveness.

Freedom Through Forgiveness

There is a great quote from *Healing with The Angels*, written by Doreen Virtue, PhD: "Forgiveness does not mean, 'What you did is okay to me.' It simply means, 'I am no longer willing to carry around the pain in response to your actions.'" Forgiveness releases you from the "prison" of another person's choices and actions and the effects they have on your life. When you are finally free, you can move forward to experience more peace, joy, and happiness.

The angels want you to experience this freedom and they want to help you every step of the way. They know how difficult it can be to forgive, especially when it involves someone close to you. Be patient with yourself and ask the angels for the courage and support you need to persevere. Be honest with the angels, and if you are having a hard time forgiving, tell them. Ask them to stay by your side until you reach that point of freedom where the pain is released and you feel peace once again.

Benefits of Forgiveness

Have you ever taken a long trip in the car that was uncomfortable and almost painful at times but, once you reached your destination, it was all worth it? The same is true about the journey to forgiveness. It can be uncomfortable and painful at times, but once you get there, the freedom you experience is well worth the ride.

When you choose to forgive you receive the following gifts:

- You receive the gift of peace by letting go of old resentment and anger.
- You receive the gift of health when you heal painful emotions.
- You receive the gift of healthy relationships when you heal past ones.
- You receive the gift of compassion when you choose to understand why the other person may have hurt you.
- You receive the gift of freedom by letting go of the past and being able to move forward.
- You receive the gift of empowerment as you take back control of your life and its destiny.

Knowing that these gifts are waiting for you on the other side of forgiveness is encouraging. It might take time, but it's worth the effort. Ask the angels of forgiveness to guide you and carry you until you reach the finish line, where you can finally experience freedom.

Angels of Forgiveness

The following angels and archangels have the specific role of helping humanity heal through forgiveness. When you ask, they will give you the strength and courage you need to let go of painful emotions so you can heal your heart and be free to experience the gifts of forgiveness: peace, joy, and love. Read about each one and see which of these divine helpers can help you in your life right now. Then use the prayers further along in the chapter so they can help you heal through the power of forgiveness.

Archangel Zadkiel Provides Forgiveness for Self and Others

Archangel Zadkiel is the archangel who stopped Abraham from sacrificing his son Isaac. Zadkiel's name means "the righteousness of God" and he is known as the archangel of benevolence and mercy. Call on Zadkiel when you are ready to let go of judgment and guilt and heal through forgiveness and compassion. He will help you heal on all levels—mind, body, and spirit—so you can be free to experience acceptance and unconditional love.

Prayer to Archangel Zadkiel

Archangel Zadkiel, I am ready and willing to forgive myself and others for any past pain. Help me heal so I can have peace once again. I know you can do this with me, and with your help I am ready to experience full freedom and move forward with compassion and understanding.

Archangel Chamuel Provides Healing of the Heart Through Forgiveness

Archangel Chamuel is often referred to as pure love in winged form. Chamuel's name means "he who seeks God" and he is listed as one of seven core archangels. When you call upon his loving energy you may see or feel yourself embraced in a beautiful pink loving energy. Call on Chamuel when you need to forgive and heal your heart from any hurtful relationship, breakup, or loss of any kind. Ask him to help you find love for yourself and everyone involved. Pray with Chamuel for compassion and forgiveness so you can heal your heart and move on to experience more love.

Prayer to Archangel Chamuel

Archangel Chamuel, please come into my heart and help me heal my wounded heart. Heal it with divine love so I can feel safe and trust love once again. Give me the courage to forgive and open my heart to love once again. I feel my heart whole, and filled with your compassionate pink healing energy.

Archangel Zaphiel Provides Healing of the Heart Through Forgiveness

Archangel Zaphiel is the leader of the choir of cherubim. If you have trouble with forgiving and you don't know how you can get to that point of forgiveness, call on Zaphiel. He helps heal even those who have the angriest of hearts. He has the power to heal and resolve any problem so you can love yourself and others in order to experience the freedom of forgiveness.

Prayer for Archangel Zaphiel

Archangel Zaphiel, release and heal the anger in my heart. I cannot find forgiveness yet but I am willing to reach out for your help. I know you have the power to help me move past the hurt and I accept your help. Heal the anger so I can set myself free to feel at peace with myself and those that I need to forgive.

Bath Kol Provides Help with Finding Forgiveness

Bath Kol is known as the angel with a heavenly voice from the Old Testament. She is symbolized by the dove and she has the ability to help you connect with spirit (the dove symbolizing the Holy Spirit) so you can forgive and deepen your experience of love. If you are having a difficult time forgiving yourself or others, call upon Bath Kol. Ask her for the gift of grace so you can open your heart to heal through the power of forgiveness. Listen to her beautiful voice and allow your heart to be filled with love once again.

Prayer to Bath Kol

Dearest Bath Kol, I accept the gift of the Holy Spirit. I am willing to forgive so I can deepen my experience of love for myself and others. I trust the Holy Spirit can perform this miracle of healing and I surrender and open my heart to receive.

As you can see, this is a powerful team of healing angels. As soon as you ask for their help, they will be by your side. Trust that no matter what the situation is, they will assist in every way they can until you reach a state of peace and forgiveness.

Steps to Forgiveness

Archangel Zadkiel, Archangel Chamuel, Archangel Zaphiel, and Bath Kol are waiting in assistance to help you reach forgiveness. They will stand by your side in unconditional love. Together as a team, they will empower you with healing so you can be free. Use the following steps if you are ready to forgive another or if it's time to forgive yourself:

1. Acknowledge you are suffering from not being able to forgive.
2. Declare to the angels and yourself that you are willing to forgive.
3. Tell your angels how you want to feel and what you want to experience on the other side of forgiveness (remember, you do not have to figure out how it's going to happen).
4. Ask Archangel Zadkiel, Archangel Chamuel, Archangel Zaphiel, and Bath Kol to help you let go, heal, and forgive.
5. Pay attention to your emotions, your dreams, and any guidance you receive that will help you reach forgiveness.
6. Ask the angels to help you be patient and persistent until you reach a place of compassion, understanding, and peace.

As you take these steps toward healing, be patient with yourself and trust the angels are working with you. They know how hard it is to forgive when you've been hurt by another, especially if it's someone you've loved or trusted. You will know when you've reached true forgiveness because you will no longer feel resentment, anger, or revenge. You will experience a feeling of acceptance and an inner peace; then you can move forward. You will no longer be triggered by the hurt from your past and you might even feel compassion for the one who has hurt you. Imagine if you could feel peace, acceptance, and compassion. Wouldn't it be worth working with the angels of forgiveness?

Use the following prayer when you are willing to forgive another. Remember to give yourself time and use it until you feel free and ready to move forward.

Archangel Zadkiel, Archangel Chamuel, Archangel Zaphiel, and Bath Kol, I am ready and willing to forgive _____ (state the person's name) so I may be free. Help me heal so I can let go of the painful emotions of my past. Chamuel and Zaphiel, please heal my heart so I can feel compassion and understanding. I surrender and trust in your love as you guide me to my freedom through the power of forgiveness.

QUESTION

What if I have a hard time forgiving someone?
Remember that forgiveness is about you and your desire to free yourself from any past pain. Go into meditation and ask the angels to help you understand why those who hurt you made the choices they did. If all else fails, surrender daily and ask them to lead you to forgiveness.

Add the following statement if you are having trouble with forgiveness:

Angels and archangels of forgiveness, I will be honest with you: I am having difficulty forgiving the one who has hurt me. Help me understand why so I can move forward. Please free me from my resistance, knowing that I am the one who benefits from forgiveness.

Self-Forgiveness

When you're unwilling to forgive yourself for something you did in your past, you hold onto toxic emotions: resentment, guilt, and feelings of unworthiness. The angels can help you, even if you don't know how to forgive yourself.

Take the following steps with the angels to heal through forgiveness:

1. Acknowledge your feelings of remorse and the mistakes you've made.
2. Declare to the angels that you are willing to heal and forgive yourself.
3. Contact someone you feel you need to make amends with. (Be cautious. If you feel it would cause more pain and hurt, then don't do it, just heal with the angels.)
4. Admit and accept your mistakes. Have compassion for yourself.

5. Learn from your mistakes and use them as knowledge for your future.
6. Ask Archangel Zadkiel, Archangel Chamuel, Archangel Zaphiel, and Bath Kol to help you heal and forgive yourself completely so you can experience inner peace.

The angels of healing and forgiveness can help you become one with self-love and acceptance. They know it does not serve you or anyone else involved when you choose not to forgive yourself. So open your heart and be willing to heal and forgive yourself. You will discover that as you do this, your heart will expand with the feelings of peace, compassion, and loving kindness.

ALERT

If you feel you need someone to forgive you in order for you to forgive yourself, stop and remember that you can't force someone into forgiveness. They need to come to it on their own and the truth is, it may never happen. Keep in mind that you need to forgive yourself.

Prayer for Self-Forgiveness

Use the following prayer when you're ready to forgive yourself. Remember to practice compassion toward yourself as you journey to forgiveness.

Archangel Zadkiel, Archangel Chamuel, Archangel Zaphiel, and Bath Kol, I am ready and willing to forgive myself. Help me take responsibility for the choices I have made and help me move forward with the lessons and wisdom learned. Give me the courage to make amends when it's in the highest and best of all concerned. Please heal my heart completely and fill it with self-love and compassion. Allow me the grace to accept myself with compassion and give me everything I need to move forward with inner peace.

Meditation for Forgiveness

Use the following meditation when you need help with forgiveness. Call on the angels of forgiveness and set your intention that you are open and willing for healing to take place. Ask for a full healing to take place so you can forgive and move forward to peace, compassion, and understanding.

ESSENTIAL

Remember, you can always record your meditation beforehand. It might be easier than going back and forth between reading and meditating.

Find a quiet and comfortable place where no one will bother you. Put some nice soothing music in the background and set your intention. If you choose, you can write to your angels beforehand, expressing your feelings and requesting the help you need.

Now take a deep breath and close your eyes. Ask Archangel Zadkiel, Archangel Chamuel, Archangel Zaphiel, Bath Kol, and all the healing angels to surround you in a beautiful circle of love, healing, and protection. (Pause) Affirm to them, "I am open and willing to experience a full healing and to forgive myself and everyone involved. (Pause) Angels of forgiveness, give me everything I need to become one with this prayer.

Now imagine yourself being surrounded in a green emerald healing light that brings healing and protection. (Pause) See a chair or a couple of chairs being placed in front of you. It's time to initiate forgiveness. It is important to remember you do not have to forgive the act that has been done, you just need to free yourself from any pain it's caused you.

Call forth anyone whom you need to forgive and ask them to sit in the chair in front of you. If you do not feel safe, ask Archangel Michael to protect you so no harm can come to you. Then say to that person,

"I am choosing to forgive you so I can free myself from any pain that you've caused me. (Pause) What you did to me hurt me and it's not okay. (Pause) Yet, it's time for me to heal, and in order to do that, I need to forgive you. (Pause) I am ready to send you healing so you can choose to act in a positive way in the future. (Pause) Imagine the angels of healing and forgiveness surrounding the other person with a light of compassion and healing. (Pause) Hand them a symbolic rose that signifies your willingness to forgive and shows that you are choosing to practice compassion. (Pause) Then release them completely and ask the angels to complete the healing between you. Affirm, "I am free. You are free. I release you. I release me. I forgive you. I forgive me." (Pause)

Now ask the angels to heal you heart, mind, body, and spirit so you are freed and healed of any past emotions that hold you back from full forgiveness. (Pause) Imagine Archangel Chamuel filling your heart with a radiant pink light symbolizing love and compassion. (Pause) Then imagine every cell and thought being illuminated in this beautiful healing pink light. (Pause)

Close the meditation affirming, "I am free. I forgive myself and _____ (state the names of anyone you forgave). We are all free to move forward in healing, compassion, and love.

Angels of forgiveness, please help me move forward with the gifts and lessons from this experience and help me remember the wisdom learned. Thank you for this healing, the gifts of forgiveness, and your loving assistance."

Take some nice deep breaths and imagine yourself illuminated in the pink light. Breathe in gratitude and the peace you feel. Ask the angels to continue to guide you and embrace you in their love. Slowly and gently come back into the present moment knowing it's a new beginning.

When you choose to forgive you make the decision to heal your past. Forgiveness takes courage because you are dealing with the raw emotions of pain and hurt. It's not easy to forgive when you've been hurt by someone you've loved or trusted. This is why you need help from the angels of forgiveness. When you invoke the divine you invite healing into your life. You free yourself from the pain of your past so you can experience the gifts of peace, compassion, and healthy relationships. So ask these loving helpers for the courage you need to forgive yourself or others so you can live a life of peace and happiness.

CHAPTER 18

Creating Abundance and Prosperity with the Angels

God and the angels want you to be prosperous. They know it's your divine right as a child of God to receive abundance on every level. When you experience abundance, you feel an overflowing fullness or you have great plenty of what you need and desire. This can encompass love, fulfilling relationships, meaningful work, and yes, financial abundance. When you experience prosperity you are thriving, successful, and you have financial well-being and good fortune. Get ready to invoke the angels of prosperity and abundance into your life so you receive all these gifts and more. Are you ready to receive and enjoy?

Understanding Abundance

When you look up the definition of abundance, you discover the following meanings: "having more than an adequate quantity or supply," "an overflowing fullness," and "great plenty." The angels will remind you that the meaning of abundance is about living in the fullness and richness of life and experiencing the abundance of life's gifts—love, joy, happiness, peace, fulfillment, and prosperity.

The angels know that one of the biggest blocks to receiving abundance is if you have the core issue of feeling unworthy and undeserving of receiving the best in your life. If this resonates with you, ask the angels to open your heart so you can heal this issue. Abundance is your natural birthright and when you decide to accept it for yourself, you attract the gifts of abundance into your life.

Another issue you might struggle with is the old belief that if you receive abundance and you have a great plenty, then it's selfish. In truth, having abundance provides you with the opportunity to share with others. You can teach others how to receive it for themselves when you've learned how to accept it for yourself.

ESSENTIAL

Use this prayer to open your heart to receive abundance: "Dearest angels, open my heart and help me heal and recognize that I am worthy and deserving of receiving God's gifts of abundance into my life. Help me remember there is more than enough and it is my divine birthright to experience abundance in all ways: love, joy, happiness, health, wealth, and fulfillment."

Once you understand the principles of abundance you learn to accept it with grace, and as you do, you open the channels for it to flow easily into your life. The angels know that everyone deserves the gifts of abundance, including you. So say yes and welcome these gifts into your life.

Understanding Prosperity

The meaning of prosperity is more specific than the diverseness of abundance. Prosperity is more about being successful and flourishing and thriving in financial respects. When people are prosperous in their businesses or careers, they experience a feeling of success and fulfillment and they are financially rewarded for their efforts. On a personal level, when you experience prosperity all your financial needs and desires are taken care of: your bills are paid, you have financial security, and you can enjoy the comforts of life.

The angels witness your pain, worry, and stress when you go through financial difficulties. Trust that they know when you're unfulfilled in your work or career. They also understand when you're feeling stuck and you don't know what to do. During these challenging times the angels want to help you turn your life around so you can experience the gifts of prosperity. They know you deserve ease, peace, and joy. When you ask, they will provide you with the opportunities to create financial security and abundance.

How You Can Help Yourself

Before the angels can help you create abundance and prosperity in all aspects of your life, you need to help yourself. Your first step is to take responsibility for your thoughts and beliefs about prosperity. Ask yourself the following questions:

- Do I really believe in abundance and prosperity and can I believe there is more than enough?
- Do I really believe that God will provide me the opportunities to experience an abundance of love, happiness, joy, fulfillment, and prosperity?
- Am I worthy and deserving of receiving abundance and prosperity?
- Do I believe I can change my situation now?

If you cannot answer yes to these questions, then you need to change your thoughts about abundance and prosperity. Remember, your thoughts create your reality. So in order for you to receive what you want, you need to believe and affirm that it's possible. As you do this, you naturally attract and magnetize to you the opportunities to create and experience the manifestations of abundance and prosperity.

ESSENTIAL

If you are challenged with recognizing your limiting beliefs or thoughts, ask the angels to help you. Ask them to help you heal and transform *anything* blocking your flow of abundance and prosperity and trust that they will.

These affirmations can help you transform your thoughts to create your true desires:

- I am worthy and deserving and I accept abundance and prosperity into my life now!
- I believe that there is more than enough in God's universe.
- God loves me and takes care of me and I am grateful that all my needs are met and more.
- The angels continuously show me the endless opportunities to experience abundance and prosperity.
- The channels of abundance are open now and the gifts of love, fulfillment, joy, happiness, and prosperity flow easily into my life.
- An abundance of money and wealth flows consistently into my life.
- I am blessed with the riches of life and I love to share with others.

You can use these affirmations or you can choose to create your own. Repeat them daily until you know them as your new truth. As you transform your belief system and you focus on what you desire, you open the gates of manifestation so that the angels can help you. Together you create opportunities, attracting everything you need so you can experience the gifts of abundance and prosperity.

How the Angels Can Help You

When you transform your old beliefs into positive intentions, you set things into motion. You have initiated a powerful energy where the angels can help you cocreate and manifest your new desires. Your next step is to ask the angels for what you need and then trust they are working behind the scenes to help you.

How can the angels help you? Here are some examples:

- The angels can connect you with the people you need to meet. Examples: clients, customers, boss, investor, referrals.
- The angels can provide you with the resources you need to fulfill your desires. Examples: financing, time, supplies, education, location.
- The angels can present you with unexpected opportunities that will allow you to manifest prosperity. Examples: a new job, funding or money showing up, a learning opportunity to create future abundance, an investment opportunity.
- The angels can provide you with the people who can help you. Example: accountant, financial adviser, teacher, counselor, or any expert you need to accomplish your desire.

These are just some of the examples of how the angels can help you create more abundance and prosperity. Think about your own personal life and ask yourself, "How can the angels help me with what I need right now?" Share your desires with the angels and imagine what it would feel like to have a team working behind the scenes helping you along your journey. Your choice is to struggle in it alone or call on the support of the angels so you can experience grace and ease in your life. Which do you choose?

Angels of Abundance and Prosperity

The following angels and archangels have the pleasure of assisting you in any way they can so you can experience more prosperity and abundance in your life. When you ask, they will gift you with unexpected blessings. They will provide you with the opportunities you need to attract and create more prosperity. These angels want you to be financially abundant and successful.

As you read about each of the angels, invoke them into your life and ask them for the help you need. Then use the prayers so you can experience ease, peace, and joy as you receive the gifts of abundance and prosperity from God and the angels.

Archangel Raziel Helps Manifest Abundance and Prosperity

Archangel Raziel's name means "secret of God." They say he stands by the throne of God and records everything He says and discusses. Supposedly, Raziel wrote all this information down in the well-known book called the *Book of the Angel Raziel*. From this wisdom he knows all the mysteries of the universe. So when you invoke his help, he will use his divine magic to help you manifest the abundance and prosperity you are seeking.

Prayer to Archangel Raziel

Archangel Raziel, you hold the wisdom and gifts of the universe, therefore you know exactly how to help me fulfill my wishes for increased abundance and prosperity. Teach me what I need to know about manifesting. Allow me to witness and receive the gifts of your divine magic so I may experience miracles in my everyday life.

Gadiel Releases Negativity and Provides Direction

Gadiel's name means "God is my wealth." He is known as one of the holiest of angels and his name has great power. To enhance this power, say his name repeatedly when asking for assistance. Gadiel will show you the best direction to take in your life so you can create abundance. If you ask, he will release you from any negativity that blocks your ability to create abundance in your life.

Prayer to Gadiel

Gadiel, Gadiel, Gadiel, please assist me in my life right now. Release me from any conscious or unconscious blocks I have about being abundant and prosperous. Help me know that I am worthy and deserving of the best. Give me the clarity I need and the direction to take so I may follow and walk the path that will lead me to abundance and prosperity.

Barakiel Brings Good Fortune

Barakiel is an ancient angel and he is the ruler of the order of the Seraphim. His name means "God's blessing." He is the angel of good fortune and he will assist you in opening your heart so you can receive the gifts of abundance. He will also help you keep a positive outlook and encourage you to expect abundance in your life.

Prayer to Barakiel

Barakiel, open my heart so I can receive the blessings and good fortune that await me. It's here and it's now and I am inviting these gifts of abundance into my life. Help me stay positive so I can be a magnet of attraction, drawing everything into my life so I can experience my heart's desires.

Gamaliel Provides Gifts and Miracles

Gamaliel's name means "recompense of God." He is known as one of the most generous angels and is referred to as the gracious gift giver. He is a very powerful angel and he will help you create heaven on earth. Expect unexpected gifts and miracles from Gamaliel. He is here to serve you and help you create more money, joy, and happiness.

Prayer to Gamaliel

Gamaliel, you are the gracious gift giver and I call upon you now. I am asking for your help in fulfilling the following desires (share your desires). I know you have the power to perform miracles and I believe in miracles. I am open to receive and I allow unexpected opportunities and gifts to show up in my life. Thank you, Gamaliel, for your graciousness.

Pathiel Opens the Gates of Manifestation

Pathiel's name means "the opener." He is the one to call on if you want to open the gates of manifestation to create abundance and prosperity. Write a request and ask Pathiel for your wishes and desires. Then surrender your list to Pathiel and trust that your prayers have been heard and will be answered.

Prayer to Pathiel
Pathiel, I surrender my wish list to you, knowing that you have the power to manifest abundance and prosperity. Please assist me in opening the gates of manifestation so everything can flow freely and easily into my life. I trust in you and that my prayers have already been answered.

Invoke these angels one at a time or call on them as a team. You don't necessarily have to remember their names; just pray to the angels of abundance and prosperity. Be honest in your prayers and ask for your needs and desires to be met. Understand that they want to help you and they already know you deserve to live a rich life. The question is, are you ready and willing to receive this for yourself?

Steps to Create Abundance and Prosperity with the Angels

Realize that as you take the following steps with the angels, you will be igniting a powerful energy into motion that will bring forth the manifestation of miracles into your life. Once you ask, know that the angels will assist you in any way they can so you can experience your highest and best, better than you could ever imagine. Take the following steps to create abundance and prosperity in your life:

1. Decide and be specific about what you desire. Write it down. For example: If you want to make more money, be specific and tell the angels how much more (always state afterward, "I am open to receive this amount or more").
2. Take responsibility if you have any limiting beliefs or thoughts that contradict and may block what you desire. For example: Do you believe you are worthy of receiving what you asked for? Do you believe it's possible?

3. Write an affirmation claiming what you desire. Include changing your old beliefs to reflect what you want to believe. For example: "I am worthy and deserving of the best. I receive my perfect job opportunity and they offer me at least 25 percent more in pay."

4. Pray and ask the angels of abundance and prosperity to help you in any way they can. Example prayer: "Archangels Raziel, Gadiel, Barakiel, Gamaliel, and Pathiel, please present me the perfect job opportunity that brings me fulfillment, balance, joy, and a 25 percent increase in pay or more. I am grateful that it comes easily, quickly, and for my highest and best, better than I could ever imagine."

5. Believe it's possible and pay attention to your dreams, intuition, signs, and synchronicities.

6. Take action accordingly when your intuition guides you. For example: Someone speaks of an opportunity that could be a lead from the angels. Your job is to follow through on the opportunity and see where it takes you.

7. Say thank you to the angels when your prayers are answered.

When you team with the angels and follow these steps, you become a powerful magnet of attraction. You draw to yourself everything you need to manifest abundance and prosperity. Your wishes and desires are fulfilled and you begin to realize the power of teaming with your angels. Be open, and practice these steps so you can become one with the gifts of abundance and prosperity. It's all around you and the angels just want you to accept it for yourself.

Prayer for Financial Freedom

Use the following prayer if you need help with your finances:

Archangels Raziel, Gadiel, Barakiel, Gamaliel, and Pathiel, please gather around me and support me in your unconditional love. Please help me believe and experience that God's universe is abundant. I affirm that, as a child of God, I deserve financial freedom. I am open and willing to receive everything I need to pay all my bills on time, in full, and I have more than enough left over to put in savings and to enjoy the good things in life. Thank you, angels, for showing me the way and blessing me with the gift of financial freedom.

Prayer for Success and Good Fortune

Use the following prayer when you want to increase your opportunities to create success and good fortune:

Archangels Raziel, Gadiel, Barakiel, Gamaliel, and Pathiel, please open the gates of manifestation so prosperity can flow easily, consistently, and abundantly into my life. With your help, I joyously receive everything I need and I am especially grateful for the unexpected opportunities that come my way. I am happy, fulfilled, successful, and prosperous in everything I do. As I continue to receive good fortune in my life, I graciously share it with others who are in need.

Meditation for Creating Abundance and Prosperity

Taking time out of your busy schedule to meditate and pray with your angels about your desires for abundance and prosperity can be very valuable. It's one thing to pray for your intentions, but it takes on a whole new energy when you sit in meditation with the angels. You raise the vibration of your desire with focused intention and visualization. Because of this valuable time spent in meditation, you become a magnet of attraction, drawing to you everything you need to fulfill your desires.

Find a quiet place to sit, and if you choose, you can put some soft music on in the background. Write out your prayers to the angels. Share with them your desires for abundance and prosperity and be specific.

Now, take a deep breath and let go of everything that happened before you closed your eyes. Then take another nice deep breath and let go of everything that is going to happen after your meditation. Now, breathe into the present moment where all transformation occurs.

Call in the angels of abundance and prosperity, Archangels Raziel, Gadiel, Barakiel, Gamaliel, and Pathiel. Ask them to create a beautiful circle of sacred light around you. (Pause) Breathe one with their love as they embrace you in divine love, light, and protection. (Pause) Imagine within this sacred circle the abundance of God already exists. All that you desire is already here and now in the circle. The kingdom of heaven is here on earth. Take a moment and imagine this to be true and breathe into the abundance that surrounds you. (Pause)

Now imagine that you have already received what you have asked for. You are living your desires right here and right now in this sacred circle. It's already done and it manifested into your life. What are you doing as you experience your desires? (Pause) What do you feel? (Pause) How are you enjoying your life and with whom? (Pause) Take it all in. Breathe into it and feel the experience in every cell of your being. (Pause)

Now, ask the angel to help you become one with your desires. Feel yourself in the center of this sacred circle and realize you are a magnet attracting to you everything you need to fulfill your desires. The angels of abundance and prosperity are working behind the scenes and playing their part perfectly to help you become one with all that you desire. Take a moment and thank them and feel the energy of joy and gratitude. You deserve it. (Pause)

Know that God and the angels are blessing your desires. Your job is to trust and affirm that it is already done and it's just a matter of timing.

Thank the angels and take a deep breath. Affirm that you are open to your highest and best, better than you could ever imagine. After you open your eyes, you will still remain in the sacred circle where all your manifestations will transform from the spiritual plane into the physical plane. When you're ready, open your eyes and come back into the present moment.

Work with the angels of abundance and prosperity and be open to the miracles that are waiting for you. They feel blessed and honored to help you and they want to shower you with many blessings from the divine. Always remember that you are a child of God and you deserve the best. Just ask, believe, and expect to receive.

CHAPTER 19

Enhancing Your Relationships with the Angels

Being in relationships with others is part of the divine plan. God gifted you with family, friends, coworkers, and lovers so you could experience many different expressions of love. God sent you some relationships to help you grow in love, others to teach you about love, and some so you could let go in love. God knew that some relationships would be joyful and easy and others would be challenging and heartbreaking. He sent the angels to assist you in both good times and bad. Read ahead and discover how the angels can help you enhance all your relationships.

How the Angels Can Help with Relationships

Relationships can be joyous, but they can also be complicated; this is why God sent you the angels, to assist you on your journey down the path of love and relationships. God wants humanity to live in harmony and cooperation, and if you want this for yourself, be willing to ask for the help you need.

ESSENTIAL

A beautiful quote by Ella Wheeler Wilcox is, "There is only one happiness in life: to love and be loved."

Here are some ways the angels can help you enhance your relationships:

- Ask the angels for help when you feel disconnected from someone you love or admire. Ask for healing to take place so you can feel reconnected and close once again.
- Ask the angels for help when anger or resentment exists in relationships. Ask that everyone involved experience peace through healing and forgiveness.
- Ask the angels for help if you would like new loving friendships to come into your life.
- Ask the angels for help if you want to meet your soul mate.
- Ask the angels for help if you would like more romance and passion in your marriage.
- Ask the angels to help you heal from a divorce or separation.
- Ask the angels for any help you need to have a loving relationship with your children.
- Ask the angels to help you with clear and honest communication.

These are just some of the ways the angels can help you when you choose to heal your relationships or experience more love. Whatever the situation is, know the angels are waiting in unconditional love to assist you.

Angels of Relationships

The following angels are here to help you discover new relationships and to heal and enhance your current relationships. They want to assist you in any way they can because they know you deserve a life filled with peace, love, joy, and happiness. Share with them your desires and ask for the help you need so you can experience the highest expression of love in all your relationships.

Archangel Chamuel Helps with True Love and Improving Relationships

Chamuel's name means "he who seeks God." He is a powerful archangel in the hierarchy. Chamuel helps those seeking true love. When you ask him, he will help you find a long-lasting, love-centered relationship. If you are already in a relationship, he will help you with communication, compassion, and strengthening the foundation of your relationship. Chamuel will always remind you that if you learn to love yourself first, it will be easier to accept and love others.

Prayer to Archangel Chamuel: Finding Love

Archangel Chamuel, I am requesting your help in finding true love. Please help me remember that I am lovable and that I deserve true love. Guide me to my ideal partner who is loving, supportive, committed, and cause our union to serve our greater good. God knows who my ideal partner is and I trust that you will bring us together at the perfect time.

Prayer to Archangel Chamuel: Existing Partnership

Archangel Chamuel, I call on you to help me in my relationship. Help us come together so we can reconnect and reignite our love and understanding for each other. Help us listen and speak from the heart so we can communicate with compassion. Teach us how to love ourselves so we can easily love one another. You know exactly what we need to deepen our love for each other and I am open to these miracles. Thank you for your assistance.

Archangel Sariel Helps Create Loving Relationships

When you ask Sariel, he will help you create loving relationships through the power of forgiveness, compassion, and acceptance. He will open your heart so you can heal and enhance all your relationships.

Prayer to Archangel Sariel

Archangel Sariel, please come into my heart and heal my heart from any past hurt and misunderstanding. I am ready to let go of the past so I can love more fully in the present. Fill my heart with compassion and loving acceptance of what was and will be. Fill my heart with the light of God and show me the meaning of true love.

Archangel Ariel Brings Relationship Harmony

Ariel's name means "lioness of God." Ariel is the master at bringing balance and harmony into any situation, even if it's in chaos. If you have relationship problems, call on Archangel Ariel and trust that she will help you with her gifts of divine magic.

Prayer to Archangel Ariel

Archangel Ariel, I am struggling with the following relationship issues and I would love for you to step in so peace and harmony can be created by using your gifts of divine magic (share you challenge). You have the ability to bring harmony and balance into any situation and I trust you will work your miracles so we can experience (state what you desire to feel when all is resolved). Thank you.

Archangel Haniel Helps Make New Friends

Haniel's name means "glory of the grace of God." Haniel is the archangel who delivers grace to all those who ask. If your desire is to meet new people and create new friendships, then call on Haniel for help. Haniel can also help when you want to experience an amazing love life with your ideal partner. Just ask for her assistance and she will gift you with grace.

Prayer to Archangel Haniel

Archangel Haniel, you bring grace into the lives of all those who ask. I am asking to be blessed with these graces in the form of new relationships and friendships. I ask that these relationships be loving, supportive, fun, and that we equally feel the connection with one another (share any other qualities you desire). I know with your help these lasting relationships will easily flow into my life.

Gadiel Helps Repair a Relationship

Gadiel's name means "God is my wealth" and he is considered one of the holiest of angels. He will help you heal and release any negative feelings you may have toward others or they may have toward you. He will help all involved transform disagreements into forgiveness and compassion. He will always answer your prayers and turn negative situations into loving experiences.

Prayer to Gadiel

Gadiel, I know you are the angel that transforms difficult situations into loving experiences. I call on you to help me with the following situation (share your concerns and desires). Please bring healing to myself and any others involved so we can release any negative feelings between us. Let us be enlightened through forgiveness and compassion so we can reunite in love and understanding.

As you can see, these powerful divine helpers can assist you with all aspects of your relationships. Use these prayers to invoke them so they can help you by creating more harmony, peace, balance, and joy in all your relationships. It is an honor for them to help you and they receive back the gift of witnessing your relationships enhanced with love.

Enhancing Your Relationships with Family

What if someone told you that you chose each and every one of your family members before you birthed into this lifetime? There is a divine plan and the family dynamics you chose and continue to take part in were all designed for your soul to grow and evolve. No matter if you believe this or not, throughout your lifetime you will experience great joy and heartache when it comes to family. The angels were gifted to you by God so you could reach out and ask for their help, especially when it relates to family.

ALERT

It's important to remember that you have the power to surrender the issue and your relationship to God, but you do not have power to change the other person and who they are. Peace will come when you stop trying to change the other person and instead pray, surrender, and change your *reaction* to the situation at hand.

Take a moment and reflect. Are you feeling any stress, tension, or disharmony between yourself and any family members? If so, the angels encourage you to surrender your relationships for healing to God and the angels. They know exactly what needs to take place in order for peace to occur. After you surrender your relationship issue to the angels, be open to their loving guidance so miracles can happen. They may ask you to practice forgiveness or they may direct you to step into the other person's shoes and see the situation from a different perspective. Don't be surprised if the phone rings and the person you have been in conflict with makes amends with you. God wants unity in the family unit. When you choose to surrender and let go and let God, miracles happen.

Prayer for Enhancing Relationships with Family

Say this prayer whenever you feel the need to shift a negative situation with a family member to a more positive and loving experience. Surrender the issue to God and ask the angels to guide you to a peaceful and harmonious relationship.

Archangel Chamuel, Archangel Sariel, Archangel Ariel, Archangel Haniel, and Gadiel, please come to me now. I surrender this situation with myself and _____(state the names) and I ask for healing and a quick and peaceful resolution for all involved. Bless us with the miracles of peace, harmony, love, and cooperation. Please help me understand what I need to do in order to create peace. I trust that you already know the resolution and all are becoming one with its truth.

Creating Cooperative and Harmonious Relationships

Outside of family, you have many other relationships that affect your day and your life in both positive and sometimes challenging ways. This can involve friends, neighbors, coworkers, customers, and even strangers. Life seems to be in the flow when you attract people into your life who are positive and cooperative. However, the road can get bumpy and the day can seem long when you encounter people who are challenging and who push your buttons.

QUESTION

How do I stay positive if I work with very negative people?
Before you go into work, ask Archangel Michael to surround you in a bubble of white light and protection and ask him to fill it with positive energy. Then imagine during the day that all the negativity from others bounces off your bubble and you stay protected and filled with positive energy.

First of all, ask the angels of relationships to send more people into your life who are positive, joyful, and cooperative. Then ask the angels to gently remove those people from your life who drain your energy and no longer serve your highest and best. Give the angels some time to manifest this prayer and then see if there are still people left in your life who are challenging. Trust that they are still around because you have more healing to do and there are lessons to be learned. Your soul has called them forth in order for you to evolve and grow. When this happens, ask the angels of relationships to help you learn the soul lesson needed in order to heal. Then pray for peace and harmony to coexist in the relationship.

Prayer for Harmonious Relationships

Archangel Chamuel, Archangel Sariel, Archangel Ariel, Archangel Haniel, and Gadiel, help me attract loving and supportive people with positive attitudes into my life. Help me let go or release me from any relationships that are unhealthy and not serving my highest and best. If there are lessons to learn from difficult relationships, help me learn them quickly so I may heal and the relationship can transform into a peaceful and harmonious experience. Thank you, angels, for your loving help and support.

Healing with the Angels After a Breakup or Divorce

Healing and grieving from a loss in a relationship is hard for everyone involved. There is a tremendous amount of emotion that one has to deal with after a breakup or a divorce: sadness, confusion, depression, anger, grief, and aloneness. The angels want to step in and assist you in as many ways as they can during these challenging and emotional times. Even though these times may be difficult, with the angels' help you can get through it more quickly and you can emerge from it with more strength, healing, wisdom, and empowerment. There are different ways the angels can help you after a breakup or divorce:

- Ask the angels to help you heal your heart and all those affected by the breakup.
- Ask the angels to help everyone involved with forgiveness so you can move on and be free.
- Ask the angels for the resources you need after the breakup—money, housing, insurance, etc.
- Ask the angels to help you heal your emotions so you can find peace again.
- Ask the angels for clarity and wisdom so you can grow and accept the gifts and lessons learned from the relationship.
- Ask the angels to open your heart again so you can love and be loved.

The angels want to help you transition through loss and grief so you can take your power back and move forward in independence, joy, happiness, and freedom to love again. Ask for the help you need and realize you do not have to go through it alone. There is a team of divine helpers ready to carry you when you need it and give you the courage to walk in strength and independence.

Prayer for Healing and Opening Your Heart

Use this prayer if you've experienced a breakup or divorce and you want help from the angels to heal your heart and move on:

Archangel Chamuel, Archangel Sariel, Archangel Ariel, Archangel Haniel, and Gadiel, please fill my heart with divine healing light so I can heal my emotions and find peace once again. Please bring healing to all those affected by the end of this relationship. Help me forgive and let go of the past so I can move forward. Give me the strength, courage, and empowerment I need to take care of myself (and my children). Please provide me with everything I need to live in comfort, peace, joy, and happiness. When I am ready, help me open my heart to love and being loved once again. Thank you for all your loving support.

Meditation to Create Harmonious Relationships

You can use this meditation to create harmonious relationships wherever you need it in your life: with family, coworkers, friends, past relationships, and even new people you meet.

Go to your sacred space where you can be alone with the angels. Call on your team of divine helpers: Archangel Chamuel, Archangel Sariel, Archangel Ariel, Archangel Haniel, and Gadiel. Ask them to support you in fulfilling your heart's desires. Relax and breathe with the loving energy that surrounds you. Know that you are not alone and you are very loved. (Pause)

Now, set your intention with the angels: "My desire is to create peaceful and harmonious relationships with _____ (state their names). (Pause) Dearest angels, help us break down any walls of fear so we come together in understanding, compassion, and love."

With your eyes closed, call forth the person or persons you wish to create harmony with in your life. Now imagine the walls of fear coming down between all involved, including you. (Pause)

Now feel or see love flowing back and forth from each person's heart. (Pause) Ask the angels to heal all involved and to initiate peace and harmony back into your lives. (Pause)

Move forward into the future and see the relationship peacefully resolved. (Pause) Imagine and feel everyone living in harmony and cooperation. (Pause) Feel gratitude and thank everyone involved, including the angels. When you're ready, slowly and gently come back into the present moment and trust that all is well.

Witness how this meditation creates change, which brings peace. Open your heart to the healing and miracles coming your way. Trust that the angels are working with all involved and your job is to believe that anything is possible with the help of God and the angels.

Finding Your Soul Mate

The angels will help you find the love of your life when you ask them for assistance. They wish for you all the experiences of love and communion that can only take place when two souls come together in partnership.

The first step is to sit with your angels and make a wish list of your desires and what you want to feel and experience in your partnership. If you have had previous experiences with other relationships, then you have more wisdom and knowledge to clarify what you do want and what you don't want. When making your list, only affirm and list what you do want to experience, the positive not the negative.

Here are some ideas when creating your wish list to the angels:

- What does your soul mate look like? Examples: handsome, athletic, tall, short, dark or light hair, awesome eyes, great dresser.
- What does it feel like when you are with him? Examples: warm, connected, happy, fulfilled, spontaneous, comfortable, genuine, fun.
- What are the characteristics of your soul mate and your relationship? Examples: committed, trusting, honest and open communication, supportive, fun, passionate.
- What's important to you? Examples: someone spiritual, likes to travel, likes to work out, loves good food, good with kids, supportive of your career, likes to have a good time, conversational, good around the house.
- What is your life like after you get together? Examples: we have financial security and abundance, we spend quality time together, we are passionate, we easily communicate, we appreciate each other, we laugh together.

ALERT

Spend some time in your sacred space when you create your wishlist. Be specific and only state the positive. If you choose, you may review it with a friend. She might have suggestions for additions to your list.

Your list is going to be very individual to who you are and what you like. Be honest and specific with the angels. Create your wish list and then surrender it to your angels. They will work diligently behind the scenes to bring you together at the perfect time and in the perfect place. Your job is to believe, affirm, and visualize your soul mate in your meditation and imagine your wish list coming true.

Prayer for Finding a Soul Mate

Archangel Chamuel and Archangel Haniel, I ask for your assistance in meeting and connecting with my true love, a soul mate who is destined for me. I share with you my wish list and desires, and I trust that you will work behind the scenes to bring us together. I am ready and willing to open my heart to give and receive the gifts of love through partnership and to meet my mate who is ready to do the same. Grace me with the gifts of this soul-connected relationship and help me recognize who he is when I see him.

Meditation for Connecting You with Your Soul Mate

This is a powerful meditation that works to help you connect and meet your soul mate. Get ready for miracles if you choose to invite her into your life.

Find a quiet place to sit and bring your soul mate wish list with you. If you choose, you can put some quiet music, in the background, get comfortable, and place your wish list on your lap. Take some nice deep breaths and set your intention that you are going to work with the angels to connect with your soul mate.

Call in your guardian angels and your soul mate's guardian angels and ask Archangel Chamuel and Archangel Haniel to join you. Ask them to create a beautiful circle of divine light, love, and power around you. Breathe in and believe they are going to help you become one with your true love on a soul level and on a physical level. (Pause)

Now imagine your soul as a star in the sky. Now send a call out to your soul mate. There are many stars in the sky, but one seems to shine very bright and it twinkles more than the others. Look for it or feel it—it's there! (Pause)

Now see that star coming toward your star until they merge and become one big, brilliant, bright star. (Pause) Now ask your soul and your angels to call out to your physical beings on the earth plane. Imagine you are both stars on the earth and you attract each other until you finally merge on the earth plane. Just like the two stars came together on the soul plane, they come together on the earth plane. See or feel that happening. (Pause) Through the help of the angels you easily find each other, you are drawn to each other, and you are destined to be together.

Now imagine, or pretend if you need to, that you are living together in happiness, commitment, joy, peace, and harmony. Imagine and feel it in every cell of your being. (Pause) Thank your soul and your angels for bringing you together and for the miracles of your love. (Pause)

Feel the gratitude and then slowly breathe back into the moment, holding on to your vision and the feeling of true love.

CHAPTER 20

Enhancing Career and Finding Life Purpose with the Angels

You deserve to have a job or a meaningful purpose that fulfills you. Can you imagine loving what you do and being rewarded for your efforts and hard work? If this isn't true for you, then believe you can have it all and ask the angels for help. The angels will guide and help you discover your life's work, get the best paying job, and empower you to be successful and confident in all that you do.

God Wants You to Be Happy

God created you as an individual with special gifts, skills, and talents. You were placed on this earth for a reason and a purpose. You are meant to discover who you are and to express yourself in your own unique way. When you live from your authentic self you know who you are and what you're good at; therefore, it's easier to find the perfect job. God and the angels want you to be passionate about what you do for work. They want you to find your life's purpose so you can help and serve others.

If you're searching and you feel there's something more for you but you haven't found it yet, reach out and ask the angels to show you the way. God wants you to spend your days here on earth happy, fulfilled, and living in purpose. As you shine in your magnificent light and you live with passion and purpose, you illuminate all those around you. You brighten their day, you empower them, and you share with them the gifts of your unique expression. In truth, you have an effect on the world and all those around you. Allow God and the angels to help you discover your purpose or find your ideal expression of work so others can benefit from your gifts and talents.

Prayer to God
God, I know I am here on earth for a reason and a purpose. Help me discover who I am and how I can best express myself. Help me get in touch with my unique gifts and talents and show me how I can best serve others and the world. Give me the confidence I need to follow my heart, my passion, and to be who I am.

Angels of Career and Life Purpose

God sent you a special team of angels to help you find your way. The following angels can help you discover your life's purpose and give you the courage to live it. They can also assist you with your current job and anything you need in regards to your career. They want you to be fulfilled, balanced, and prosperous in everything you do. Invoke and invite them into your life and allow them to work their magic.

Archangel Chamuel Helps with Career and Life Purpose

Chamuel's name means "he who seeks God." He is a powerful archangel in the hierarchy. Chamuel is a protector of your personal world and he will help you with all aspects of your career. If you are searching, he will help you connect with your life purpose and work that is meaningful and long lasting. He wants you to be happy and fulfilled in your career while making more than enough money to fulfill all your desires.

Prayer to Archangel Chamuel

Archangel Chamuel, I am ready to find the perfect work that fulfills all my heart's desire and I need your help. I trust that you know what's in my highest and best and what I am destined to do and you will easily lead me to this work. I ask that it not only be meaningful, but that the rewards of pay and benefits are beyond my expectations. Thank you, Chamuel, for the perfect match.

Archangel Michael Helps with Courage, Direction, and Life Purpose

Archangel Michael is the leader of the archangels and the order of the angels known as the Virtues. His name means "he who is like God." Throughout history Michael has assisted famous leaders such as Joan of Arc. He is here to help all those that choose to help and lead through spiritual teaching and healing work. Michael will guide you, direct you, and give you all the courage you need to follow your life's purpose. When you are stuck, he will free you from your fear so you can feel worthy and deserving of having a career that is fulfilling, joyful, and abundant.

Prayer to Archangel Michael

Archangel Michael, you know my fears and what might hold me back from fully owning my true power. Release me from my fears and give me the courage to be all of who I am and do what I love to do. Show me that it's possible and help me feel worthy and deserving of receiving everything I need to live my life's purpose. I am ready now to step into my life's work where I am fulfilled, joyful, passionate, abundant, and prosperous. And so it is!

Archangel Jehudiel Helps with Direction and Getting a Great Job

Jehudiel is the archangel of divine direction. He is a powerful leader who can help you build your self-esteem and confidence so you can find work that you are passionate about. He will lead you in the direction of success and he will make it easy for you to follow the path of your true desires.

Prayer to Archangel Jehudiel

Archangel Jehudiel, you know the path of my true desires and I ask you to lead me in this direction. You know how I can be successful with my gifts, talents, and abilities. Provide me with the self-esteem I need in order to believe in myself and feel confident in whom I am. Show me the divine direction where I may serve for the greatest good of all and where I can experience the most joy, happiness, and fulfillment.

Gazardiel Helps with Starting a New Career and Raises

Gazardiel is also known as "the illuminated one." In the Jewish tradition, he is known as the angel who has dominion over the rising and setting of the sun. He will illuminate the way for anyone who asks. Call on him if you are seeking new beginnings or if you want to start a new career. If you are ready to receive a well-deserved raise in pay, invoke Gazardiel's help.

Prayer to Gazardiel

Gazardiel, I am ready for a new beginning. Please illuminate the path for me and show the opportunities and possibilities waiting for me. I deserve a career I love and a salary that's better than I could ever imagine.

Hasmal Helps You Connect With Your Life's Purpose

Hasmal is known as "the fire-speaking angel" who guards the throne of God. He will burn away your limited beliefs holding you back from living your divine purpose. He is the keeper of ancient wisdom and he knows what life purpose will benefit you and others. He will gladly help when you ask him to connect you with your life's purpose.

Prayer to Archangel Hasmal

Archangel Hasmal, you have the power to release me from my limiting beliefs. Please do this for me so I may create from my highest potential. You have access to divine wisdom and you know what my purpose is. Help me live it fully so I can benefit myself and others with my natural gifts, talents, and abilities. Thank you, Hasmal, for your continued support.

Help with Your Career

Think about how much time you spend at your job daily, weekly, and yearly. Then add to that the amount of time you spend after work just thinking about your job. When you add it all up, you spend a great deal of time on the job. If you're content with your job it can be rewarding, but if you're unhappy, the days can seem very long. The angels want to help you spend this valuable time in the most fulfilling way.

Here are some different ways the angels can help you in your career:

- Ask the angels to help you experience harmonious and cooperative relationships at work.
- Ask the angels to help you when negotiating compensation (hint . . . ask for better than you could ever imagine).
- Ask the angels for a positive attitude so you can recognize the blessings during your day.
- Ask the angels to help you with balance between work, family, and play.
- Ask the angels to help you create a new business or be inspired with new ideas.
- Ask the angels for confidence when speaking with others or presenting your ideas.
- Ask the angels to release you from any stress and provide you with peace and ease.

These are just some of the ways the angels can assist you in your career. If there is something specific going on and you would like the angels' help, then sit with them in meditation or pray with them in your car before you go to work. Share with them what you would like to feel once everything is resolved and then trust that they will do everything they can to assist you. Remember, you are not alone on the job. The angels can be your team in spirit, helping you every step of the way.

Prayer for Help with Your Career

Archangel Chamuel, Archangel Michael, Archangel Jehudiel, Gazardiel, and Hasmal, I invite you into my life and I ask for your loving assistance. I would like help with the following situation (state the circumstances and what you desire). My wish is to experience (state the feeling outcome you desire) when this is all resolved. I know you will help me and I will stay open to your guidance. I expect a miraculous resolution and an outcome better than I could ever imagine. Thank you, angels.

Finding a New Job

Are you looking for a new job or career? If so, this is your chapter. The angels are eager to help and they want you to have a fulfilling job where you can experience happiness, pride, joy, and even take home a rewarding pay. They know you deserve the best and now it's time for you to expect it and accept it.

The first step to take with the angels is to sit down and create a wish list of what you want to experience in your ideal job. Get clear about what you want and what you don't want and then state on your wish list only your true desires.

Here are some questions to ask yourself while creating your list:

- What are you passionate about? What do you love to do? Examples: I love to work with people. I love to be creative. I love working with numbers. I love helping other people. I love creative solutions.
- What is your schedule of hours and days you work?
- What are the people like with whom you interact or do you work independently? Examples: cooperative, fun, lighthearted, hard workers, successful, team players.
- How far away is your work or do you work at home?

- How do you feel when you're working at your new job? Examples: happy to go to work, productive, creative, enthusiastic, grateful, easy, content.
- How much are you getting paid or how much are you making? What are your benefits?
- How does it benefit your personal life? Examples: I come home happy from work. I have balance between my work, family, and play. I have more than enough time and money to go on vacation. My family is well provided for.

Now, take all your desires and create a positive affirmation for each intention. Write it with feeling and emotion and state it in the present tense as if it was happening right now. For example, "I am so grateful I am working with people who are supportive, enthusiastic, and helpful. Everyone enjoys their job and we are well taken care of by the company."

ESSENTIAL

The gift of having experiences in a not-so-good job is this: If you know what you don't want you can figure out what you do want. So make a list of your don't wants and turn them into your do wants.

After you create your list, call on the angels of career and purpose and share with them your list of desires. Then surrender your wish list to the angels and trust that they will do everything in their power to help you create what you want. Your job is to hold the vision of your perfect job and believe it's possible and already done. Remember to stay open and pay attention to the signs and synchronicities and also your dreams and intuition. The angels will use all of these forms of communication to lead you to the perfect job.

Prayer for a New Job or Career

Archangel Chamuel, Archangel Michael, Archangel Jehudiel, Gazardiel, and Hasmal, with your help I am ready, willing, and open to make a change and step into a new job that's perfect for me and my intentions. I surrender my wish list to you, trusting that you will lead me to my ideal job that matches this list and is better than I could ever imagine. Help me recognize the clues you give me and give me the courage to follow my intuition and make the changes I need to make. I know the perfect job is waiting for me now for my highest and best, better than I could ever imagine. Thank you for leading me to my perfect job with ease and grace.

Your Life's Purpose

What does it mean, to live your life-purpose? When you are expressing who you are and doing what you love to do from your authentic self, you are living in purpose. You share with others your gifts, your talents, and what you feel passionate about. When you're in purpose, you feel good about yourself because you know you're making a contribution to enhance or help others in some way.

If you enjoy pumping gas and greeting your customers with a smile on your face, you are in purpose. If you are a nurse and you feel compassionate and helpful assisting others along their journey of wellness, you are in purpose. If you spend your day on the front porch waving to all those that pass by, you are in purpose. If you love staying home with your children and you love being a mom, you are in your purpose.

ESSENTIAL

Take a moment and reflect back to your childhood. What did you always say you wanted to be when you grew up? What did you love to do and what brought you great joy? As you reflect upon this, you might discover some clues leading you to your purpose.

Purpose is what brings you joy, happiness, peace, and fulfillment. It's not living the expectations of others or doing what you have to do or are supposed to do. When this happens, you feel stuck and trapped in something that's not who you are. This creates unhappiness, resentment, depression, and stress.

You decided a long time ago, before you birthed into this world, what your purpose would be. You, God, and the angels all sat down and designed a plan, deciding what that special purpose would be that would fulfill you and help others. It really doesn't matter if you believe this or not. What matters is, you have the opportunity to be fulfilled, happy, and abundant in all that you do.

Discovering Your Life's Purpose

If you have not yet discovered what living in purpose feels like and you have a desire to know what it is, ask the angels for help. They know who you are, why you're here, and what your true potential is. Ask them to help you recognize it for yourself.

Take time to gather your information or your clues, which will lead you to unfolding your life's purpose.

Ask and write your answers to the following questions:

1. What do you love to do? If you had an unlimited amount of time and money and you could enjoy everything you love, what would you be doing or how would you be spending that time?
2. What do you feel passionate about? Is there a cause, an organization, or something that has meaning that you feel passionate about?
3. What comes naturally to you? Is there anything you do or certain characteristics you have that seem very natural? (For example; putting things together or figuring things out, speaking or communicating with others, wood working, singing, seeing things in a way that others can't see.)
4. Is there anything you've experienced or gone through in your life that enables you to help others with the life lessons learned and the experience/wisdom gained?
5. If you had only ten years left to live, would you do anything differently?
6. If you could envision your perfect life without any limitations, what would it look like?

When you take time to answer these questions, you emerge with some beautiful insights, understanding more fully the truth about who you are, what makes you happy, and why you're here. Once you enlighten yourself with this wisdom you can ask the angels of life purpose to help you. You can ask them to help you release the fear and gain the courage you need to follow this path. You can ask them for the resources and the connections you need to make it happen. They know exactly what it takes to make it your reality. You have to want it and believe it's possible and as you do, they will bring into alignment all the miracles and manifestations needed to make it happen easily, effortlessly, and naturally.

Prayer for Becoming One with Your Life Purpose

Archangel Chamuel, Archangel Michael, Archangel Jehudiel, Gazardiel, and Hasmal, my desire is to know and live from my divine purpose. You know exactly what it is that will bring me happiness, fulfillment, purpose, and joy. Help me unfold it for myself. Give me the direction, courage, and guidance I need to become one with my divine purpose. I have reflected, and these are all the things that I love to do and I feel passionate about. Help me bring it all together and show me the possibilities to live it fully and create all the abundance I need and desire. Thank you.

Angel Reading for Life Purpose and Career

You can use the angel cards to do a specific reading in order to gain insight about career and life purpose. The cards can help you see what you may not be able to hear or understand for yourself.

Before you pick your cards, you want to set your intention with the angels. Ask for specific guidance on what you need to know about your career or life purpose and ask for the highest guidance to come through. If you have a specific situation you need clarity on, then pick your cards with the intention of getting an answer or clear insight into what you need to know.

Shuffle your deck of angel cards and call on the angels of career and life purpose. Ask them to give you the guidance you are seeking through the cards. Then spread them out in front of you and pick two cards. See if your answer is immediately shown by the cards chosen. If you are confused and you need more clarity, ask the angels to clear the confusion with the next card you pick. Then choose that card. Write your cards down in your journal or keep them out for a couple of days. You will be surprised how accurate they really are as the day unfolds. Remember, the angels want you to receive the clarity you are searching for, so expect the answers to be revealed.

Your career and living your life purpose are two important aspects of living a full and prosperous life. It is your divine right as a child of God to be happy and fulfilled as you serve others and humanity. You are here on earth as a unique expression of the divine and you have your special place in the big picture. Have the courage to discover what that place may be if you haven't already remembered it for yourself. The angels will help you in the most amazing ways if you call out and ask for help. Remember, you deserve to be in a place where you love what you do and you live abundantly and prosperously as you express your unique and special self.

CHAPTER 21

Manifesting Your Dreams with the Angels

What if miracles were an everyday experience? Can you imagine how magical your life would be? The angels can deliver these miracles to you as long as you hold the belief that anything is possible. Together as a team, you and your angels can cocreate your heart's desires. It's time to think outside of the box and step into the reality of heaven on earth. It's here and it's now and you can experience it with the help of the angels.

Miracles

The *Merriam Webster Dictionary* defines a miracle as "an extraordinary event manifesting divine intervention into human affairs" or "an extremely outstanding or unusual event, thing, or accomplishment." Often, when you think about the word miracle you think of Jesus. When He was here on earth He demonstrated to humanity that miracles really do happen. Jesus turned water into wine; He healed the lame and the blind; He walked on water and He even raised Lazarus from the dead.

FACT

A *Course in Miracles* says, "Miracles should inspire gratitude, not awe. You should thank God for what you really are. The children of God are holy and the miracle honors their holiness, which can be hidden but never lost."

Jesus tried to show you that the power of God is within you and around you if you only believe. How do you get to the point where you can see the miracles and expect them in your everyday life? Believe as Jesus did in the power of God and the angels and know that you are a child of God just like all those that have experienced miracles: Jesus, Moses, Buddha, and Mary, to name a few. You are no different than they were. The only difference is that they believed and they had faith and trust in God.

To witness or experience miracles in your life, be willing to accept and initiate the following:

- Understand you are a child of God and you were created in the likeness of God. You are one and the same.
- Open your heart and your mind and believe miracles really do happen.
- Imagine that all that you are seeking is already here and it's here right now.
- Know that you are worthy and deserving of receiving miracles.
- Visualize or imagine the miracles you desire.
- Believe and have faith in yourself, God, and the angels.
- Expect and allow the miracles to appear.

Small blessings and significant miracles happen every day throughout the world. When you open your awareness to experience heaven and earth as one and the same, you will witness miracles on a daily basis. The angels will show you that there are no limitations to what you can create.

Prayer for Initiating Miracles

Say the following prayer to invite miracles into your life on a daily basis:

God, help me remember the power of your love is within me and around me. Fill me with the same faith that all the enlightened ones had which gifted them the ability to manifest and experience miracles. I know I am your child and I deserve the same. Help me to see, feel, and experience these miracles every day in every way and remind me to thank you for each of these blessings.

Manifesting with the Angels

Manifesting is about creating what you want in your life and knowing you have the power to do it. It's no longer true that only the mystical saints and the "gifted ones" have this ability to perform magic or miracles. You have the power within you, and with the help of the angels you can manifest your dreams into reality. The following steps will help you own your power to manifest your true desires:

1. Get clear about what you desire. Make a wish list and release any limited thinking or negative beliefs while making your list. Believe that anything is possible.
2. Write positive affirmations, enhancing them with feeling and emotion. Claim what you desire now in the present moment.
3. Spend time in meditation visualizing what you truly desire. Match your visualizations with the feeling that it's already done.
4. Call on the angels and ask them to help you manifest your desires and then surrender your wishes to God and the angels.
5. Feel worthy and deserving and be open to receive your highest and best and the highest and best of all, better than you could ever imagine.

These steps are very powerful. You initiate a powerful energy by aligning your thoughts, beliefs, feelings, and visions to a desired outcome. This energy becomes the law of attraction, which draws to your reality the manifestation of what you requested.

The Law of Attraction

It's important to understand what the law of attraction means. The simple definition is "like attracts like" or as Proverb 23:7 says, "As a man thinks in his heart, so is he." It works like this: Your focused thoughts, feelings, and emotions are charged with energy or vibration, which acts as a magnet that attracts into your life exactly what you're focused on. So if your desire is to create prosperity but you're focused on thoughts of lack, then you will continue to experience situations that reflect lack. When you focus your intention and attention on thoughts and feelings of being prosperous while imagining yourself financially free, then you begin to draw to your reality a mirror reflection of this.

ESSENTIAL

Be kind to yourself as you reflect on the thought, "I am creating my reality." Be willing to take responsibility for what's not going right in your life and seek to change it. First, decide on a possibility that could bring you more peace and happiness and then ask the angels to empower you with everything you need to change it.

After you take this important action of owning your thoughts and feelings and matching them to your desires, then you need to let go of how it's going to happen or when it's going to happen. Release it to the angels and the universe and allow it to happen. Expect what you desire and then accept the miracle as it unfolds. Always pay attention, listen to your divine guidance, and take inspired action when it feels right. You will witness with gratitude the miracles of your manifestation coming into form. What was once a thought and a feeling will become your reality.

Divine Magic and Alchemy

These are two additional terms you will see when you read about the different angels and how they can help you manifest your dreams and desires. Remember, they all come from the intention of love; they just represent different expressions of divine intervention and the miracles of manifestation.

Divine magic is a magical occurrence as a result of divine intervention. Mysticism and mystical experiences have been a part of Judaism and the Kabbalah since the early days. The word "magic" has been widely misinterpreted throughout the ages. When you have the desire to learn about God and the connection of mysticism or magic to the divine, then you will discover the true meaning of divine magic. It is created and used from a loving intention as one chooses to cocreate with the divine.

Alchemy is the power or process of transforming something common into something special. Have you ever heard alchemy described as "transmuting base metals into gold"? In medieval times, those who studied to be alchemists were dedicated to working on themselves in order for the process of alchemy to work. They often became hermits in their quest to pursue their desire. This desire came from the belief that if they recognized and became one with their full potential, then they could create from the power within and affect the transformation of matter. When you decide to realize your true potential as a divine being in a human body, you can become an alchemist in many ways.

When you ask the angels, they will teach you how to connect with divine power so you can experience divine magic and witness the process of alchemy. They will encourage you to own your power and use your natural gifts of divine magic and alchemy so you can live the life you were born to live— a life of happiness, joy, fulfillment, and peace.

Angels of Divine Magic, Manifestation, and Alchemy

God gifted you with the following angels to help you manifest and live your heart's desires. You deserve to have it all and to be happy in every aspect of your life. Work with these angels to create miracles and experience the power of divine magic. Down the road, when your dreams have come true, you will look back on your life and realize that the angels helped you get there. So start now and call on this team of angels so you can create your own experience of heaven on earth.

Archangel Ariel Helps with Divine Magic and Manifestation

Ariel means "lioness of God." Ariel is both a healer of the human and animal kingdom. In the Kabbalah and Judaic mysticism, Ariel is associated with conducting divine magic and manifestation. Call on her to witness and experience the gifts of divine magic so together you can manifest what you desire.

Prayer to Archangel Ariel

Archangel Ariel, I know you have the gift of divine magic and I ask for your help with the following desires and wishes (share with Ariel). Continue to show me all that I need to know so I can play my part in manifesting. Help me believe the impossible to be possible. Enhance my thoughts, feelings, and visions with positive divine energy so I can be empowered to manifest. Thank you, Ariel, for cocreating magic in my life.

Archangel Jeremiel Helps Manifest Your Heart's Desires

Jeremiel means "mercy of God" and in Judaism is known as one of the seven core archangels. He is a visionary and he will help you manifest your dreams into reality. He will inspire you to reach for your highest goals and to hold your vision of what you desire until it comes true. He wants you to experience true happiness and will assist you in any way he can so you can create harmony in all aspects of your life.

Prayer to Archangel Jeremiel

Archangel Jeremiel, you are the visionary and with your help you can assist me in manifesting my true desires. Help me feel worthy and deserving of reaching my highest goals and my greatest potential. Help me believe in myself and the visions of my dreams (you can share some of your dreams with Jeremiel). Keep manifesting the miracles into my life so I can experience true happiness. Thank you, Jeremiel.

Archangel Raziel Helps with Divine Magic, Manifestation, and Alchemy

Raziel's name means "secret of God." He has this name because he knows all the secrets of the universe and how it works. All this secret knowledge and wisdom is recorded in *The Book of the Angel Raziel*, which is also considered a book of divine magic. Raziel is like a divine wizard and he can teach you about manifestation and working with the power of divine magic.

Prayer to Archangel Raziel

Archangel Raziel, you hold the secrets of the universe and you have the gift of divine magic. Teach me the wisdom of divine magic and help me manifest divine miracles into my life. Help me understand that when I am one with God anything can happen. These are the manifestations I would like help with right now in my life (share your desires). Thank you, Raziel, for sharing this secret knowledge.

Suriel Helps Manifest Your Heart's Desires

Suriel means "God's command" and he is known as an angel of healing and an angel of death. Suriel will help you let go of limiting beliefs so you manifest your heart's desires. He has the power to manifest anything from nothing. He will help you live your wildest dreams and experience heaven on earth.

Prayer to Suriel

Dearest Suriel, you are an angel of healing and I ask you now to heal my limiting beliefs. You know better than I what holds me back from experiencing my true heart's desires. I am open and ready to experience my personal heaven on earth. Please help me believe so I can witness the miracles unfold and my dreams manifest into reality. Thank you, Suriel, for all your help.

Archangel Uriel Helps with Divine Magic and Alchemy

Uriel's name means "God is light" or "fire of God" because he brings illumination to all situations. In the Book of Enoch, Uriel is considered "one of the holy angels, who is over the world . . . the leader of them all."

He is known for having the gift of prophecy and it was said that he warned Noah of the impending floods. Uriel has the knowledge of alchemy and he has the ability to manifest things out of thin air. If you want to learn about alchemy and the power of manifestation, call on Uriel and ask him to teach you and help you believe in the power of divine magic and alchemy.

Prayer to Archangel Uriel

Archangel Uriel, you carry the light of God and I ask you to illuminate the following situations in my life (share your desires). You have tremendous gifts of alchemy and divine magic and I am eager for you to teach me about these gifts. I am ready to experience the power of alchemy and divine magic in my life so I can manifest my true desires and intentions. Thank you, Uriel, for these gifts and for sharing your knowledge and wisdom.

As you can see, this is a team of angels who can help you manifest your true desires. Their role is to help you believe that anything is possible and miracles really do happen. Take some time to pray and meditate with them and invoke them into your life so you can experience the magic of the divine.

Creating the Experience of Heaven on Earth

In the Bible, Matthew 6:10 says, "Thy kingdom come, Thy will be done in earth, as it is in heaven." It can be translated different ways, but what if it meant that the kingdom of heaven is already here and it's possible to experience heaven on earth? If this were true, you would be able to see and communicate with the angels, you would have everything you need, and the beauty and peace you imagine experiencing after death would be yours, right here and right now.

This might be farfetched to you in this moment, but wouldn't it be worth finding out if it's true? Notice how it feels to think about the possibility of experiencing heaven on earth. Imagine what it would be like if you were living the life of your dreams. Your relationships would be harmonious and loving, you would be in a job that you loved, you would live in a home that was filled with beauty and tranquility, your body would be healthy, your mind would be peaceful, your spirit would be alive, and there would be interconnectedness with all of humanity. The angels know it's possible and heaven on earth already exists all around you. Open your heart and your mind to experience the miracles waiting for you and ask the angels to help you live your personal expression of heaven on earth.

Manifesting Your Heaven on Earth

In heaven there is no time between a thought and its manifestation. When Jesus focused His thoughts on water, it transformed into wine instantaneously. This is the reality of heaven on earth. When you set your intentions and you focus your attention on your desires, they become your reality. The ultimate and most powerful place to be when you set your intentions is one with God, the Creator of all things.

FACT

"Heaven is not a place or a condition. It is merely an awareness of perfect oneness."—*Course in Miracles*

Spend some time journaling or visualizing in meditation what your personal heaven on earth would look and feel like. What dreams and desires would you like to manifest in the following areas in your life?

- Relationships and family
- Body and health
- Emotional and spiritual well-being
- Job, career, or life purpose
- Financial
- Home
- Fun, travel, and creativity

After you are finished with your list, give it to the angels and say the following prayer:

Archangel Ariel, Archangel Jeremiel, Archangel Raziel, Suriel, and Archangel Uriel, I come to you sharing my dreams and desires. You are already one with God and have the power to create miracles. Help me become one with God and believe in the power of miracles and divine magic. I am open, I deserve, and I allow myself to experience heaven on earth in all aspects of my life. Deliver to me the gifts of manifestation and empower me to become a magnet so I can draw into my life everything I need to live my personal heaven on earth for my highest and best and the highest and best of all, better than I could ever imagine.

Become the Magnet of Your Desires Meditation

Once you have created your wish list and surrendered it to the angels, you can do the following meditation to enhance and accelerate the law of attraction. As you raise your vibration and focus your energy on your desires with positive thoughts, feelings, and visualizations, you become a powerful magnet. Effortlessly, you attract everything you need to live your heart's desires and in a short period of time you will look back and realize what was once a thought became your reality.

Take some quiet time and find a place where you will not be disturbed. Bring your wish list of your dreams and desires with you. Get comfortable and take a deep breath and let go of everything that happened before you closed your eyes. Then take another nice deep breath and let go of everything that's going to happen after you open your eyes. Now breathe into the present moment and believe that anything is possible when you open your heart and come into union with God and the angels. Now affirm to yourself and God that you are open to your highest and best and the highest and best of all, better than you could ever imagine.

With your eyes closed, ask Archangel Ariel, Archangel Jeremiel, Archangel Raziel, Suriel, Archangel Uriel, and any other angels to gather around you and ask for their help in manifesting your wish list. (Pause) Ask them to create a beautiful and sacred circle of divine light all around you. Know that in this circle heaven on earth already exists and all the miracles you are asking for are already done. Imagine and feel the angels gather on the edge of the circle supporting you, loving you, and holding the energy of your sacred space. (Pause)

Start with the first area of your life you would like to manifest your dreams and desires. Imagine with as much feeling and emotion as you can that it's already done and you are experiencing it right now. (Pause) Now imagine yourself as a magnet and you are drawing to yourself everything you need to fulfill the manifestation of your desire. See or imagine the angels working behind the scenes making it all possible. Feel or imagine the magnetism of the energy field all around you, active and powerful. (Pause) After you finish with that area of your life, move to the next dream and desire and repeat the process.

When you have completed your wish list, affirm "and so it is" and thank the angels. This affirms your belief and faith in God and the angels. Trust in the power of the universal law of attraction and believe that miracles are on their way. Take a deep breath of gratitude and slowly and gently breathe yourself back into the present moment. Periodically look at your list and keep the feeling alive that you experienced in meditation until you are actually living it.

CHAPTER 22

Angel Stories and Miracles

You have read throughout this book about the power of working with God and the angels. Now you can read for yourself the stories about divine intervention and the miracles people experience when they invite the angels into their lives. These stories are placed in the book to inspire you and to share with you how the angels work. Invite the manifestations of miracles into your life and trust that the angels love you dearly and they want to help you in any way they can.

Jeannie's Near-Death Experience

This story is about Jeannie and her near-death experience at nine years old. She believes this experience was a blessing in her life and to this day it still affects her outlook on life. As you read her story, notice how it touches your heart and reflect on its message for your personal life.

My story is a true experience that happened to me when I was a little girl, age nine. I was home sick for three days running a high temperature. When I got worse, my parents brought me to the emergency room. After the ER doctor saw me, he immediately sent me up to the operating room. I'll never forget when he said the word "stat." My appendix had ruptured and the doctor caught it just in time, right before it burst; however, the poison peritonitis set in. I was in a coma for a week and given my last rites.

During my time in a coma I took an amazing journey. I felt the love of God as my spirit left my body and I moved slowly through a tunnel of light. I was enveloped by divine light. It was like a warm red glowing sensation, a sensation of love. As I moved forward toward the light at the end of this tunnel, I could see all around me but I could also see me, if you can understand that. Pictures of my life were flashing before me in constant motion. With every picture of my life, good or bad, I could feel every feeling of that experience.

As I got closer to the end of the tunnel, I felt so happy. I was almost through the opening when I could see at the end a couple of white doves flying, a beautiful blue sky, and tall grass with flowers. It looked like heaven. The grass started parting as if it was welcoming me home and I felt love everywhere. All of a sudden I heard this deep voice behind me saying, "Go back, go back, your mother needs you." I didn't want to do any such thing. I was feeling love beyond what I could ever imagine, but the voice continued. I felt myself turning around (no body), and in the far distance I noticed a silhouette person with no face, just a long robe. I listened to the voice and went back to my body in the hospital.

I woke up from my coma and about five weeks later I returned home. To this day, my mother has needed me both emotionally and financially. I know this was divine intervention, and to this day I still remember that voice. It reminds me of the important role I play in my mother's life and I will always be there for her.

I truly believe that each day is a blessing. Don't take it for granted. Thank God for your little miracles and blessings of each day. I do, and now have a second chance to make a difference.

If you choose, you can learn from Jeannie's experience and seek the blessings in your everyday experiences. Life is too short, so try not to take it for granted and live it to its fullest.

Erin's Miraculous Dream

This story is Erin's miracle, but it can also remind you about the power of prayer and to pray for your own personal miracles.

I was praying to the Blessed Mother Mary and Archangel Rafael, but mostly to Mary, about a friend of the family's little girl who was going through chemo and was running temps of 105°F and over. She couldn't battle the temperatures because her immune system was so low due to the chemo. So every time I thought of the little girl, I asked Mary and Archangel Raphael to help her and watch over her. This went on for four to five days. Then one night before I went to bed, I asked Mary again to help this little girl. I never remember my dreams, but this one I will never forget.

I was at my house when an angel came to see me. The angel took me to the hospital room of the little girl. I had never been to the hospital to see her because she was so sick and we didn't want to give her any germs to make her worse. When I got there, the whole room was filled with angels. So many were there that I didn't know how I was going to get in the room. Then the angels cleared a path for me so I could get to the bedside, where I saw Mary sitting beside the bed. Mary looked at me and said, "Don't worry, everything is going to be all right." I said thank you and I felt calmed. I woke up at this point and I felt very peaceful and went back to sleep.

When I woke up the next morning, I went and checked the website of the hospital where the family posted messages on how the little girl was doing. When I read it I got all filled up. It said that the little girl's fever broke and she was doing much better. One week later, the doctors took a spinal tap and some blood tests and shortly after we found out that the little girl is now in remission! Thank you, Mary, Archangel Raphael, and all the angels, for helping this little girl! She is home now from the hospital and doing much better! Thank you! Thank you!

Hopefully, Erin's dream will inspire you to pray for others when they are in need of healing. The angels will be right by their side comforting and healing them. Your prayers are more powerful than you imagine and when you feel helpless and you don't know what to do, turn to prayer. Know that all will benefit, including yourself and the one you are praying for.

Ninety Miles Per Hour Miracle

Pat's story is a powerful example of divine intervention. When it comes to sudden life and death situations, there is no time to ask the angels for help. If it's not your time to go they will always intervene without your permission. Trust that they are always watching over you, even when you are unaware of their presence.

When I lived in the mountains of New Mexico, I would occasionally go back and forth to the Dallas area of Texas to see my children and grandchildren. This was a thirteen-hour drive across eastern New Mexico and west Texas, the wide-open spaces of our country.

The temperature was around 100°F when I was returning home and I wanted to get back to my cool mountain home. I had been driving for about eight hours and going approximately ninety miles per hour. This speed is not unusual for that part of the country. I was approaching an eighteen wheeler and moved over to the left lane to pass. As I was about half way into passing the truck, my right front tire exploded. It seemed as if time stood still. I could see the black pieces of the tire hitting the windshield. My thought was to try to pull over to the median on my left. I heard, "Don't touch the brakes. Don't touch the brakes. Keep the steering wheel steady!" I felt very calm, didn't touch the brakes, and kept the steering wheel steady. All of a sudden, I was stopped on the right side of the road and the truck was in back of me. How I got in front of the truck, I don't know. My first thought was to say thank you to all of the angels who helped me. My next thought was why? Why was I saved? I had to assume there was a reason.

By then, the truck driver was at my window asking me if I was okay. He said he couldn't figure out how I had got in front of him and off to the side of the road. He kindly replaced my front tire with the donut and I thanked him and off he went. The rest of the way home I continued to thank my angels and pondered the thought of why that all just happened.

Hopefully, Pat's story will teach you the valuable lesson that it's not safe to drive at ninety miles per hour, but also that your angels are close by watching over and keeping you from harm. So if you ever hear that voice telling you what to do, pay attention and follow your inner guidance. It might save your life.

The Easy-Bake Oven Miracle

This story is Karen's miracle after she asked God and the angels for financial support to follow her life purpose. If it's meant to be and it's for your highest and best, the angels will work behind the scenes to make it happen.

In 1997, I discovered the power of hypnosis to help me heal after being diagnosed with thyroid cancer. I believed in it so much that I wanted to get certified as a hypnotherapist. I found someone in my area who taught the certification course, but I put the brakes on and stopped myself from moving forward when I discovered the tuition fee was $1,200.

I could feel my soul nudging me to sign up for the course, but my fear set in and my bank account statement confirmed that I didn't have the money to pay for the course. So I sat down with my angels and I said to them, "If this is meant to be and it's in my highest and best to become a hypnotherapist, then show me the money."

A couple nights later my daughter asked me if she could use her Easy-Bake Oven that had been in the basement for over a year. I explained to her that she could get it from the basement, but I wasn't sure if there were any mixes left to make the desserts. When she brought the box up from the basement and I pulled out the oven, out came a check with it. It was a check, dated a year prior, that I never cashed from my sales commission, for $655.22. Not only that, the check was dated 11/11, which is a number which signifies the angels' presence. I called my boss and confirmed that I never cashed the check and he said he would gladly reissue it.

I followed the call of my soul, and with the help of the angels I signed up for the course and was certified as a hypnotherapist. The rest of the money came and by the end of the course I had paid it off in full.

After that experience, I framed the old check so I would never forget the truth—that the angels are watching over me and if I ask and it's meant to be, they will make it possible.

When you ask the angels for help, be willing to let go of how it's going to happen. As you witnessed in this story, money can appear out of nowhere. Believe in the impossible and trust that miracles happen when you invoke the angels. Ask for the help you need to follow your heart and manifest your dreams into reality.

I Manifested a Soul Partner

You have discovered in this book that the angels will help you find true love. Here is a story validating the power of creating your wish list to manifest your ideal partner, and how teaming with the angels can make miracles happen.

After taking an eight-week course focused on the book *Excuse Me, Your Life is Waiting* by Lynn Grabhorn, I decided to work on manifesting my soul partner. I sat down with the angels and I made my wish list of what I really wanted in a relationship. I knew what I didn't want after experiencing my past relationship, and therefore I had more clarity about what I did desire.

I shared with the angels what I wanted to feel emotionally and physically with my partner. I asked for someone special who was spiritual, playful, supportive, financially secure, committed, honest, and open with communication. I allowed myself to ask for everything I wanted with no boundaries. My wish list was very detailed and it included our future family life, our home, travel plans, and shared interests as we got older. After three days of working on my wish list, I completed it by including my prayers of surrender to God and the angels. I prayed that my soul partner would enter my life for the greatest good of all, better than I could ever imagine.

Three weeks later he walked into my life. It took me a while to figure out that it was him, but once I did, I went back to my wish list and I checked everything off on my list. My angels listened, and it was worth the three days I spent getting clear about what I wanted and what I deserved. It's been seven years now and it's better than I could have imagined.

This story is a perfect example of how miracles really do happen. It also illustrates the truth, "Ask and you shall receive." Notice how she took the time to sit and create her wish list and then she trusted enough to surrender it to her angels, asking for help. Are you looking for a soul mate? If so, allow this story to inspire you and believe it can happen for you, too.

Donna's Sign from Her Angel

Donna's story is a perfect example of how powerful it can be when you ask for a sign from your angels. Read and try to put yourself in Donna's shoes and notice the comfort and reassurance you feel as you read her story.

> I was diagnosed in March with inflammatory breast cancer. After undergoing chemo, a mastectomy, and radiation, I am doing very well! A few weeks ago I went for my first mammogram. You can only imagine how scared I was. I had prayed to my angel the day before to please show me a sign of a star so I would know that she was around me. After having the mammogram *three* times, the third time I just burst into tears, thinking the cancer was now in my other breast, the radiologist came in to tell me that everything was fine.
>
> When we got off the elevator to go to our car, the parking attendant saw us, and he took something off the hood of our van. As we walked closer to him, he held something out to us in his hand and asked, "Is this yours?" It was a little charm, a *star*! I just stood there with my mouth open in shock. My husband responded, "I guess so." I shared with him my prayer about asking my angel for a sign of a star and he was just amazed. I guess that was my angel letting me know that she was with me throughout that whole thing! I feel so blessed!

Next time you need confirmation or reassurances from the angels, ask for a sign. Remember, it can be a specific sign like Donna's star or you can ask for any significant sign that you would understand. When you receive your sign you will be comforted in the truth that you are not alone and you have a whole team of divine helpers watching over you.

The Day We Saw the Angels

This is an amazing story about an angel encounter that was reprinted many times in various publications, including *Guideposts* and *Spiritual Frontiers Fellowship*. The story, entitled "The Day We Saw the Angels," is by Professor S. Ralph Harlow of Northampton, Massachusetts. It took place during the 1930s.

It was not Christmas, it was not even wintertime, when the event occurred that for me threw sudden new light on the ancient angel tale. It was a glorious spring morning and we were walking, my wife and I, through the newly budded birches and maples near Ballardvale, Massachusetts.

Now I realize that this, like any account of personal experience, is only as valid as the good sense and honesty of the person relating it. What can I say about myself? That I am a scholar who shuns guesswork and admires scientific investigation? That I have a BA from Harvard, an MA from Columbia, a PhD from Hartford Theological Seminary? That I have never been subject to hallucinations? That attorneys have solicited my testimony, and I have testified in the courts, regarded by judge and jury as a faithful, reliable witness? All this is true and yet I doubt that any amount of such credentials can influence the belief or disbelief of another.

In the long run, each of us must sift what comes to us from others through his own life experience, his view of the universe, his understanding. And so I will simply tell my story.

The little path on which Marion and I walked that morning was spongy to our steps and we held hands with the sheer delight of life as we strolled near a lovely brook. It was May, and because it was the examination reading period for students at Smith College where I was a professor, we were able to get away for a few days to visit Marion's parents.

We frequently took walks in the country, and we especially loved the spring after a hard New England winter, for it is then that the fields and the woods are radiant and calm yet show new life bursting from the earth. This day we were especially happy and peaceful; we chatted sporadically, with great gaps of satisfying silence between our sentences.

Then from behind us we heard the murmur of muted voices in the distance, and I said to Marion, "We have company in the woods this morning."

Marion nodded and turned to look. We saw nothing, but the voices were coming nearer—at a faster pace than we were walking—and then we knew that the strangers would soon overtake us. Then we perceived that the sounds were not only behind us but above us, and we looked up.

How can I describe what we felt? Is it possible to tell of the surge of exaltation that ran through us? Is it possible to record this phenomenon in objective accuracy and yet be credible?

For about ten feet above us, and slightly to our left, was a floating group of glorious, beautiful creatures that glowed with spiritual beauty. We stopped and stared as they passed above us.

There were six of them, young beautiful women dressed in flowing white garments and engaged in earnest conversation. If they were aware of our existence they gave no indication of it. Their faces were perfectly clear to us, and one woman, slightly older than the rest, was especially beautiful. Her dark hair was pulled back in what today we would call a ponytail, and although I cannot say it was bound at the back of her head, it appeared to be. She was talking intently to a younger spirit whose back was toward us and who looked up into the face of the woman who was talking.

Neither Marion nor I could understand their words, although their voices were clearly heard. The sound was somewhat like hearing but being unable to understand a group of people talking outside a house with all the windows and doors shut.

They seemed to float past us, and their graceful motion seemed natural—as gentle and peaceful as the morning itself. As they passed, their conversation grew fainter and fainter until it faded out entirely, and we stood transfixed on the spot, still holding hands and still with the vision before our eyes.

It would be an understatement to say that we were astounded. Then we looked at each other, each wondering if the other also had seen.

There was a fallen birch tree just there beside the path. We sat down on it and I said, "Marion, what did you see? Tell me exactly in precise detail. And tell me what you heard."

She knew my intent—to test my own eyes and ears to see if I had been the victim of hallucination or imagination. And her reply was identical in every respect to what my own senses had reported to me.

I have related this story with the same faithfulness and respect for truth and accuracy as I would tell it on the witness stand. But even as I record it I know how incredible it sounds.

Perhaps I can claim no more for it than it has had a deep effect on our own lives. For this experience of almost thirty years ago greatly altered our thinking.

This is a validation that the angels can be seen with your physical eyes open, if you only believe. One of the lessons you can choose to receive from this story is the angels can make their presence known even to the greatest of skeptics. Even if you are a skeptic by nature, choose to open your eyes to the possibilities of witnessing heaven on earth.

Archangel Michael the Firefighter

This story is a wonderful illustration describing the role of Archangel Michael. He is the protector and he will watch over you, your loved ones, and your home. Pamela's story is also a great example of how your intuition or your angels might try to get your attention before something occurs in the near future.

One night, I was going through my angel card decks looking for an Archangel Michael card. I have several decks, and after looking through all of them I was drawn to one in particular. The picture of him was so beautiful, his wings were stunning. I made a color copy of it and returned it to my room. I sat staring at the card and quickly fell asleep.

At 11:00 P.M., my oldest son, Wally, came running into my room saying, "The candle's on fire!" He had come upstairs for something to drink and he saw the candle in the living room out of the corner of his eye. It was not something he could simply blow out. It was a fairly good size candle in a clay pot. The wax was boiling and the entire surface was in flames. We went back in the living room and with great effort we put out the fire. The candle was on our computer desk and the shelf above the candle was black with soot and starting to singe.

When things calmed down, I sat down at my kitchen table, speechless. I sat in silence for a very long time. The reality of how close we came to having a major house fire was more than I could take in. We had been just seconds away from a major disaster. But nothing happened.

I eventually went back to my room and again looked at the Archangel Michael card and it reads: "YOU ARE SAFE" Archangel Michael, "I am protecting you against lower energies, and guarding you, your loved ones, and your home."

I had my answer and I knew Archangel Michael was watching over and protecting us. Thank you, Michael, and also thank you to my son for following his divine guidance.

Call on Archangel Michael often to watch over your home and your loved ones. He will protect you from all types of harm and he will assure your safety no matter what the circumstances are. Can you imagine how you or your loved ones would feel if you always knew this powerful and strong archangel was watching over you?

An Angel on the Edge of a Cliff

Children are very open to the presence of the angels. The veil is thinner for children because their belief system is not as tainted as adults.

> When my sister and I were little girls, maybe eight or nine years old, our parents took us to New Hampshire for vacation. My mom decided we should visit the Flume. It's a very beautiful, very old passage, carved into the rock by the water. You climb and climb until you reach the top, where you can look back and see an amazing view. As we reached the top, my parents stopped to talk and my sister and I walked approximately twenty feet away from them. We were on a round overlook that jutted out over the steep edge of the Flume. It was completely surrounded by a two-rail wooden fence.
>
> She and I stood together looking over the top rail. To get a better view, I stood on the bottom rail and held onto the top one. I can still remember how the damp wood felt against my hand. Suddenly, I lost my footing and slid between the top and bottom rail. I instantly found myself on my back, sliding down the cliff. I heard my sister scream as I reached over my head and caught the bottom rail with my hand. I was completely terrified and could feel the earth slipping below my feet. In that same moment, I felt a hand grab me by my wrist and pull me back up to safety. My sister saw the man who saved me. She watched as he pulled me to my feet. My sister and I hugged for a moment and turned to speak to my hero. He somehow vanished as quickly as he arrived. As we looked back, we saw my parents in the exact spot we left them and there were a few other people standing at the rail. None of them had seemed to move. When we explained to our parents what happened, they told us we should be more careful, but they also couldn't find the man who grabbed my wrist to thank him.

I'm not sure if my sister and I used the term angel on that day, but even as small girls we knew that whatever happened, it was profound, magical, and life changing. Now as women, we sometimes reflect back on that event, knowing that we were not only blessed by the presence of an angel but we had each other to witness the experience together.

An angel can appear as a human if needed. Imagine if Crystal had seen an angel instead of a human being. It might have scared her even more and made the situation worse. Take a moment and think back on your life experiences. Have you had a human angelic encounter where someone appeared with a message or the help you needed? It's possible and it happens more often than you think.

Bebe Joey and the Tiny Shamrock

Sometimes it's hard to trust when you don't have control and you're searching for an answer that has not yet revealed itself. Jean struggled with this during her daughter's pregnancy, but she called on her angels for help and she asked them to renew her faith.

My daughter Brenda was two months pregnant. Blood tests indicated that she may not have a viable pregnancy. My son-in-law, Joe, was unfazed by the tests. He was convinced that all was well. Joe is blonde, blue eyed, and a huge Boston Celtics fan. Being a nurse, I knew that the outcome was very uncertain. I was worried about my daughter and her unborn child. I asked my angels for a sign that all was well.

Later that day I was in a gift shop, not looking for anything in particular, just sort of browsing around. I looked down and there was my sign. On the shelf in a beautiful gold box was a newborn onesie. It was pure white and its only decoration was a tiny green shamrock. The tag read "Bebe Joey." I was filled with relief and gratitude and cried as I paid for that beautiful white onesie with its tiny shamrock. Seven months later, blonde, blue eyed, baby Joey wore that onesie home from the hospital.

How often do you find yourself in the mystery of the unknown, feeling afraid, confused, and worried? This is the perfect time to call on the angels for help. Ask for a sign like Jean did, so you can be reassured that all is well. Then pay attention and expect its delivery. They are here to comfort you and bring you peace in any way they can.

Bethaney's Miracle of Healing and Forgiveness

Moving toward healing and forgiveness is a choice. You can hold onto your anger and resentment or you can work with the angels to free yourself from the pain of the past. Bethaney and her husband decided to use the tools you have in this book to practice forgiveness. They called on the angels for help and miracles happened.

For the past two weeks I have been working with the angels of healing and forgiveness. My husband and I had a wedding this past Saturday for his cousin, and it was an uncomfortable and difficult situation for us. There is major anger and fighting in the family. We contemplated not attending the wedding, but we decided to be there to support his cousin. Since I was working with the angles of healing and forgiveness, I called on them specifically for this day. I asked them to be with the entire family and I prayed for peace. My husband and I set the following intention for the wedding: To support his cousin and his new wife.

To make a long story short, after the wedding and during the reception there were tears, apologies, and talk of regret. It was crazy! We were caught completely off guard and my husband was dumbfounded.

After the wedding, we were invited to an after-party and we decided to go, to further the healing process and to speak our peace. We called on the angels again, especially Archangel Michael and Archangel Gabriel, for courage and clear communication to speak our truth. I reminded my husband that there was also an opportunity for him to heal as well as his family. He opened up to the opportunity so he could let go of his anger, move toward forgiveness and have compassion for others' pain as well. And he did: it was so amazing! The healing for all was incredible! We are grateful to be taking these steps forward. It was miraculous! Today we feel freer and we are experiencing more peace than we have had in a long time.

As you can see, forgiveness is not easy. It requires effort and a choice to move beyond the pain and experience life differently. Bethaney and her husband made this choice as they stepped into the uncomfortable in hopes of healing. With the help of the angels, miracles happened and they experienced compassion, peace, and forgiveness.

A Gift of Grace

This is a story of courage and trust. It's about sharing the messages of divine guidance when you receive them. There is a definite feeling and knowing that comes with strong message from the angels. If you pay attention to it and deliver the message, you gift others with an opportunity to experience a miracle. Read on about Carroll's courage as she gives a difficult but healing message of divine guidance.

This story is about a young woman, twenty-four years old, and a friend of the family who was dying from a brain tumor. I am an occupational therapist and I worked with her since her evaluation at the hospital where I worked on 9/11/01 (a bad day for many reasons). I worked with her weekly until she died on February 2, 2008.

The night before she died, I was asked by the family to bring a splint over for her left hand because it was painful and it needed support. The patient at this point was nonverbal and clearly in need of "going home." Her eyes said more to me than any conversation I had with her the past fifteen years since I've known her. It was very clear to me that she didn't want to let her parents down and die. I knew her parents had to be told to "allow" her to go. As I was walking from their family room to the front door to leave, a very clear voice in my head said, "Tell them. You must tell them!" It was gentle but firm and absolutely unmistakable who it was. I was thinking in my head, "I cannot do that, I cannot tell these people to let their daughter die." There was now fifteen feet between me and the door. I had to make my decision as the voice got louder and firmer. As I walked to the door, many thoughts went through my head. These folks were long-standing family friends as well as business associates. What could I possibly say? What right did I have to tell these parents, Let your beloved daughter die?"

As I turned to say goodbye at the door, I looked directly in the mother's eyes. When I opened my mouth to speak, I had no idea what would come out. The voice made one last pitch, "TELL HER." I simply said, "It's time for Cheryl to go home." I waited for her mom to whack me and throw me out the door. Instead, she just collapsed in my arms and sobbed. I then said, "You must tell her it's alright to go home." As she agreed, still hugging and thanking me, I thought, "Where did that voice come from?" I then turned and left the house. As the door closed behind me, I heard that voice say, "Well done." I sobbed all the way home. Cheryl died the next day after her parents told her she fought a good fight and they were proud of her.

Later, when I thought about this profound experience, I realized that all those Sundays I went to Cheryl's home to work with her were not for her at all. They were, in fact, for me. All those Sundays prepared me to be at Cheryl's home at that exact moment in time, to listen to the voice and follow those instructions with faith. I recognized that I had heard that divine voice many times in my life. I chose this time to listen. I have been listening ever since.

How often do you hear that voice guiding you, and most importantly, how often do you pay attention to it and follow its guidance? Even though Carroll was afraid of the reaction of others, she acted upon her guidance and she received back a tremendous gift of grace. Remember her story the next time you hear that persistent voice guiding you. You never know what miracles may unfold.

A Book about Angels

Hopefully this angel book woke you up to the possibilities of working with the angelic realm. Evelyn found a similar book some years ago and it changed her life and the life of her family. May you be inspired by her story, and hopefully it will encourage you to use this book in the same way, to help you in all aspects of your life.

Some people see, hear, feel, and know angels at an early age. They communicate with imaginary friends and know that they are not alone.

My journey did not start as a child, but as a parent of a child who began to make some very bad decisions. Upon discovering the choices my son was making, I became desperate. There was no avenue I would not try to get help. Nothing seemed to be helping.

Then one day, I was in a bookstore looking for something to read. I was drawn to a book that really surprised me—it was an angel book. The next surprising thing that happened was I bought the book. I had no clue about angels, the angelic realm, or anything to do with angels. But something inside of me said, "Here's your help."

That book gave me the courage to move forward in getting help for my son and healing for our family. I learned to call on angels and ask for divine intervention. And guess what? Things actually began to get better. I began to trust that the right people would help us at the right time. And they did.

I began to ask Archangel Michael to surround my son with 1,000 angels, and I trust that he did, because things got better. As time went on and I read and learned more about angels, I put into practice what I had learned. I realized that God's unconditional love is also the angels unconditional love, which became my unconditional love. It was this realization that turned the tides for my son and our family.

To this day, I firmly believe that the angels, archangels, and divine intervention got us to where we are today, happy and healthy. I am grateful for the love that we now appreciate and cherish. Thank you, God and the angels, for your help and support.

Evelyn learned how to work with the angels and it changed her life. She gained courage, she asked for help, she met the right people to help her during a time of need, and she leaned about unconditional love. What you have learned in this book can help you in more ways than you could imagine. Are you ready to invite divine intervention into your life and live a life that you appreciate and cherish? Now is the time, and you have everything you need to do it right here in this book.

As you can see, miracles happen in both subtle and profound ways. The angels were there for each and every person who shared their story. They are there for you as well. It is a choice of free will to invite them into your life and to ask them to help you. However, as you have witnessed in these testimonials, they will intervene without your permission when necessary.

The angels love you unconditionally and they were sent to you by God. He gifted you the angels so you would remember you are never alone and you always have help from God if you choose to ask for help. God wants you to experience a life filled with peace, love, protection, joy, and fulfillment. Invite the angels into your life and use the tools from this book to create your own personal miracles. The gifts of grace are all around you and heaven on earth is here and it's now. Say yes to it all.

APPENDIX A

Additional Resources

Books

Berkowitz, Rita and Deborah S. Romaine. *Empowering Your Life with Angels*. Royersford, PA: Alpha. 2004.

Foundation of Inner Peace. *A Course in Miracles*. New York: The Penguin Group, 1996.

Grabhorn, Lynn. *Excuse Me, Your Life is Waiting: The Atonishing power of Feelings*. Charlotte, VA: Hampton Roads, 2003.

Gregg, Susan. *Encyclopedia of Angels, Spirit Guides and Ascended Masters: A Guide to 200 Celestial Beings to Help, Heal, and Assist You in Everyday Life*. Beverly, MA: Fair Winds Press, 2008.

Hicks, Esther and Jerry. *Ask and it is Given*. Carlsbad, CA: Hay House Inc., 2004.

Mark, Barbara. *Angelspeake: How to talk with your Angels*. New York: Simon & Schuster, 1995.

Paolino, Karen. *What Would Love Do? A 40-Day Journey to Transform your Fears into Miracles of Love*. Abington, MA: Heaven on Earth, 2006.

Stratton, Elisabeth. *Seeds of Light: Healing Meditations for Body and Soul*. New York: Simon & Schuster, 1997.

Virtue, Doreen and Lynnette Brown. *Angel Numbers*. Carlsbad, CA: Hay House Inc., 2005.

Virtue, Doreen. *Archangels and Ascended Masters: A Guide to Working and Healing with Divinities and Deities*. Carlsbad, CA: Hay House Inc, 2003.

Virtue, Doreen. *Fairies 101: An Introduction to Connecting, Working and Healing with Fairies and other Elementals*. Carlsbad, CA: Hay House Inc., 2007.

Virtue, Doreen. *Healing With The Angels*. Carlsbad, CA: Hay House Inc., 1999.

Virtue, Doreen. *How to Hear Your Angels*. Carlsbad, CA: Hay House Inc., 2007.

Angel Cards

Angel Therapy Oracle Cards by Doreen Virtue
www.HayHouse.com

Archangel Oracle Cards by Doreen Virtue
www.HayHouse.com

Angel Blessings by Kimberly Marooney
www.angelblessingscards.com

Daily Guidance from Your Angels Oracle Cards by Doreen Virtue
www.HayHouse.com

Messages from Your Angels by Doreen Virtue
www.HayHouse.com

Healing with the Angel Oracle Cards by Doreen Virtue
www.HayHouse.com

Guided Meditation CDs

Angel Attunement by Karen Paolino
www.createheaven.com

Chakra Workout Meditations by Elizabeth Harper
www.sealedwithlove.com

Spark the Light by Karen Paolino
www.createheaven.com

Meditation Music

Liquid Mind CD series
www.Liquidmindmusic.com

Steven Halpern's Inner Peace Music
www.innerpeacemusic.com

Personal Readings

My center, *Heaven on Earth*, is located in Massachusetts, but I work with clients over the phone. When I do an angel reading, I connect with the client's angel, guides, and loved ones from spirit. During a reading I can see, hear, and feel the angels and guides around you.

They share their messages of divine guidance with you and they explain why they are here to help you. Possible messages of divine guidance that come through a reading relate to relationships, finances, career, physical and emotional well-being, and life purpose. The readings are always insightful, uplifting, and filled with divine love and healing. I also do a variety of workshops about the angels and I facilitate an *Angel Messenger Certification Program*.

If you are interested in booking a reading or a workshop, please e-mail me at *Heavenonearth444@aol.com* or visit my website at *www.createheaven.com*.

Reverend Rita Berkowitz, MS

Rita is a gifted spirit artist and medium. She can see, draw, and communicate with those who have passed to the higher side of life. Spirit guides working with Rita's artistic talent allow her to draw a portrait of a spirit guide or spirit loved one that is around you. Her gifts will also allow the spirit communicator to make known the message they have come to give. If you are interested in booking a reading with Rita, e-mail her at *Spiritrita@aol.com* or visit her website at *www.thespiritartist.com*.

APPENDIX B

Glossary

Abundance

Having more than an adequate quantity or supply; an overflowing fullness and great plenty.

Affirmation

Declaring the truth through a positive statement.

Alchemy

A power or process of transforming something common into something special.

Angel cards

A deck of cards used for doing angel readings. The cards have various illustrations of the angels and they each have a message of divine guidance.

Angel reading

A method of divination where you connect to the angels to receive messages of divine guidance about all aspects of your life.

Angelic realm

A spiritual realm of pure love where God's divine helpers reside.

Angels

Messengers of love who serve as guardians and helpers between heaven and earth.

Apparition

When an angelic being or a deceased loved one becomes visible and you can see them with your eyes open.

Archangels

A higher order of angels that oversee the angels. They have the ability to be with everyone simultaneously.

Ascended masters

God's divine helpers. These beings of light walked before you on this earth and during their lifetimes they were great teachers. They have now ascended into heaven and their role is to help all those that need them.

Ascension

When in reference to Christ, it means the rising of his body into heaven. In New Age terms, it means transforming your energy from a lower vibration into a higher vibration.

Attunement

To adjust or harmonize your vibration with the angels.

Beliefs

A mental acceptance or conviction that something is true.

Chakras

The seven spiritual energy centers of the body.

Chanting

To recite something in a repetitive tone or to make melodic sounds with your voice.

Cherubim

The guardians of the fixed stars, keepers of the heavenly records, and bestowers of knowledge. Cherubim are in the first triad of the hierarchy.

Clairaudience

Clear hearing. This is when you experience or hear clear thoughts or words flowing through your mind and no one is physically there talking to you.

Claircognizance

Clear knowing. When you have an inner knowing you feel very strong that something is true or you know beyond any doubt that you need to take action.

Clairgustance

Clear taste. When you experience this, you have a clear taste of something in your mouth without any explanation of why it's happening.

Clairolfactory

Clear smell. When you use this ability, you can smell something even though it's not physically in your presence.

Clairsentience

Clear feeling. This is when you receive information as a feeling in your body.

Clairvoyance

Clear vision. This is when you have visions, images, or symbols presented to you through your inner vision.

Coincidence

When two things happen at the same time for no apparent reason.

Discernment

To gain insight or understanding about something that might have been confusing.

Divine guidance

Receiving clarity, direction, or inspiration from a divine source.

Divine inspiration

When you are guided or motivated by the divine to take action and express the inspiration.

Divine intervention

When the angels intervene and perform a miracle.

Divine magic

A magical occurrence as a result of divine intervention.

Divine resolution

When a problem or an issue is resolved miraculously by the divine.

Dominions

Angels in the second triad of the hierarchy. They are the divine leaders who regulate the angels' duties. They are the angels of intuition and wisdom and the majesty of God is manifested through them.

Earthbound spirits

Deceased humans who are hanging around the earth plane. Some people refer to them as ghosts.

Ego

The part of your personality self that sees itself separate from God. It usually wants to be in control and it focuses on fear.

Energy

An immeasurable universal source and power.

Faith

A firm belief in something for which there is no proof; a belief and trust in God.

Guardian angels

Your personal angels. Everyone has at least two guardian angels who were gifted to you by God.

Guided meditation

A meditation that is guided by the voice of the facilitator.

Heaven on Earth

Having all the experiences of heaven here on Earth: bliss, unity, abundance, miracles, wholeness, joy, peace, and unconditional love.

Hierarchy

An order of holy beings organized in a successive ranking order of power.

Icon

A religious image or symbol that is sometimes painted on a wooden panel.

Intention

Focusing your thoughts and feelings on what you desire to create and experience with determination.

Intuition

The instinctual knowing you get when you listen to your inner senses.

Invocation

Asking for help or support from God and the angels.

Kabbalah

A secret doctrine of mystical teachings based on the esoteric interpretation of the Hebrew Scriptures.

Law of attraction

When your focused thoughts, feelings, and emotions are charged with energy or vibration and it acts as a magnet that attracts into your life exactly what you're focused on.

Life purpose

When you've found a way to express yourself and it feels meaningful and significant to you. It's fulfilling and you feel passionate about it.

Manifestation

A materialized form that was created from a thought or a prayer.

Meditation

To engage in reflection, prayer, or contemplation.

Medium

Someone who communicates with deceased loved ones to deliver messages of healing and love.

Miracle

An extraordinary event manifesting divine intervention into human affairs or an extremely outstanding or unusual event, thing, or accomplishment.

Nature angels

The angels of Mother Nature; the fairies.

Near-death experience
When someone is close to death or they are pronounced clinically dead and they have an experience of life after death.

New Testament
The second part of the Christian Bible that includes the book of Acts and Revelation and the canonical Gospels and Epistles.

Old Testament
The first part of the Christian Bible including the books of Jewish canon of Scripture.

Powers
The angels in the second triad of the hierarchy. These angels are the defenders and protectors of the world. They keep track of human history and they are the organizers of world religions.

Precognition
When you receive visions or information about a future event.

Principalities
The angels in the lowest triad of the hierarchy. They are the protectors of politics and religion.

Prosperity
Being successful and flourishing and thriving in financial respects.

Quantum physics
A science that deals with the effects of invisible energy. It studies the fundamental nature of the universe and it describes the universe as very different from the world we see.

Sacred space
A place of retreat where you can step away from the busyness of your everyday life and experience peace and relaxation.

Seraphim
The highest order of God's angelic servants who sit closest to the throne of God.

Shamanism

The religion of the indigenous people of Northern Europe and Asia. They practice communicating with the spirit world, prophecy, shape shifting, and divine healing.

Sign

A confirmation from your angels.

Spiritual toolbox

A place in your mind where you hold all your spiritual teachings.

Spirituality

Your personal and private relationship and connection with the divine.

Synchronicity

A coincidental occurrence of two or more events that have no relevance to one another, yet when it takes place, it has great meaning to the person who is witnessing or experiencing it.

Third eye

The spiritual eye that receives intuitive information and spiritual visions. This energy center is located behind the forehead between the eyes.

Thrones

The angels in the first triad of the hierarchy, they bring God's justice to Earth. They create and send positive energy to the earth and all its inhabitants.

Vibration

A characteristic emanation, aura, or spirit that infuses or vitalizes someone or something and that can be instinctively sensed or experienced.

Virtues

The angels in the second triad of the hierarchy. They are known as the miracle angels. they are sent to Earth to bestow grace and valor.

Wish list

A list of desires and intentions you would like to manifest into physical form.

The Archangels and Angels

ARCHANGELS

Name	Meaning of Name	Type of Assistance
Archangel Ariel	"lion or lioness of God"	Protecting the environment, animals, and the waters, protection if you travel by water, helps with sick or lost pets, relationship harmony, divine magic, and manifestation
Archangel Azreal	"whom God heals"	Comforting the dying and grieving, helps with transition from this life into the afterlife, helps you communicate with loved ones who have passed
Archangel Chamuel	"he who seeks God"	Finding lost items, healing of the heart, compassion, relationship healing including forgiveness, finding true love, enhancing your current relationship, career, and life purpose
Archangel Gabriel	"God is my strength"	Clear communication with God, life purpose involving the arts, adopting a child, fertility or child conception, communicating with spirit or your unborn child
Archangel Haniel	"glory of the grace of God"	Grace, meeting new people and creating new friendships, finding true love, discovering and enhancing your spiritual gifts, developing clairvoyance and your psychic abilities
Archangel Jehudiel		Divine direction, build self-esteem and confidence, get a job
Archangel Jeremiel	"mercy of God"	Manifesting your heart's desires, creating your best future, understanding prophetic information, understanding and interpreting your dreams, and life reviews to take an inventory of your life
Archangel Michael	"he who is like God"	Protecting children, protection during travel, protection of all kinds, mechanical difficulties, patron saint of policemen, releasing and shielding from negativity, chakra clearing, courage, strength, self-esteem, motivation, direction, and life purpose
Archangel Raphael	"God heals" or "God has healed"	Healing of all kinds, animals, protecting travelers, protects and watches over pets
Archangel Raziel	"secret of God"	Divine magic, manifestation, alchemy, abundance, prosperity, spiritual growth, enhancing psychic abilities, understanding esoteric information, and sharing the wisdom of the universe
Archangel Sariel	"light of God"	Creating loving relationships, healing and enhancing relationships, guidance in your dreams, and interpreting your dreams
Archangel Uriel	"God is light" or "fire of God"	Weather, prophecy, bringing light to a situation, manifestation, divine magic, and alchemy
Archangel Zadkiel	"the righteousness of God"	Healing guilt, emotional healing, releasing judgment, healing with acceptance and compassion, and helps with forgiveness for self and others
Archangel Zaphiel		Protecting and watching over children, healing of the heart, forgiveness of self and others, healing anger, and weather conditions
Archangel Zerachiel		Finding lost items, healing addictions, and helping children affected by parents of addiction

ANGELS

Name	Meaning of Name	Type of Assistance
Barakiel	"God's blessing"	Good fortune, abundance, maintaining a positive outlook and encouragement
Bath Kol		Forgiveness of self and others and healing of the heart
Gadiel	"God is my wealth"	Releasing negativity, abundance and prosperity, finding life direction, transforming disagreements into compassion and forgiveness
Gamaliel	"recompense of God"	Miracles, experiencing more joy and happiness, gifts of all kinds, abundance and prosperity
Gazardiel	"the illuminated one"	Finding a new career, getting a raise, illuminates your path ahead, and opportunities
Hasmal	Known as the fire-speaking angel who guards the throne of God	Releasing limiting beliefs, discovering your divine purpose, and creating your highest potential
Laylah	An angel of the night; his name comes from the Hebrew word meaning sleep	Watching over newborn children and new mothers
Pathiel	"the opener"	Opening the gates to manifestation, abundance and prosperity, wishes and desires, and computer problems
Suriel	the angel who rules over the earth	Protecting your home and possessions, manifesting your heart's desires, letting go of your limiting beliefs, experiencing heaven on Earth

Index

A

The EVERYTHING® Series!

BUSINESS & PERSONAL FINANCE

Everything® Accounting Book
Everything® Budgeting Book, 2nd Ed.
Everything® Business Planning Book
Everything® Coaching and Mentoring Book, 2nd Ed.
Everything® Fundraising Book
Everything® Get Out of Debt Book
Everything® Grant Writing Book, 2nd Ed.
Everything® Guide to Buying Foreclosures
Everything® Guide to Fundraising, $15.95
Everything® Guide to Mortgages
Everything® Guide to Personal Finance for Single Mothers
Everything® Home-Based Business Book, 2nd Ed.
Everything® Homebuying Book, 3rd Ed., $15.95
Everything® Homeselling Book, 2nd Ed.
Everything® Human Resource Management Book
Everything® Improve Your Credit Book
Everything® Investing Book, 2nd Ed.
Everything® Landlording Book
Everything® Leadership Book, 2nd Ed.
Everything® Managing People Book, 2nd Ed.
Everything® Negotiating Book
Everything® Online Auctions Book
Everything® Online Business Book
Everything® Personal Finance Book
Everything® Personal Finance in Your 20s & 30s Book, 2nd Ed.
Everything® Personal Finance in Your 40s & 50s Book, $15.95
Everything® Project Management Book, 2nd Ed.
Everything® Real Estate Investing Book
Everything® Retirement Planning Book
Everything® Robert's Rules Book, $7.95
Everything® Selling Book
Everything® Start Your Own Business Book, 2nd Ed.
Everything® Wills & Estate Planning Book

COOKING

Everything® Barbecue Cookbook
Everything® Bartender's Book, 2nd Ed., $9.95
Everything® Calorie Counting Cookbook
Everything® Cheese Book
Everything® Chinese Cookbook
Everything® Classic Recipes Book
Everything® Cocktail Parties & Drinks Book
Everything® College Cookbook
Everything® Cooking for Baby and Toddler Book
Everything® Diabetes Cookbook
Everything® Easy Gourmet Cookbook
Everything® Fondue Cookbook
Everything® Food Allergy Cookbook, $15.95
Everything® Fondue Party Book
Everything® Gluten-Free Cookbook
Everything® Glycemic Index Cookbook
Everything® Grilling Cookbook
Everything® Healthy Cooking for Parties Book, $15.95
Everything® Holiday Cookbook
Everything® Indian Cookbook
Everything® Lactose-Free Cookbook
Everything® Low-Cholesterol Cookbook

Everything® Low-Fat High-Flavor Cookbook, 2nd Ed., $15.95
Everything® Low-Salt Cookbook
Everything® Meals for a Month Cookbook
Everything® Meals on a Budget Cookbook
Everything® Mediterranean Cookbook
Everything® Mexican Cookbook
Everything® No Trans Fat Cookbook
Everything® One-Pot Cookbook, 2nd Ed., $15.95
Everything® Organic Cooking for Baby & Toddler Book, $15.95
Everything® Pizza Cookbook
Everything® Quick Meals Cookbook, 2nd Ed., $15.95
Everything® Slow Cooker Cookbook
Everything® Slow Cooking for a Crowd Cookbook
Everything® Soup Cookbook
Everything® Stir-Fry Cookbook
Everything® Sugar-Free Cookbook
Everything® Tapas and Small Plates Cookbook
Everything® Tex-Mex Cookbook
Everything® Thai Cookbook
Everything® Vegetarian Cookbook
Everything® Whole-Grain, High-Fiber Cookbook
Everything® Wild Game Cookbook
Everything® Wine Book, 2nd Ed.

GAMES

Everything® 15-Minute Sudoku Book, $9.95
Everything® 30-Minute Sudoku Book, $9.95
Everything® Bible Crosswords Book, $9.95
Everything® Blackjack Strategy Book
Everything® Brain Strain Book, $9.95
Everything® Bridge Book
Everything® Card Games Book
Everything® Card Tricks Book, $9.95
Everything® Casino Gambling Book, 2nd Ed.
Everything® Chess Basics Book
Everything® Christmas Crosswords Book, $9.95
Everything® Craps Strategy Book
Everything® Crossword and Puzzle Book
Everything® Crosswords and Puzzles for Quote Lovers Book, $9.95
Everything® Crossword Challenge Book
Everything® Crosswords for the Beach Book, $9.95
Everything® Cryptic Crosswords Book, $9.95
Everything® Cryptograms Book, $9.95
Everything® Easy Crosswords Book
Everything® Easy Kakuro Book, $9.95
Everything® Easy Large-Print Crosswords Book
Everything® Games Book, 2nd Ed.
Everything® Giant Book of Crosswords
Everything® Giant Sudoku Book, $9.95
Everything® Giant Word Search Book
Everything® Kakuro Challenge Book, $9.95
Everything® Large-Print Crossword Challenge Book
Everything® Large-Print Crosswords Book
Everything® Large-Print Travel Crosswords Book
Everything® Lateral Thinking Puzzles Book, $9.95
Everything® Literary Crosswords Book, $9.95
Everything® Mazes Book
Everything® Memory Booster Puzzles Book, $9.95

Everything® Movie Crosswords Book, $9.95
Everything® Music Crosswords Book, $9.95
Everything® Online Poker Book
Everything® Pencil Puzzles Book, $9.95
Everything® Poker Strategy Book
Everything® Pool & Billiards Book
Everything® Puzzles for Commuters Book, $9.95
Everything® Puzzles for Dog Lovers Book, $9.95
Everything® Sports Crosswords Book, $9.95
Everything® Test Your IQ Book, $9.95
Everything® Texas Hold 'Em Book, $9.95
Everything® Travel Crosswords Book, $9.95
Everything® Travel Mazes Book, $9.95
Everything® Travel Word Search Book, $9.95
Everything® TV Crosswords Book, $9.95
Everything® Word Games Challenge Book
Everything® Word Scramble Book
Everything® Word Search Book

HEALTH

Everything® Alzheimer's Book
Everything® Diabetes Book
Everything® First Aid Book, $9.95
Everything® Green Living Book
Everything® Health Guide to Addiction and Recovery
Everything® Health Guide to Adult Bipolar Disorder
Everything® Health Guide to Arthritis
Everything® Health Guide to Controlling Anxiety
Everything® Health Guide to Depression
Everything® Health Guide to Diabetes, 2nd Ed.
Everything® Health Guide to Fibromyalgia
Everything® Health Guide to Menopause, 2nd Ed.
Everything® Health Guide to Migraines
Everything® Health Guide to Multiple Sclerosis
Everything® Health Guide to OCD
Everything® Health Guide to PMS
Everything® Health Guide to Postpartum Care
Everything® Health Guide to Thyroid Disease
Everything® Hypnosis Book
Everything® Low Cholesterol Book
Everything® Menopause Book
Everything® Nutrition Book
Everything® Reflexology Book
Everything® Stress Management Book
Everything® Superfoods Book, $15.95

HISTORY

Everything® American Government Book
Everything® American History Book, 2nd Ed.
Everything® American Revolution Book, $15.95
Everything® Civil War Book
Everything® Freemasons Book
Everything® Irish History & Heritage Book
Everything® World War II Book, 2nd Ed.

HOBBIES

Everything® Candlemaking Book
Everything® Cartooning Book
Everything® Coin Collecting Book
Everything® Digital Photography Book, 2nd Ed.

Everything® Drawing Book
Everything® Family Tree Book, 2nd Ed.
Everything® Guide to Online Genealogy, $15.95
Everything® Knitting Book
Everything® Knots Book
Everything® Photography Book
Everything® Quilting Book
Everything® Sewing Book
Everything® Soapmaking Book, 2nd Ed.
Everything® Woodworking Book

HOME IMPROVEMENT

Everything® Feng Shui Book
Everything® Feng Shui Decluttering Book, $9.95
Everything® Fix-It Book
Everything® Green Living Book
Everything® Home Decorating Book
Everything® Home Storage Solutions Book
Everything® Homebuilding Book
Everything® Organize Your Home Book, 2nd Ed.

KIDS' BOOKS

All titles are $7.95

Everything® Fairy Tales Book, $14.95
Everything® Kids' Animal Puzzle & Activity Book
Everything® Kids' Astronomy Book
Everything® Kids' Baseball Book, 5th Ed.
Everything® Kids' Bible Trivia Book
Everything® Kids' Bugs Book
Everything® Kids' Cars and Trucks Puzzle and Activity Book
Everything® Kids' Christmas Puzzle & Activity Book
Everything® Kids' Connect the Dots
      Puzzle and Activity Book
Everything® Kids' Cookbook, 2nd Ed.
Everything® Kids' Crazy Puzzles Book
Everything® Kids' Dinosaurs Book
Everything® Kids' Dragons Puzzle and Activity Book
Everything® Kids' Environment Book $7.95
Everything® Kids' Fairies Puzzle and Activity Book
Everything® Kids' First Spanish Puzzle and Activity Book
Everything® Kids' Football Book
Everything® Kids' Geography Book
Everything® Kids' Gross Cookbook
Everything® Kids' Gross Hidden Pictures Book
Everything® Kids' Gross Jokes Book
Everything® Kids' Gross Mazes Book
Everything® Kids' Gross Puzzle & Activity Book
Everything® Kids' Halloween Puzzle & Activity Book
Everything® Kids' Hanukkah Puzzle and Activity Book
Everything® Kids' Hidden Pictures Book
Everything® Kids' Horses Book
Everything® Kids' Joke Book
Everything® Kids' Knock Knock Book
Everything® Kids' Learning French Book
Everything® Kids' Learning Spanish Book
Everything® Kids' Magical Science Experiments Book
Everything® Kids' Math Puzzles Book
Everything® Kids' Mazes Book
Everything® Kids' Money Book, 2nd Ed.
Everything® Kids' Mummies, Pharaoh's, and Pyramids
      Puzzle and Activity Book
Everything® Kids' Nature Book
Everything® Kids' Pirates Puzzle and Activity Book
Everything® Kids' Presidents Book
Everything® Kids' Princess Puzzle and Activity Book
Everything® Kids' Puzzle Book

Everything® Kids' Racecars Puzzle and Activity Book
Everything® Kids' Riddles & Brain Teasers Book
Everything® Kids' Science Experiments Book
Everything® Kids' Sharks Book
Everything® Kids' Soccer Book
Everything® Kids' Spelling Book
Everything® Kids' Spies Puzzle and Activity Book
Everything® Kids' States Book
Everything® Kids' Travel Activity Book
Everything® Kids' Word Search Puzzle and Activity Book

LANGUAGE

Everything® Conversational Japanese Book with CD, $19.95
Everything® French Grammar Book
Everything® French Phrase Book, $9.95
Everything® French Verb Book, $9.95
Everything® German Phrase Book, $9.95
Everything® German Practice Book with CD, $19.95
Everything® Inglés Book
Everything® Intermediate Spanish Book with CD, $19.95
Everything® Italian Phrase Book, $9.95
Everything® Italian Practice Book with CD, $19.95
Everything® Learning Brazilian Portuguese Book with CD, $19.95
Everything® Learning French Book with CD, 2nd Ed., $19.95
Everything® Learning German Book
Everything® Learning Italian Book
Everything® Learning Latin Book
Everything® Learning Russian Book with CD, $19.95
Everything® Learning Spanish Book
Everything® Learning Spanish Book with CD, 2nd Ed., $19.95
Everything® Russian Practice Book with CD, $19.95
Everything® Sign Language Book, $15.95
Everything® Spanish Grammar Book
Everything® Spanish Phrase Book, $9.95
Everything® Spanish Practice Book with CD, $19.95
Everything® Spanish Verb Book, $9.95
Everything® Speaking Mandarin Chinese Book with CD, $19.95

MUSIC

Everything® Bass Guitar Book with CD, $19.95
Everything® Drums Book with CD, $19.95
Everything® Guitar Book with CD, 2nd Ed., $19.95
Everything® Guitar Chords Book with CD, $19.95
Everything® Guitar Scales Book with CD, $19.95
Everything® Harmonica Book with CD, $15.95
Everything® Home Recording Book
Everything® Music Theory Book with CD, $19.95
Everything® Reading Music Book with CD, $19.95
Everything® Rock & Blues Guitar Book with CD, $19.95
Everything® Rock & Blues Piano Book with CD, $19.95
Everything® Rock Drums Book with CD, $19.95
Everything® Singing Book with CD, $19.95
Everything® Songwriting Book

NEW AGE

Everything® Astrology Book, 2nd Ed.
Everything® Birthday Personology Book
Everything® Celtic Wisdom Book, $15.95
Everything® Dreams Book, 2nd Ed.
Everything® Law of Attraction Book, $15.95
Everything® Love Signs Book, $9.95
Everything® Love Spells Book, $9.95
Everything® Palmistry Book
Everything® Psychic Book
Everything® Reiki Book

Everything® Sex Signs Book, $9.95
Everything® Spells & Charms Book, 2nd Ed.
Everything® Tarot Book, 2nd Ed.
Everything® Toltec Wisdom Book
Everything® Wicca & Witchcraft Book, 2nd Ed.

PARENTING

Everything® Baby Names Book, 2nd Ed.
Everything® Baby Shower Book, 2nd Ed.
Everything® Baby Sign Language Book with DVD
Everything® Baby's First Year Book
Everything® Birthing Book
Everything® Breastfeeding Book
Everything® Father-to-Be Book
Everything® Father's First Year Book
Everything® Get Ready for Baby Book, 2nd Ed.
Everything® Get Your Baby to Sleep Book, $9.95
Everything® Getting Pregnant Book
Everything® Guide to Pregnancy Over 35
Everything® Guide to Raising a One-Year-Old
Everything® Guide to Raising a Two-Year-Old
Everything® Guide to Raising Adolescent Boys
Everything® Guide to Raising Adolescent Girls
Everything® Mother's First Year Book
Everything® Parent's Guide to Childhood Illnesses
Everything® Parent's Guide to Children and Divorce
Everything® Parent's Guide to Children with ADD/ADHD
Everything® Parent's Guide to Children with Asperger's
      Syndrome
Everything® Parent's Guide to Children with Anxiety
Everything® Parent's Guide to Children with Asthma
Everything® Parent's Guide to Children with Autism
Everything® Parent's Guide to Children with Bipolar Disorder
Everything® Parent's Guide to Children with Depression
Everything® Parent's Guide to Children with Dyslexia
Everything® Parent's Guide to Children with Juvenile Diabetes
Everything® Parent's Guide to Children with OCD
Everything® Parent's Guide to Positive Discipline
Everything® Parent's Guide to Raising Boys
Everything® Parent's Guide to Raising Girls
Everything® Parent's Guide to Raising Siblings
Everything® Parent's Guide to Raising Your
      Adopted Child
Everything® Parent's Guide to Sensory Integration Disorder
Everything® Parent's Guide to Tantrums
Everything® Parent's Guide to the Strong-Willed Child
Everything® Parenting a Teenager Book
Everything® Potty Training Book, $9.95
Everything® Pregnancy Book, 3rd Ed.
Everything® Pregnancy Fitness Book
Everything® Pregnancy Nutrition Book
Everything® Pregnancy Organizer, 2nd Ed., $16.95
Everything® Toddler Activities Book
Everything® Toddler Book
Everything® Tween Book
Everything® Twins, Triplets, and More Book

PETS

Everything® Aquarium Book
Everything® Boxer Book
Everything® Cat Book, 2nd Ed.
Everything® Chihuahua Book
Everything® Cooking for Dogs Book
Everything® Dachshund Book
Everything® Dog Book, 2nd Ed.
Everything® Dog Grooming Book

Everything® Dog Obedience Book
Everything® Dog Owner's Organizer, $16.95
Everything® Dog Training and Tricks Book
Everything® German Shepherd Book
Everything® Golden Retriever Book
Everything® Horse Book, 2nd Ed., $15.95
Everything® Horse Care Book
Everything® Horseback Riding Book
Everything® Labrador Retriever Book
Everything® Poodle Book
Everything® Pug Book
Everything® Puppy Book
Everything® Small Dogs Book
Everything® Tropical Fish Book
Everything® Yorkshire Terrier Book

REFERENCE

Everything® American Presidents Book
Everything® Blogging Book
Everything® Build Your Vocabulary Book, $9.95
Everything® Car Care Book
Everything® Classical Mythology Book
Everything® Da Vinci Book
Everything® Einstein Book
Everything® Enneagram Book
Everything® Etiquette Book, 2nd Ed.
Everything® Family Christmas Book, $15.95
Everything® Guide to C. S. Lewis & Narnia
Everything® Guide to Divorce, 2nd Ed., $15.95
Everything® Guide to Edgar Allan Poe
Everything® Guide to Understanding Philosophy
Everything® Inventions and Patents Book
Everything® Jacqueline Kennedy Onassis Book
Everything® John F. Kennedy Book
Everything® Mafia Book
Everything® Martin Luther King Jr. Book
Everything® Pirates Book
Everything® Private Investigation Book
Everything® Psychology Book
Everything® Public Speaking Book, $9.95
Everything® Shakespeare Book, 2nd Ed.

RELIGION

Everything® Angels Book
Everything® Bible Book
Everything® Bible Study Book with CD, $19.95
Everything® Buddhism Book
Everything® Catholicism Book
Everything® Christianity Book
Everything® Gnostic Gospels Book
Everything® Hinduism Book, $15.95
Everything® History of the Bible Book
Everything® Jesus Book
Everything® Jewish History & Heritage Book
Everything® Judaism Book
Everything® Kabbalah Book
Everything® Koran Book
Everything® Mary Book
Everything® Mary Magdalene Book
Everything® Prayer Book

Everything® Saints Book, 2nd Ed.
Everything® Torah Book
Everything® Understanding Islam Book
Everything® Women of the Bible Book
Everything® World's Religions Book

SCHOOL & CAREERS

Everything® Career Tests Book
Everything® College Major Test Book
Everything® College Survival Book, 2nd Ed.
Everything® Cover Letter Book, 2nd Ed.
Everything® Filmmaking Book
Everything® Get-a-Job Book, 2nd Ed.
Everything® Guide to Being a Paralegal
Everything® Guide to Being a Personal Trainer
Everything® Guide to Being a Real Estate Agent
Everything® Guide to Being a Sales Rep
Everything® Guide to Being an Event Planner
Everything® Guide to Careers in Health Care
Everything® Guide to Careers in Law Enforcement
Everything® Guide to Government Jobs
Everything® Guide to Starting and Running a Catering Business
Everything® Guide to Starting and Running a Restaurant
Everything® Guide to Starting and Running a Retail Store
Everything® Job Interview Book, 2nd Ed.
Everything® New Nurse Book
Everything® New Teacher Book
Everything® Paying for College Book
Everything® Practice Interview Book
Everything® Resume Book, 3rd Ed.
Everything® Study Book

SELF-HELP

Everything® Body Language Book
Everything® Dating Book, 2nd Ed.
Everything® Great Sex Book
Everything® Guide to Caring for Aging Parents, $15.95
Everything® Self-Esteem Book
Everything® Self-Hypnosis Book, $9.95
Everything® Tantric Sex Book

SPORTS & FITNESS

Everything® Easy Fitness Book
Everything® Fishing Book
Everything® Guide to Weight Training, $15.95
Everything® Krav Maga for Fitness Book
Everything® Running Book, 2nd Ed.
Everything® Triathlon Training Book, $15.95

TRAVEL

Everything® Family Guide to Coastal Florida
Everything® Family Guide to Cruise Vacations
Everything® Family Guide to Hawaii
Everything® Family Guide to Las Vegas, 2nd Ed.
Everything® Family Guide to Mexico
Everything® Family Guide to New England, 2nd Ed.

Everything® Family Guide to New York City, 3rd Ed.
Everything® Family Guide to Northern California and Lake Tahoe
Everything® Family Guide to RV Travel & Campgrounds
Everything® Family Guide to the Caribbean
Everything® Family Guide to the Disneyland® Resort, California Adventure®, Universal Studios®, and the Anaheim Area, 2nd Ed.
Everything® Family Guide to the Walt Disney World Resort®, Universal Studios®, and Greater Orlando, 5th Ed.
Everything® Family Guide to Timeshares
Everything® Family Guide to Washington D.C., 2nd Ed.

WEDDINGS

Everything® Bachelorette Party Book, $9.95
Everything® Bridesmaid Book, $9.95
Everything® Destination Wedding Book
Everything® Father of the Bride Book, $9.95
Everything® Green Wedding Book, $15.95
Everything® Groom Book, $9.95
Everything® Jewish Wedding Book, 2nd Ed., $15.95
Everything® Mother of the Bride Book, $9.95
Everything® Outdoor Wedding Book
Everything® Wedding Book, 3rd Ed.
Everything® Wedding Checklist, $9.95
Everything® Wedding Etiquette Book, $9.95
Everything® Wedding Organizer, 2nd Ed., $16.95
Everything® Wedding Shower Book, $9.95
Everything® Wedding Vows Book, 3rd Ed., $9.95
Everything® Wedding Workout Book
Everything® Weddings on a Budget Book, 2nd Ed., $9.95

WRITING

Everything® Creative Writing Book
Everything® Get Published Book, 2nd Ed.
Everything® Grammar and Style Book, 2nd Ed.
Everything® Guide to Magazine Writing
Everything® Guide to Writing a Book Proposal
Everything® Guide to Writing a Novel
Everything® Guide to Writing Children's Books
Everything® Guide to Writing Copy
Everything® Guide to Writing Graphic Novels
Everything® Guide to Writing Research Papers
Everything® Guide to Writing a Romance Novel, $15.95
Everything® Improve Your Writing Book, 2nd Ed.
Everything® Writing Poetry Book